S0-BSR-011

IMPROVING OFFICE OPERATIONS: A PRIMER FOR PROFESSIONALS

Van Nostrand Reinhold Series
in Managerial Skills
in Engineering and Science

IMPROVING OFFICE OPERATIONS: A PRIMER FOR PROFESSIONALS

Jack Balderston

VNR VAN NOSTRAND REINHOLD COMPANY
_____ New York

Copyright © 1985 by Van Nostrand Reinhold Company Inc.

Library of Congress Catalog Card Number: 84-12006
ISBN 0-442-21310-7

Manufactured in the United States of America

Published by Van Nostrand Reinhold Company Inc.
135 West 50th Street
New York, New York 10020

Van Nostrand Reinhold Company Limited
Molly Millars Lane
Wokingham, Berkshire RG11 2PY, England

Van Nostrand Reinhold
480 Latrobe Street
Melbourne, Victoria 3000, Australia

Macmillan of Canada
Division of Gage Publishing Limited
164 Commander Boulevard
Agincourt, Ontario M1S 3C7, Canada

15 14 13 12 11 10 9 8 7 6 5 4 3 2 1

Library of Congress Cataloging in Publication Data
Balderston, Jack.
   Improving office operations.

   (Van Nostrand Reinhold series in managerial skills in
engineering and science)
   Includes bibliographies and index.
   1. Office management   I. Title.   II. Series.
HF5547.B26 1984   651.3   84-12006
ISBN 0-442-21310-7

To Phyllis

Van Nostrand Reinhold Series in Managerial Skills
in Engineering and Science

M. K. Badawy, Series Editor
Cleveland State University

Developing Managerial Skills in Engineers and Scientists: Succeeding as a Technical Manager, by M. K. Badawy

Modern Management Techniques in Engineering and R&D, by J. Balderston, P. Birnbaum, R. Goodman, and M. Stahl

Improving Office Operations: A Primer for Professionals, by Jack Balderston

Series Introduction

This book is the third volume in the Van Nostrand Reinhold Series in Managerial Skills in Engineering and Science. The series will embody concise and practical treatments of specific topics within the broad area of engineering and R&D management. The primary aim of the series is to provide a set of principles, concepts, tools, and practical techniques for those wishing to enhance their managerial skills and potential.

The series will provide both practitioners and students with the information they must know and the skills they must acquire in order to sharpen their managerial performance and advance their careers. Authors contributing to the series are carefully selected for their experience and expertise. While series books will vary in subject matter as well as approach, one major feature will be common to all volumes: a blend of practical applications and hands-on techniques supported by sound research and relevant theory.

The target audience for the series includes engineers and scientists making the transition to management, technical managers and supervisors, upper-level executives and directors of engineering and R&D, corporate technical development managers and executives, continuing management education specialists, and students in technical management programs and related fields.

We hope that this dynamic series will help readers to become better managers and to lead most rewarding professional careers.

M. K. BADAWAY
Series Editor

Preface

Again and again over the past twenty years I have seen highly trained professionals move into supervisory or administrative jobs and be completely baffled about what their new duties are and how to handle them. The puzzlement isn't just about "how to be a supervisor." Most companies provide some sort of help on this subject, and there are hundreds of courses available. The main confusion involves the office routine, the "paperwork." Education and intelligence don't seem to help; those with advanced degrees flounder as much as those without them. Even professionals holding M.B.A. or Ph.D. degrees do no better when it comes to the practical ability to handle the paper tiger.

This book is a result of watching this happen repeatedly. It comes from years of helping intelligent professionals who come up against the administrative "system." It is a practical guide for the person who moves into an office job or who assumes office duties as part of a promotion. My purpose is to make this person comfortable in a strange environment, able to work more effectively in it and to change those aspects of the "system" that he or she sees as obsolete and inefficient.

The book, therefore, is written for the professional specialist who encounters the administrative system and believes it can be improved; for the newly appointed technical or operations manager who wants to understand the system; for the seasoned manager who wants to know the practical uses of recent developments in office system technology; for the managers and professionals who are the office work force and want help in improving their operation. The focus is on improving the efficiency and productivity of office operations—of the paperwork—and on how the reader, whatever his or her position in the organization, can help to bring this about. We show how to plan, sell, and implement a change. We describe the many elements that comprise the office paper flow and provide practical suggestions on how to improve each. We cover "office automation" methods and note the circumstances in which they are helpful. Along the way, we provide tips on how the professional can significantly improve his or her own personal productivity. Throughout, the thrust is on the practical and pragmatic rather than the theoretical. This is a "how to do it" book.

The need to understand and improve office systems is not confined to business and industry. Those who hold positions in the public sector or in academe also need a background in handling information and paperwork—the public sector because it represents the pinnacle of paperwork systems, and academe because it creates a swamp of paper quicksand.

There should be no need for this book. A professional who graduates with the latest knowledge and skills in his or her chosen field should be able to start a job in industry (or a university or government position) understanding how information is generated, communicated, and acted on—in other words, how the paperwork operates. The professional is part of this paperwork system from the day he or she first crosses the organization's threshold. Within the undergraduate and graduate curricula there should be one practical course on how to work within an industrial organization. Unfortunately, there isn't. This book, therefore, addresses this need, and I hope that it will inspire some schools or professional groups to undertake training in managing office systems.

I acknowledge with pleasure the three companies for whom I worked for thirty years and whose practices, both good and bad, provided the insight and knowledge I hope to give to the reader. They are two divisions and the corporate headquarters of North American Aviation, Inc. and Rockwell International Corporation (the former having been merged into the latter); the Aerospace Corporation; and the Occidental Research Corporation.

I thank Dr. M. K. Badawy, Cleveland State University; Mr. Jeffrey Long, the Administrative Management Society; Mrs. Sylvia Savage, Rockwell International Science Center; and Mrs. Pat Petring, American Diversified Savings, for reviewing all or parts of the manuscript (the responsibility for accuracy, of course, is mine, not theirs). Thanks also to Ms. Fran Reich of Booz·Allen & Hamilton for helping me find pertinent parts of their study; to many vendors for providing current data on their products; and to the Epson Corporation and Rising Star Industries for a word processing program that let this manuscript be created and revised easily. I wish also to acknowledge the help provided by Ms. Constance McDonald in the editing of this book. Finally, I express my great love and appreciation to my wife, Phyllis, for her editing help and endless patience during sixty-hour work-weeks while this manuscript was being written and revised.

JACK BALDERSTON
Irvine, California

Contents

Series Introduction / vii
Preface / ix

1. INTRODUCTION / 1

The High Cost of Paperwork / 1
Purpose of This Book / 2
Plan of This Book / 3
Summary / 4

2. OFFICE PRODUCTIVITY / 5

Need for Productivity Improvement / 5
Functions of the Office / 11
Policies and Procedures / 12
Roles of Managers, Professionals, and Support Staff / 13
The Office-less Professional / 17
Administrative Functions / 17
Summary / 20
For Further Information / 21

3. PLANNING FOR CHANGE / 22

Know the Present System / 22
Change Within One Department / 30
Multi-function Change / 38
Cost Justification / 39
Summary / 42
For Further Information / 43

4. OFFICE ELEMENTS / 44

Dictation Systems / 44
Electric and Electronic Typewriters / 52
Word Processors / 54
Summary / 77
For Further Information / 78

5. MORE OFFICE ELEMENTS / 79

Personal Computers / 79
Data Processing / 86
Telecommunications / 88
Reprographics / 91
Micrographics / 95
Mail / 95
Files Management / 99
The Integrated Office / 104
Summary / 105
For Further Information / 106

6. TECHNIQUES FOR WORK MEASUREMENT / 108

Productivity, Efficiency, and Effectiveness / 108
Measuring and Improving the Work Process / 112
Measuring Activities / 119
Cost Considerations / 123
Forms Design / 123
Measuring Output / 124
Establishing Standards / 125
Summary / 126
For Further Information / 127

7. IS AUTOMATION FOR YOU? / 128

Value of Information, Convenience, and Time / 128
Areas to Automate / 131
The Automation Study / 145
The Decision to Automate / 148
Summary / 149
For Further Information / 150

8. IMPROVING THE USE OF OFFICE ELEMENTS / 151

How to Work with a Secretary / 151
How to Dictate / 154
How to Use Word Processing / 159
How to Revise a Document / 163
How to Run a Meeting / 164
Training / 170
Summary / 170
For Further Information / 171

9. BUDGETS AND COST CONTROL / 173

Calculating the Budget / 173
Contingency Planning / 183
Narrative Justification / 184
The Capital Budget / 186
Approval Cycle / 187
Monthly Spread of the Budget / 188
Control of Costs / 189
Summary / 193
For Further Information / 194

10. LEADERSHIP / 195

Motivation / 195
Leadership / 199
Responsibilities of Managers / 205
Summary / 213
For Further Information / 214

11. PERSON-TO-PERSON COMMUNICATION / 216

Understanding / 216
Communicating with Superiors / 221
Communicating with Colleagues / 224
Communicating with the Administrative Staff / 224
Communicating with Subordinates / 228
Interviewing the Job Applicant / 232
Summary / 235
For Further Information / 236

12. SELLING A CHANGE / 237

Inform and Educate / 237
The Key Decision Makers / 239
What Is Important to Management / 240
Cost Benefit Analysis / 242
The Presentation / 244
Summary / 246
For Further Information / 247

13. IMPLEMENTING CHANGE / 248

Handling Resistance to Change / 248
Selling the Concept / 253

Selecting Equipment / 254
Utility Needs and Problems / 256
Procedures / 258
Training / 260
User Orientation / 260
Start-Up / 261
Summary / 262
For Further Information / 262

Appendix. **KEEPING UP WITH THIS FIELD / 265**
Index / 267

1
Introduction

"The overhead costs are killing us! As a percentage of direct productive costs, they are now 20% higher than five years ago. I'd settle for keeping them even. I'm not even asking that they go down. But the cost of computers and copy machines and now word processors is driving my office costs sky high!"

A familiar lament?

THE HIGH COST OF PAPERWORK

The office represents a staggering cost. Thirty percent of the entire cost of doing business lies in the office. In a classic study done by Booz·Allen & Hamilton in 1979, it was found that about $800 *billion* a year was spent by American businesses on office functions. These are 1979 dollars. Harvey Poppel of Booz·Allen & Hamilton has estimated that office costs in 1982 were over $1,000 billion![1] One thousand billion dollars is approximately one-third our Gross National Product (G.N.P.)!

You may think that business devotes a lot of attention to this huge cost drain. If so, you are mistaken. Until the advent of data processing in the sixties and word processing in the seventies, little was done to change office functions and improve office efficiency. It is also a moot point whether these two functions have actually increased office costs rather than lessened them.

Role of the Office

Business could not operate without the office function. All planning and control takes place in the office. Sales are booked and processed. Materials are ordered. People are hired, trained, promoted, disciplined, and their needs taken care of. Research is done. Analyses are made and statistics kept. Legal and regulatory issues are reviewed and translated into company policies and procedures. Money is obtained to finance the business. The accounting books are maintained. Employees are paid, as are suppliers. Customers are invoiced. Out-

---

1. Poppel, Harvey L. Who Needs the Office of the Future? *Harvard Business Review,* 60,6 (Nov.– Dec. 1982): 147.

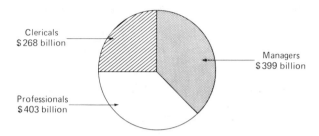

Figure 1-1. Cost of office support in the United States, 1982. Source: Booz·Allen & Hamilton, Inc.

going checks are written. Incoming checks are deposited. Cash flow is measured. Profits are determined. Complaints are handled. And there are many other functions besides these that are performed in the office.

The office does paperwork. It generates, reproduces, distributes, reads, annotates, and files paper. The numbers and words on the paper lead managers to make decisions. The making of decisions, and the record of what each decision is and how it was made, is the purpose of the paperwork. So what is wrong with paperwork? Nothing, if its content is pertinent, and its handling is efficient. That is where the problem lies. That is what this book is about.

Lack of Training

The office is the brain of the business. Most if not all managers and professionals supervise, influence, or are affected by the way in which the office is run. And yet few businesses provide any form of training or help for the manager who has to run an office. Nor does the professional trained in engineering, science, accounting, law, or any other field of specialization get help in learning how to work with office systems.

Nor does any major university, to this author's knowledge, prepare its graduates to run an office, to improve the way it is run, or even to know how to work effectively within the office structure.

PURPOSE OF THIS BOOK

This book aims to help the manager, the professional, or the paraprofessional who works in or with an office to improve his or her personal productivity. It also shows how office systems can be improved and how a significant part of the 30% of G.N.P. that represents business overhead can be turned to profit.

It is written for the person in the business world who is part of an office, supervises some or all office functions, or simply interacts with office personnel. It is for the person who wishes a better understanding of why the "system" appears so cumbersome—and what he or she might do to improve the situation.

We mentioned the paraprofessional. This term needs definition. Paraprofessionals are people without business degrees whose jobs are much more than clerical. This is the position that the secretary will have when technology eliminates much of his or her typing and telephone-answering chores. Paraprofessionals are part of the base of "knowledge workers" with whom we are concerned. They will relieve the business professional of much of the routine analysis and follow-up that require judgment and take time.

Office management as a pragmatic discipline is probably not appropriate for an undergraduate curriculum. You have to be in the business world to appreciate the pervasiveness of the office influence and to understand how ineffective office systems can be at times. There are few people who have not screamed at the blip paperwork and figured that there must be some way to make it easier. Undergraduates will not appreciate the extent of this problem. But this does not excuse the continuing education divisions of universities and colleges from offering the business world some help.

This book, therefore, is also written with a continuing education class in mind. It is divided by chapter into bite-size chunks, each of which can be absorbed in a 2½-hour class segment.

The reader can consider each chapter to be independent of those both ahead of and behind it. If only a few of the subjects covered are pertinent to your needs, head straight to the appropriate parts of the book. But if you supervise an office function, or have ambitions along these lines, read each chapter in sequence.

PLAN OF THIS BOOK

The book is organized as follows: Chapter 2 describes the tremendous improvement in business profits that even a small increase in office effectiveness will produce. This involves the personal effectiveness of managers, professionals, paraprofessionals, and the clerical support staff, as well as improvement in systems and procedures. This chapter closes with a section describing office functions and the roles of those who supervise, interact with, or are buried under those functions.

Chapter 3 describes the process of planning a change and shows the steps necessary to improve the system you find yourself a part of. Chapters 4 and 5 describe many of the elements that comprise the office system—elements that you can influence. Chapter 6 describes work flow and concepts for its measurement and simplification. Chapter 7 looks at automation, and where its use does and does not make sense. Chapter 8 provides specific techniques for improving your own productivity within the office system. Chapter 9 shows how to create budgets and control costs. It is for the professional who has been put in charge of a group or project.

Chapter 10 discusses motivation, an essential element of any effective system. It also covers styles of leadership and the importance of a flexible style. Chapter 11 is about oral communications, the pulsing heart of any office operation. Because any change to a system requires the approval of higher management, Chapter 12 addresses how to sell a change. Chapter 13 looks at implementing change, with emphasis on resistance and how to overcome it. At the close of each chapter is a brief list of recent books and articles that give additional information on the subjects covered by the chapter. This list does not try to show all or even most references to a subject; it provides one or two references that will start the reader digging deeper into the subject. The appendix provides a list of useful magazines and meetings.

SUMMARY

Thirty percent of the cost of doing business lies in the office functions. These functions are vital to business. They perform planning, control, staffing, purchasing, accounting, financing, legal, research, and many other activities. However, despite the size and cost of the office, relatively little attention has been given to it.

This book is written for the newly appointed or seasoned manager who is responsible for some office functions. It is intended also for all other professionals who must work with administrative support groups. It provides pragmatic advice on improving office operations and personal productivity.

2
Office Productivity

Inefficiency seems to abound. Most if not all workers see their own organizations as inefficient. You look at other prosperous companies and wish yours were as well run as the others. Of course, the employees of the other companies are looking at your company and thinking the same thing. The grass *is* always greener on the other side of the chain-link fence. Most employees believe they could improve the situation if given the opportunity. And most employees are right. Office productivity can be improved significantly.

NEED FOR PRODUCTIVITY IMPROVEMENT

Booz·Allen & Hamilton Study

The Booz·Allen & Hamilton study mentioned in Chapter 1 states that "U.S. businesses could achieve an annual (office) productivity improvement of between 13% and 18% within five years. . . . Potential cumulative annual value in the United States alone amounts to $270 billion!"[1] That's a huge number. It is more than $1000 per year for every man, woman, and child in the United States! It is also more than the projected national budget deficits. Think of the effect of a savings, or an increase in business efficiency, of this size!

How did Booz·Allen & Hamilton reach their conclusion? The study covered office-based white collar workers. Looking at compensation and fringe benefit costs, the 1982 update to the study, using 1981 data, showed managers representing 37%, nonmanagerial professionals 42%, and clerical support 21% of office costs. Managers and professionals together are the "knowledge workers." They represent almost four-fifths of the salary costs of the office.

Despite the dominance of knowledge workers in the office cost picture, efforts to improve office productivity have concentrated thus far on clerical operations and the work flow. Much more attention needs to be directed at helping the knowledge workers and at improving their effectiveness. For most of this book, that will be our goal.

What do knowledge workers do? The Booz·Allen & Hamilton study covered

---

[1] *Business Week*, Mar. 21, 1983: 62

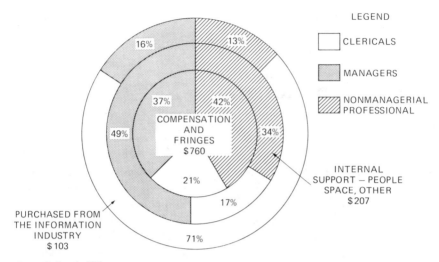

Note: Dollars In Billions.
Source: Booz, Allen estimates based on published sources for 1981.

Figure 2-1. In the United States alone, businesses spend over $1 trillion annually on their office-based white collar workers. Source: Booz·Allen & Hamilton Inc. estimates based on published sources for 1981. (Dollars in billions.)

this point too. Their findings show that a very minor fraction of time—about 8%—is spent on analysis, on using the little gray cells to solve a problem. Most, 40% to 60%, is spent in communication, either through meetings or by telephone. A large amount of time, 30% in the case of the professionals, is spent on activities described as "less productive." The results are shown in Figure 2-2.

Less Productive Activities

What are these "less productive" activities? Booz·Allen & Hamilton divides the category into three parts:

1. The totally unproductive.
2. The quasi-professional.
3. The activities that represent managers and professionals doing work at a clerical level.

Totally Unproductive. The totally unproductive time includes:

1. Travel time
   (a) To a meeeting outside the building or city. "On average, each hour

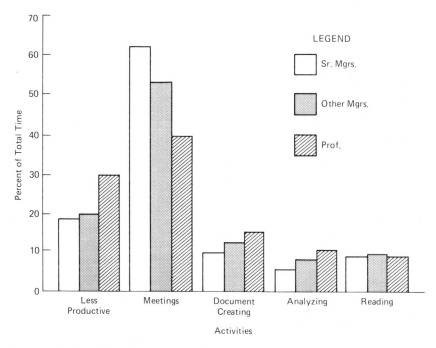

*Less productive activities include waiting/idle, organizing work, scheduling, seeking a person, seeking information, expediting, filing, copying, transcribing, and "other."
*Meetings includes listening, talking, discussing and observing.
*Document creating includes composing, dictating, editing and drawing/designing.
*Analyzing includes analyzing and calculating.
*Reading includes annotating/routing and reading.

Figure 2-2. Knowledge worker activity profile. Reprinted from the Special Advertising Section in the Mar. 21, 1982 issue of *Business Week* by special permission. © 1983 by McGraw-Hill, Inc., all rights reserved. Source: Booz·Allen & Hamilton Inc.

spent at an external site requires an additional 40 minutes of idle travel time." [2]

    (b) To another office or conference room within the building.
  2. Waiting time
    (a) For a meeting to start.
    (b) For someone to be off the telephone.
    (c) To reach someone on the telephone, playing telephone tag.
    (d) For a copy machine.

---

[2] Poppel, Harvey L. Who Needs the Office of the Future? *Harvard Business Review*, 60,6 (Nov.–Dec. 1982): 149.

(e) For a dictating machine or typewriter.
(f) For a computer terminal.

Quasi-professional.   This element includes:

1. Getting hold of information.
2. Expediting work.

These activities require some professional knowledge or judgment. This type of work can often be done by the paraprofessional who has been given an understanding of what the manager or professional needs to do. These functions also lend themselves to automation, particularly computer-assisted retrieval of information.

Clerical Activities.   This third element represents managers and professionals doing clerical work. Do you find this surprising? Examples are:

1. Filing documents.
2. Retrieving documents from the files.
3. Transcribing data from one document to another (e.g., from computer printouts to personal work sheets).
4. Typing a report because secretarial help is unavailable.
5. Making one's own reservations.
6. Making one's own appointments.

The reader can add to this list from his or her own experience.

The above "less productive" activities comprise about one-quarter of the knowledge worker's time. It is not practical to eliminate all of them from the manager's and professional's schedules, but it is quite possible to cut this wasted time in half. Some activities, such as waiting for meetings, should be eliminated altogether. This just takes planning and discipline. Travel time can be reduced. Other activities can be delegated to paraprofessionals or to the clerical support staff. Paraprofessionals and clerical support should be available in sufficient numbers and be trained well enough that they can handle the issues that are delegated.

The "less productive" activities represent 30% of the professional's time. Cutting this waste in half will not cut office costs by 15%; the number and cost of the support staff will probably rise. But savings of 10% or so of total office costs are quite possible just by reducing the less productive time of knowledge workers. This should be one of our goals.

Meetings

Refer back to Figure 2-2. Meetings, both face to face and by telephone, comprise between 40% and 60% of the knowledge worker's time. Who has not sat in a conference and thought it a waste of time? Some conferences and meetings should never be held. Others should be better organized. The list of attendees should be chosen carefully so that those who are not needed do not attend. The duration of a meeting should be as short as is necessary for the business at hand; a meeting should not continue merely because the conference room has been reserved until a certain hour.

Individual face-to-face meetings between two people are usually handled more efficiently than conferences. But when you set up a meeting with someone, does that person always know the subject of the meeting so that he or she can come prepared?

Telephone calls should stick to the information one wants to receive or impart. The social content need not be eliminated, but often it can be reduced. Telephone tag can be reduced considerably by message-handling techniques.

Improving all forms of meetings may provide the greatest potential for saving time. If meetings represent 40% of the time of professional knowledge workers, at least one-quarter of this 40% can be saved. This translates to 10% of the knowledge worker's time.

Creating Documents

Refer again to Figure 2-2. Document creation is a necessary part of analyzing an issue. As such, it is a proper part of that small 29% of the knowledge worker's time that represents intellectual activity. But have you ever had to write a report that you considered unnecessary? Not all documents created in the office are required!

Final reports on a study are important. Conclusions, and the arguments and data that underlie them, must be recorded. They may be required at a later date when you no longer remember all the facts. Or someone else may inherit your position and need to know what happened and why.

What about progress reports? The need for mandatory weekly activity reports should be looked at very carefully, especially if one is obliged to write something when there has been no significant accomplishment during the week. Most progress reports are better given orally to one's superior. Only on large projects of great interest to many people is there a reason for periodic written reports. Even here, they should be spaced so that significant change is likely to occur between report dates.

Better than periodic reports are milestone reports. These reports are written only when significant accomplishments happen or milestones are met. They could be a few weeks apart or several months, or even the better part of a year.

Being stingy with reports may cut out about a quarter of those being generated, saving another 4% of the knowledge worker's time.

The Savings of Time

Is the reader convinced that significant savings in time for the knowledge worker are possible? The author suggests that the following is quite practical:

1. Cut the less productive activities in half, and save 15% of work time.
2. Cut meeting and telephone time by one-quarter, and save 10% of work time.
3. Cut report preparation by one-quarter, and save 4% of work time.

This totals 29% of the working time of each knowledge worker!

The 29% savings in time translates directly to a 29% increase in knowledge worker productivity. It does not, however, translate to a 29% savings in office cost. For one thing, some of the time saving will be possible only because of additional paraprofessional and clerical support. Also there will be a cost involved to automate certain information functions. But the savings in office costs

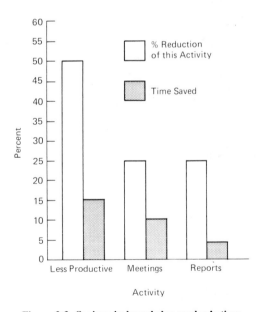

Figure 2-3. Savings in knowledge worker's time.

of 13% to 18% per knowledge worker estimated by Booz·Allen & Hamilton and quoted earlier in this chapter seems quite feasible.

What does this mean to business in terms of profits? Booz·Allen & Hamilton estimate a profit improvement (savings as a percent of operating income before taxes and dividends) of 10% to 50%, depending on the type of business. The amounts are shown in Figure 2–4.

FUNCTIONS OF THE OFFICE

What is an office? It is any location where business transactions take place. Decisions are made in the office. Information is acquired, analyzed, used, communicated, recorded, stored, and retrieved.

The administrative support functions of a business all take place in the office. These include the activities of the employee relations department, of purchasing, of finance, of engineering, of facilities, of the legal department, and of the executive function. Also such administrative support activities as the secretarial functions, mail, reprographics, word processing, records management, and communications take place in the office.

What is not part of the office? The production facilities, the warehouse, the shipping and receiving dock, and the sales floor in a service business or store are not. These are the areas where the principal goods and services of the business are produced, stored, and shipped. This gives a clue to the definition. The office handles the paperwork of the organization, in contrast to the areas that handle the organization's output of goods or services.

The distinction is not always clear. In an engineering company, the endless

INDUSTRY	GROSS SAVINGS/ KNOWLEDGE WORKER* ($000's)		LARGE BUSINESS GROSS SAVINGS*	AS A PERCENT OF OPERATING INCOME BEFORE TAXES AND DIVIDENDS
	GROSS	%		
Manufacturing	$8.2	13.1%	1.3%/ Net Sales	10%–15%
Finance	8.3	18.9	0.25%/ Total Assets	35%
Insurance	7.4	13.7	2.4%/ Premium	30%–50%
Federal Government	9.8	14.0	N.A.	N.A.

*Based solely on case study results, assumes 8% inflation.
**Based on various published Department of Commerce, Federal Reserve, A.M. Best and World Almanac Statistics.

Figure 2-4. Five-year savings potential by type of business. Reprinted from the Special Advertising Section in the March 21, 1983 issue of *Business Week* by special permission, (c) 1983 by McGraw-Hill, Inc., all rights reserved. Source: Booz·Allen & Hamilton Inc.

rows of drafting boards and the rows of desks or cubicles where engineers establish specifications are not considered to be part of an office. The engineering area is called the drafting room or engineering floor. This is the engineering company's main line of activity. This is the "production" of that company. The space occupied by the engineers is that company's equivalence to the manufacturing floor.

Actually, the office is not a location or a series of locations. It is an activity. It is anywhere that the office work or paperwork of the organization is handled. This can be in a room with four walls, the way we usually think of an office. It can be in a partitioned space or in a "bullpen." It can also be in a small area within the warehouse or next to the production floor.

Henceforth in this book we will not discuss the office as a place. We will discuss office activities or functions. It is these functions that the professional interacts with. It is to their improvement that each chapter is addressed.

POLICIES AND PROCEDURES

Office functions are built around policies and procedures, which are designed to simplify the office processes. They are essential to effective office performance.

Policies provide a standard decision to a recurring set of circumstances. There are policies about when you get paid, how many vacation days you get each year, how your performance is rated, how materials are bought, and so on. Based on these policies, the working staff makes decisions on routine actions without having to ask a member of management every time. The policies define the rules of the game. If you work within the policies, you are doing what the organization desires.

The procedures are the specific actions to be followed in implementing a policy. Procedures avoid the need to instruct people on how to perform a function every time the issue comes up.

A few examples will make the difference between policies and procedures clear. The statement "The Purchasing department is the only function permitted to commit the Company to the purchase of materials and equipment" is a policy. The statement "Fill out a Purchase Requisition, form number xxxx" is one step in the procedure that implements this policy. "Overtime requires the approval of a supervisor" is a policy. "To request overtime, submit form xxxx showing the following information . . ." is a procedure to implement that policy. "Hard hats will be worn in the construction area" is a safety policy. "Any employee not wearing a hard hat will be disciplined" is a procedure for enforcing that policy.

Policies and procedures are a vital part of making office systems efficient. They are a very powerful tool. Properly designed, understood, and used, they relieve the office managers of making routine decisions. They allow the managers to concentrate on the exceptional cases. They give managers the time to do the necessary planning and the other important parts of their jobs.

Because of this power, policies and procedures can be abused. Poorly written policies or, worse, those that do not really represent what higher management wants, promote inefficiency. If published policies are incorrect and are therefore ignored, this situation promotes a disregard for organizational discipline and will make improvement more difficult to achieve. Poorly designed procedures waste time. They also promote disrespect for the system of which they are a part.

Policies and procedures handle the routine of the office. They should never be considered as cast in concrete. Policies, by their nature, are more fixed than procedures. But if there is a good reason to make an exception, the issue should be raised with higher management. Procedures, also, can be altered for a good reason. Some procedural steps may not apply to the situation you are facing. The intelligent office professional ignores such inappropriate steps. This professional also keeps his or her manager aware of what has been done in case the action was improper. In later chapters we discuss improving work flow and office procedures.

ROLES OF MANAGERS, PROFESSIONALS, AND SUPPORT STAFF

Managers

The managers are, or should be, the leaders. It is important that the professional understand the role of his or her manager. The manager does not do the day-to-day work; the professionals and the support staff do that. The manager has a unique set of duties. These exceed what many professionals visualize as their boss's job.

The traditional functions of a manager are:

1. Planning: deciding what needs to be done and how it will be done.
2. Organizing: deciding who does what.
3. Staffing: hiring and maintaining a superior staff.
4. Directing: guiding the staff; giving orders.
5. Controlling: making sure that plans and actions are carried out.

That list is somewhat abstract. The following is a more specific breakdown of supervisory or managerial (we use the terms interchangeably) concerns.

1. Planning
   (a) What are the forthcoming workloads: tomorrow? next month? next year?

(b) What do we need in order to handle these workloads: number of people? skills of people? equipment? overtime? outside help?

(c) What is the purpose of our group: today? next year?

(d) What performance levels should we have: now? next month? next year? (and what does higher management expect of us?)

(e) What should we do to achieve or exceed the performance levels?

(f) How can we improve efficiency? effectiveness?

(g) What funding do we need (i.e., budget) this year? next year? long term?

(h) How do we justify additional funds, people, and equipment now? next year? long term?

2. Organizing

(a) What are the best procedures to accomplish each task or function?

(b) Who should be assigned the responsibility for repetitive tasks or functions?

(c) How should the work area be laid out to make the work flow easiest to handle?

(d) With what other groups or functions should work be coordinated? How?

3. Staffing

(a) How does one set job specifications? skill levels needed? experience levels needed?

(b) How does one interview applicants to find out who is good and who isn't?

(c) How does one select and hire the most appropriate person?

(d) What training does the staff need? does the supervisor need?

(e) How are individuals motivated to do their best?

(f) What staff performance characteristics should be rated? How? When?

(g) Who should get salary increases? How much? When?

(h) How can morale be improved?

4. Directing

(a) When are direct orders appropriate? How should they be phrased?

(b) When is a less direct form of guidance appropriate?

(c) How does one know when orders have been understood? accepted?

(d) How much counseling should be done? How?

(e) When are exceptions to procedures appropriate? to policies?

(f) What tasks take priority over other tasks?

(g) Who should be given an incoming task?

(h) When should each task be finished?

5. Controlling

(a) How do you stay aware of all activities in the group? in the department? in other functions that interact?

(b) How can group output be measured? individual output? accuracy?

(c) How do you read budget and cost reports?

(d) What actions can be taken to hold costs within budget? How soon? Who else is involved?

(e) What actions must be taken to meet other commitments?

(f) What actions by subordinates call for disciplinary measures?

(g) How can disciplinary action be taken in a positive way?

(h) What actions require you to consult your manager ahead of time? to consult staff in other departments?

(i) What conditions require immediate attention? can wait a few hours? can wait for days?

(j) What degree of freedom does a manager have? in what circumstances?

(k) Who should be informed when direction is given? discipline taken? problems arise?

(l) When should information be in writing? be verbal? interrupt someone?

(m) What performance measures should be shown regularly to your manager? in what form? how often?

These are the specific issues that a manager or supervisor faces daily. It is the job of the manager to handle them promptly and correctly.

Professionals

For the purpose of distinguishing roles, we restrict the term professional to the person without managerial responsibilities as described above. The professional may direct a technician, aide, or junior professional in performing a mutual task, but the remaining functions of the manager are not part of the professional's job.

The professional is a specialist in some discipline. Years of special education and experience give this person the expert knowledge and skills needed to perform a task or set of tasks in his or her area of specialty. Each professional is a specialist in some aspect of a field, the breadth of this specialty depending on the person's ability and the nature of the subject area. The organization relies on each professional's combination of skills and knowledge to provide the expertise necessary for the jobs to be done.

Professionals are the backbone of an engineering or research organization. They perform analyses, determine specifications, and recommend solutions for a variety of technical problems. Other professionals form the backbone of the office support groups. Their specialties may be accounting, marketing, law, employee relations, purchasing, education, or business administration. They perform the support tasks that require specialized knowledge or analytical skill. The knowledge, ability, and advice provided by professionals determine the worth of many decisions that managers make.

Professionals, often more than managers, interact directly with the office systems. They write the first drafts of reports and have them typed, revised, duplicated, and sent to others through the company mail. They request materials, equipment, and outside services. They fill out time sheets. Managers interact with the support staff primarily through their secretaries or their professional aides. Thus the professional often is more aware of and more frustrated by inefficiencies in the office systems than the manager.

This book is written primarily for those who are now professionals or were professionals before becoming managers. You know what you and your colleagues do. Therefore we will not dwell further on this role.

Support Staff

The support staff is an essential part of the organization, one whose abilities usually are not utilized to the fullest extent. To a large degree, improving office productivity and the speed with which an action is completed depends on better use of the abilities of the support staff.

The key member of the support staff is the secretary to the group or the manager. Increasingly, the secretary's role is that of operating an information center, rather than just using a typewriter and a telephone. The secretary's role is evolving toward that of a general assistant to the manager and to the professionals.

The secretary should be the first person you see to find out how to do something in an organization, or to find out whom to see to get a decision made. Traditionally, this knowledge resided with the manager. As managers became busier and less accessible, this became part of the role of an "assistant to" or administrative aide. As technology makes the handling of correspondence and telephones less time-consuming, the jobs of the secretary and administrative aide are merging into one. In many organizations this has already happened.

The good secretary is a paraprofessional, a person who relieves the manager and professional of much of the quasi-professional and clerical activities that Booz·Allen & Hamilton identified.

The remaining office support staff come in all varieties. There are clerk-typists, accounting clerks, employee relations clerks, legal clerks, filing clerks, computer input clerks, and operators of special machines including word processors, reproduction machines, telephones, and many others. Often they are not called "clerks" or "operators" but by some other title such as "specialist." Such titles are meant to suggest more dignity and responsibility, but the dignity and responsibility are not always given.

These support jobs will acquire more status and become more efficient as the human beings who fill them are given the respect they deserve. They can be helpful if given the opportunity. This is the key to improving professional and managerial efficiency and thereby the productivity of the office functions.

The new, fancy titles may turn out to be quite appropriate if we learn to structure the office support functions correctly and use the talents of the existing support staff.

THE OFFICE-LESS PROFESSIONAL

What of the engineer, sales representative, or shop foreman who does not work in an office? What does this book provide for that person?

Some professionals may not have "an office" in the physical sense, but all perform office functions. It is these functions, not the walled space, with which we are concerned. Paperwork flows from and to all professionals in an endless stream.

The person whose work place is away from the traditional office area is often more frustrated than the professional who sits within the office building. Both distance and infrequent personal contact makes it harder for this person to get explanations and have his or her needs understood and taken care of.

Knowing the roles of each office function and how to work with each will solve a lot of this office-less professional's frustration. Unfortunately, these facts of life are rarely explained. One is supposed to learn by asking questions, or by experience. This works only if you know what questions to ask, and if your experiences are successful. It does not work when the experiences are universally bad. We cannot provide the experience, but we do provide the questions.

ADMINISTRATIVE FUNCTIONS

Here are the office departments or functions that the professional interacts with frequently.

There is, first, the department in which you, the professional, reside. It does not matter if this is an administrative department or an engineering group or a sales department. You must know how to handle the administrative routine of your department.

Then there are the departments that you must use to get your job done. These departments can help you in the following matters:

1. Accounting
   (a) To establish and understand budgets.
   (b) To read and understand cost reports.
   (c) To find your missing paycheck.
   (d) To find out if a vendor has been paid.
   (e) To estimate future costs on your project.
   (f) To learn what all the paycheck deductions are for.
   (g) To check time sheets.
   (h) To examine property records.

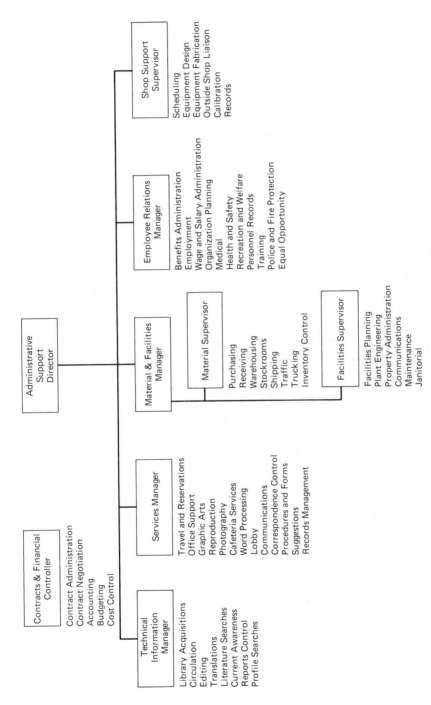

Figure 2-5. Typical functional organization chart.

2. Data processing
    (a) To read and understand production, sales, and inventory reports.
    (b) To learn how to input data to the main computer.
    (c) To learn how to program or use your own computer.
    (d) To request special analyses of the data you work with.
    (e) To prepare a ''model'' of the routines used frequently in your job so you can ask the computer ''what if'' questions.
3. Purchasing
    (a) To buy the materials you need less expensively and with assured quality and delivery schedule.
    (b) To receive, inspect, and deliver the material.
    (c) To handle the paperwork so that the supplier is paid.
    (d) To have the common supplies you need in a stockroom nearby.
4. Facilities
    (a) To lay out an area for improved work flow.
    (b) To modify utilities.
    (c) To tear down or install walls.
    (d) To move partitions, desks, and terminals.
    (e) To maintain equipment in good condition.
    (f) To fix the air conditioning.
    (g) To change your office location.
    (h) To change your telephone's features.
    (i) To change your furniture.
    (j) To fix broken items and change burned-out lights.
    (k) To clean the rooms and empty the ash trays.
5. Employee relations
    (a) To place advertisements for staff.
    (b) To screen applicants.
    (c) To conduct salary surveys.
    (d) To keep personnel records.
    (e) To advise on salary increases and performance measures.
    (f) To advise on issues involving unions and legal regulations.
    (g) To conduct training.
    (h) To provide medical support.
    (i) To explain employee benefit plans such as medical insurance, sick leave, vacation policy, etc.
6. Office support
    (a) To prepare documents through word processing.
    (b) To draw charts for briefings.
    (c) To copy documents.
    (d) To operate a central document file on film or tape to assure good indexing and fast retrieval.
    (e) To make airline and hotel reservations.

(f) To send and receive electronic messages and regular mail.

(g) To operate vending and food services.

(h) To take messages when you are out or tied up.

These are the office functions with which you interact. In the remaining chapters we will describe how to do so in a way that increases your productivity and reduces your frustration level.

SUMMARY

A classic study by Booz·Allen & Hamilton suggests that U.S. businesses can achieve a productivity improvement of between 13% and 18% by improving the productivity of office workers. Almost 80% of office costs represent managers and professionals, the knowledge workers. The study found that knowledge workers spend only 8% of their time on analysis. Thirty percent is spent on "less productive" activities, 40% to 50% on meetings, and 15% in creating documents.

The less productive category includes time spent in travel and waiting, looking for information or expediting work, and filing, retrieving, and copying data. We suggest that the amount of time spent on these activities can be cut in half. We also suggest that time spent in meetings can be cut by one-quarter, as can the document preparation time. This would make an additional 29% of the knowledge worker's time available for productive activities.

The office is not a physical space; it is an activity. It is the origination, handling, analysis, and use of the paperwork that supports a business and is performed anywhere that these pursuits take place. Office functions are built around policies and procedures. Policies provide a standard decision to a recurring set of circumstances. Procedures are the specific actions to be followed when implementing a policy.

Managers plan, organize, staff, direct, and control. This chapter lists specific issues in each of these categories that the manager faces daily. Professionals perform specialized tasks to accomplish the work of the organization. The support staff assist, and can assist a lot more than they usually do. A key member of the support staff is the department secretary. Much improvement in office productivity will come from using paraprofessionals for most of the "less productive" work.

This chapter closes with a list of the administrative support functions—office functions—with which the professional comes in frequent contact. The more common matters that require such contact are listed.

FOR FURTHER INFORMATION

Productivity Improvement

Information Technology Management, special advertising supplement in *Business Week,* Mar. 21, 1983.

Poppel, Harvey L. Who Needs the Office of the Future? *Harvard Business Review,* 60,6 (Nov.–Dec. 1982). 146–155.

Paraprofessionals

Murphy, Elizabeth R. *The Assistant: New Tasks, New Opportunities.* New York: AMACOM, 1982.

Office Functions

Keeling, B. Lewis, Kallaus, Norman F., and Neuer, John J. W. *Administrative Office Management,* 7th ed. Cincinnati: South-Western Publ., 1978.

Quible, Zane K. *Administrative Office Management: An Introduction,* 3rd ed. Reston, VA: Reston Publ. Co., 1984.

3
Planning for Change

"If only I were in charge of this crazy operation, I'd straighten out this mess in fifteen minutes!"

Have you ever said this? Or heard a colleague say it? We all know ways to improve the operation we're a part of, or to improve someone else's operation that we deal with frequently. It seems so easy. But is it? What should you do to initiate change—a change for the better?

In this chapter we examine how to plan and justify a significant change. By significant, we mean a change that will alter policies or procedures, work flow, or an individual's job content. The principles apply to changes affecting any of these.

You, the reader, will be in one of three situations:

1. You are in charge of a group or function in which you want to make a change.
2. You are a member of a task force or an advisory group looking at a function that is a candidate for change.
3. You are an individual with ideas on what needs to be done, but without official sanction to investigate or initiate change.

If you are in the first situation, you are in a position to follow the steps outlined below without further delay. If you are part of a task force, you should persuade the group to follow the guidelines we will outline. If you are an individual with ideas but no official status, this chapter provides concepts you can use to sell management on the idea of improving an ineffective operation.

KNOW THE PRESENT SYSTEM

Before making any type of change, know the present system! This is rule number one. It is absolutely imperative. Don't *think* that you know how things are being done now. Don't take someone else's word for where the problem lies. Don't even accept published procedures as being correct. Find out for yourself how the function operates. Be sure that you thoroughly understand the present operation.

It is essential that you know the following information:

1. The philosophy of the operation.
2. The policies under which it operates.
3. The procedures being followed.
4. The responsibilities of the people involved.
5. The flow of work within the operation.
6. The forms that are in use.
7. The reports that are generated.

We discuss each of these items in turn.

Philosophy of the Operation

This may seem to be a strange subject with which to start. It may even seem strange to bring it up at all in a pragmatic book. Yet it is very important.

All companies have a philosophy or style of operation. It is generally not stated anywhere in writing. Yet, after you have been in the organization for three to six months, you know what that philosophy is.

- Some companies are very tightly controlled from the top. Decisions are made by top-level executives, and little authority is delegated.
- Some companies operate strictly "by the book." All levels of management follow the written policies and procedures. Getting changes made is like getting a law passed in the Congress.
- Some companies encourage employee ideas and pay attention to the employees' input. They may use the quality circle concept, or a less formal method. Good ideas are considered and acted on.
- Some companies are authoritarian. One person dominates, often the founder of the company. Nothing happens without this person's blessing. Anything is possible if you can get his or her ear.
- Some companies are very open. The president knows many of the workers by their first names and sees them often. Informal get-togethers are frequent. There is a real "open door" to the president's and vice-presidents' offices.

The way in which you go about initiating change is different depending on which philosophy applies in your organization.

1. If you are in charge of the function you wish to change, the company's philosophy of operation has minimal effect. Follow the steps that we describe below. But be sure you keep your manager informed of what you are doing and how you are going about it. If you do profane one of the organization's

sacred cows, your manager can advise an alternate approach or, perhaps, agree to join you in battle with higher management.

2. If a study group or task force has been formed and you are on it, the philosophy affects the group's approach. If you are in a tightly controlled or authoritarian company, you aim your study at the person or persons who make the decisions. You must tailor the approach you present and the examples you use to the particular interests of these key people. Issues that are important and top priority to them become the key issues for the task force. If you are a "by the book" company, it is helpful to have a member of the systems and procedures group on the task force. If you are lucky enough to be in a company open to ideas, you can follow the concepts below with little concern about the politics of the situation.

3. If you are in the third of the work situations specified—an individual with concerns and ideas—the company philosophy has the greatest impact. Your approach must differ depending on which type of company you are in:

(a) In companies with tight control, you must work through your line management, convincing your superior that change is needed and persuading that individual to convince his or her superior, etc., up to the level where decisions are made.

(b) In companies that go "by the book," your objective must include getting the "book" changed. This is one step harder than convincing somebody high up in management that change is needed. Policy and procedure manuals seem to have a life of their own. By-the-book companies usually have systems and procedures groups that write and maintain the policy and procedure manuals. Besides convincing management to open up the subject, you must get to a person in this systems function and persuade him or her that your concept is valid.

(c) In companies that are open to suggestions, you have an easier time. If there are quality circles, try to become a member of one that is looking into the area of your concern. Otherwise work through your supervisor or manager to have the company initiate a task force with you on it.

(d) In an authoritarian company, find out who makes the decisions. Next find out who has the decision maker's ear. If you know one or more of the people close to the key person, work through them. If you do not, find out who influences one of this secondary group of people. Work through one of them.

(e) Finally, in companies with a true open door, take advantage of it. If your ideas are worthwhile, you will be heard.

These differences in approach are the reason why you need to consider the company's philosophy or style of management.

In each case, your intent is to be appointed to a task force or study group.

Once on it, you are in a position to improve the operation. Your next step is to examine the remaining six subjects on the "need to know" list.

Policies of the Operation

Find out what policy statements govern the operation you wish to see changed. Check the company policy manuals for everything that involves the operation you are studying. In larger firms, some administrative departments such as employee relations, purchasing, and facilities may also have departmental policy and procedure manuals. Get them.

These policy statements are the rules under which the operation is functioning.

1. Do you see a problem with the rules? Is there a policy you will want to change? It is more difficult to change a policy than to change a procedure. Policy change may require consideration at a higher level of management. It may also affect other departmental policies and procedures.
2. Is the problem in the manner in which these rules are being implemented? That is, is it in the procedures?

Procedures Being Followed

Get copies of all pertinent procedures from the company manuals and any departmental manuals. Informal procedure statements may also exist, written by the supervisor or by some of the staff themselves. Such informal procedures are sometimes prepared as a help in training new employees, or to assist temporary-help-agency people, or simply as a self-help tool for the employees themselves. Obtain copies of all of them.

Talk to the individuals doing the jobs. Ask them what they do and how they go about it. If you're looking at purchasing, ask the buyer the steps he or she goes through in placing an order. Go into as much detail as the procedure does. Don't assume anything. Be as ignorant as an extraterrestial. Keep probing until you can answer all these questions:

1. What is the sequence of steps?
2. Who does each step?
3. How is each done?
4. What information is needed for each step?
5. What forms are used?
6. What documentation is made?

Check what you learn from the interviews against the procedure manual. Don't be surprised if the actual procedure sequence differs from what the manual describes. Procedures are written carefully when an operation is first established. When the employees have learned the procedures, the manuals frequently are forgotten, and are not updated as events cause procedures to change.

There is nothing wrong with having obsolete procedures in a manual as long as everyone knows that they are obsolete. To change a formal procedure manual every time a minor change is made would be a waste of time and paper. But a procedure manual should not be allowed to lie fallow for long. At some point it should be brought up to date or else be laid to rest.

The worst sin is to have a set of procedures that management and the heads of other functions believe are being followed, but which no longer represent the way the operation functions. This can be a source of misunderstanding about what is being done, and of confusion about who is responsible for an activity. If you find this situation, look into it carefully. It may be the source of the inefficiency you wish to change.

Responsibilities of Individuals

Find out who is responsible for each part of the operation. Next to each step in the procedure put the name or the job title of the person who performs it. The buyer places an order; the secretary records and files it; the expediter follows up at a preset time; and so on. Answer these questions:

1. Is every step covered by somebody?
2. Is there a gap?
3. Is there double coverage? As on a baseball team, each person has an area to cover, and all parts of the field must be covered by someone. When no one goes after the ball, inefficiency results. If two people go after the ball, someone must decide who makes the play. This person's authority to make the decision must be agreed on in advance. You know what happens otherwise.
4. What are the limits on each person's authority? There are usually dollar limits. Mr. A can sign for items of value up to $10,000, Ms. B up to $1,000, Mr. C only to $100, etc.
5. Are the signature limits consistent with the responsibilities of people's jobs?
6. Who can set priorities when several important jobs are stacked up waiting?
7. Who can make an exception to the function's policies and procedures?
8. What happens if the people listed in (6) and (7) above are absent? Lack of contingency plans for the absence of key players is a frequent problem.
9. Have people been made specialists in one segment of the job? Does one buyer handle only electronic parts, another office supplies, and a third forgings and castings? Does one staff member in employee relations do

only applicant interviewing, and another handle salary matters? Sometimes this specialization improves efficiency because an individual becomes a true expert in a limited field. But it can be overdone. It leads to inefficiency if more than one person must be involved to complete a single action, e.g., to purchase an electromechanical system or to negotiate special employment terms with an applicant.

Flow of Work

The initial question under "Procedures" was: What is the sequence of steps? The field of work flow analysis is one of the oldest parts of industrial engineering. If a work flow chart exists, get it. You may want to draw one (techniques are described in a later chapter), but usually this is not necessary. Few operations are so complicated that a list of the steps won't suffice. Consider these questions:

1. Is the work flow balanced? Does each person in the chain of activity have about the same quantity of work? If not, the person with the most work or longest segment of the task will be a bottleneck. This problem is easily solved by redistributing the work.
2. Where, physically and geographically, is each step performed? If paperwork can simply be handed to the next person or placed at the next work station, the work sequence will be fast. If the paperwork must move by company mail or courier from one step to the next, the sequence will be slow.
3. How does the paperwork get from one location to the next? Within the work room, does paperwork go from desk to adjacent desk, or are people walking across the room and down the hall each time they retrieve, type, review, sign, copy, or file a piece of paper? The latter pattern slows down an operation.

Forms in Use

Forms serve a valuable purpose. A properly designed form assures that all the necessary information is at hand when an action is taken. Use of forms also makes the job easier for the person who has to take the action. A particular item of information is always at the same location on a form. This makes it easy and fast to find the item. Do you need a telephone extension number? Or the name of the requester? You know exactly where to look to find these items.

A well-designed form also lists information in the sequence in which it will be needed. This keeps your eyes from jumping all around the form. It speeds up the action.

Some forms are so poorly designed that they negate the promised efficiency. Some do not have spaces for information essential to the action. Others contain spaces for unnecessary information. Many have spaces so small that the necessary words do not fit. The latter type encourages users to make their handwriting so small that it is illegible, or to provide inadequate descriptions.

Forms are important in repetitive operations. Examples include purchasing, maintenance requests, repair orders, time cards, salary reviews, and changes of address. In each action, the individual data are different, but the operation being performed with these data is the same, or close to being the same. The buyer goes through the same steps regardless of what is bought. Time cards are processed in the same way regardless of whose cards they are. Forms simplify these operations. Forms should not be used for one-of-a-kind situations. Answer these questions:

1. Are forms are being used where they should be, and only where they should be?
2. Is the necessary information requested, and only the necessary information?
3. Are the forms well designed, easy to read and to use?

Adequacy of Equipment

Examples of supporting equipment include typewriters, copy machines, word processing equipment, facsimile equipment, data processing equipment and terminals for access to it, microfilm reader-printers, and telephones. Having appropriate equipment that is reliable improves efficiency; poor equipment can detract from productivity. Other equipment problems that could cause inefficiency are inadequate or awkward file cabinets, poor desk design, and poor chair design. We discuss ergonomics in a later chapter.

Find out what equipment supports the staff of the function.

1. Is it the proper equipment for the job?
2. Is there enough of it?
3. Is it in good repair?
4. Does the staff know how to use it?

Deciding if equipment is proper for the job can turn into a big task by itself. Before devoting a lot of time to this, decide if the particular item of equipment is really crucial to the job. A typewriter, for example, is extremely important to the secretary or to the clerk who spends much of the day typing. A manual typewriter would decrease a secretary's efficiency enormously. An electric typewriter without a correcting key and ribbon also reduces efficiency significantly. But using an old-fashioned typewriter makes little difference to the professional who does hunt-and-peck on the keyboard for an hour or so a month or to a clerk who uses it only to type address labels. Techniques are presented later in this chapter for determining if the cost of a piece of new equipment is justified in terms of time and salary saved.

Other factors to consider that can significantly affect office productivity are lighting and noise levels.

Adequate Size and Quality of Staff

These two subjects are discussed together because they are interrelated. You need fewer excellent people to do a job than you need mediocre people.

1. Can the existing staff handle the work load now?
2. After changes have been made in procedures and responsibilities:
   (a) Will the existing staff be able to handle the new system? Or will the function need more people? less people?
   (b) Will it need a different mix of skills?
   (c) Will it need a different level of competence?

The answers cannot be finalized until you (or the task force) have determined your recommendations for changes. But as you discuss changes, bear in mind the effects of your findings on the number, abilities, and skills of the present staff, and what the recommendations will mean to the people.

Reports Generated

Get all the reports that are generated about the operation.

1. What reports show the status of the operation?
2. Are there productivity statistics? Examples are: number of purchase orders processed per buyer, number of applicants interviewed.
3. Are there monthly narrative reports to management?

Statistics can be dangerous. A large number of purchase orders per buyer may mean an efficient buyer. It may also mean a sloppy buyer or an overworked one who has given less thought and analysis to each purchase than it needed. A high rate of interviewing may show an efficient interviewing technique. It may also mean inadequate interviews or inadequate screening of people invited to be interviewed. There are often two explanations of a statistic. Do not accept a large number as an indication of efficiency. Dig deeper.

Summarizing the Findings

If the existing operation is complex, write yourself a report on how it operates now. When you make a change, it is always useful to know exactly what the prior condition was. Reference the existing policies and procedures. Note all deviations from them that you have found. Note who is responsible for every step. Diagram the work flow if it is complicated; otherwise describe it in words. Diagram the work area layout if you consider it to be inefficient.

If you followed the approach suggested above, you asked yourself a series of questions as you went along. Are the problems with the operation you are examining due to:

1. Obsolete or inappropriate policies?
2. Actual practice differing from written procedures?
3. Conflicting responsibilities?
4. Failure to assign responsibilities?
5. Inadequate authority given to those people who are responsible?
6. Lack of contingency planning for the absence of key people?
7. Lack of staff specialization?
8. Overspecialization, with several people being needed to reach a decision?
9. Poor work flow?
10. Poor work area layout?
11. Poorly designed forms?
12. Lack of forms where they are useful?
13. Use of forms where they are not appropriate?
14. Improper equipment?
15. Lack of training on the equipment?
16. Not enough personnel?
17. Inadequate mix of skills?

When you have finished learning how the present system works, you will have reached some conclusions about where at least a few of the problems lie.

CHANGE WITHIN ONE DEPARTMENT

Once you know what *is* being done, the next step is to determine what *should* be done.

The approach should vary, depending on whether you are planning to change the operation of one department or function only, or are looking at the entire office operation. The former is simpler. We will describe the technique for this first.

Throughout this section we use "you" to represent the person or group planning the change. The "you" may be you, the reader, acting alone. It may also represent a task force of many people acting together. This is done to avoid using the phrase "you or the task force" each time we refer to the change agent.

Determining Objectives

The temptation is to jump directly into the procedures and the work flow and correct the obvious inefficiencies that you have found. Hold off. There is one step ahead of that. Determine the objective or objectives of the operation you are studying. Get agreement on these objectives from both those who run the operation and those who use it.

This is not as easy as it sounds. Let us take purchasing as an example. Is the primary objective to buy the desired quantity and quality at the lowest price? Or is it to buy for earliest delivery at a reasonable price? Or to obtain delivery as fast as possible regardless of price? Time and price are often trade-offs. When is each the more important factor?

Take another example. In the office services function, people type, duplicate, and distribute paperwork. This paperwork may be letters, memos, invoices, receipts, orders, confirmations, specifications, reports, or whatever else is important to your business. Processing paper takes time. Also paperwork never arrives in an even flow. There is a lot of it at some times, and little of it at other times. Companies staff and equip their secretarial or word processing function, their duplicating function, and their mail function to handle average work loads or loads slightly above average. Therefore at peak times there can be lengthy backlogs. How important is time? Is the objective of the office services function to minimize clerical costs or to reduce the processing time for orders, correspondence, and so on?

What is the objective of the function you want to change? Until this is clearly defined, you cannot establish proper policies and procedures.

New Policies, Procedures, Responsibilities

Policies, procedures, and responsibilities are discussed as a single issue because they are interrelated. Assigning a responsibility to someone depends on the procedure. The procedure depends on the policy. But the procedure also depends on the availability of time of people who have certain skills and on the availability of whatever equipment is required. The costs of implementing a new policy or procedure and of operating under the new system must also be considered.

Policies. Review the policies first:

1. Do they fit the objectives agreed upon?
2. Are they appropriate to the mission of the function?
3. Do you agree with them?

If you give a negative reply to any of these questions, this is the place to start. Draft revised policies that will yield a "yes" answer to these questions. Discuss the draft with both the users of the function and the supervisor(s) of the function. Reach a consensus on the revised policy statement.

The consensus is important. If there is disagreement on a policy issue between the function's supervisor(s) and its users, no constructive action can be taken until it is resolved. The issue will have to be taken to a higher level of management for a decision.

Procedures.   Assuming the policy question is resolved, look next at the procedures. Use the data from your study of the existing system and the questions we listed earlier in this chapter to spot the problem areas.

The importance of having written procedures increases with the size of the company and the size of the function. It is unnecessary and expensive to write procedures for a small firm with an office function of less than a dozen people. In the small operation, the paperwork is not extensive. Each person can be told what to do, and there is not a great deal to learn. One person can keep track of where everything stands. You need a routine, but you do not need a written procedure manual. The larger the organization, however, the more important it is to have the procedures and responsibilities spelled out in detail.

Development of an effective procedure is largely a matter of common sense and experience. There is no magic formula. You can do elaborate work flow measurements and time studies. A whole branch of industrial engineering is devoted to just this, and we will discuss the formal techniques in a later chapter. But only in the most complex office functions are work flow measurement and time studies necessary. In 99% of the cases, an equally good set of procedures and work flow can be developed by brainstorming with the people who are closest to the work being done.

The principles for good procedures are these:

1. They are in writing and are easily accessible to those who use them or are affected by their use.
2. They are written in simple English, are clear, and are not ambiguous.
3. They are comprehensive. No steps have been omitted.
4. The steps themselves are simple, and the responsibility for each is specified.
5. There is no duplication of authority at any point.
6. The number of steps required is minimized.
7. The number of approvals required is minimized.
8. The means for obtaining exceptions to the procedures or to the underlying policies is specified.

Procedures are established using the knowledge and experience of those people who are closest to the operation. Use the principles presented above. When you have prepared a draft of the revised procedure, check it against the questions listed in the section "Know the Present System."

No two organizations will do a job in exactly the same way. There is nothing wrong with this. One procedure is not necessarily better than the other. Conditions are different. People are different. And minor changes of one or two percent in efficiency are not what we seek here. We are looking for the significant changes that result in a 10% improvement or more. Nearly all organizations can achieve this, even those that consider themselves well run.

Examples. Here are two examples from the author's experience.

A purchasing group consisted of three buyers and three support staff. They were receiving many complaints about the length of time it took to place orders and the lack of follow-up on delivery times for orders already placed. The objectives and policies of this purchasing group were acceptable. The problem lay with the working procedures and the assignments of responsibilities.

I asked the group members if they would spend their lunch hour for several days reviewing existing procedures to come up with better ways to do their work. They agreed, and the company catered a lunch for us each day during that time. We started by listing what was happening step by step. Step one was receipt by the purchasing department's secretary of a requisition in the incoming company mail. I asked: Who does what to it? This gave us step two: The secretary logged in the requisition on an 8½ × 11 tablet she kept on her desk. Question: What data were entered in this "log"? Et cetera. I took notes.

When everyone agreed on how the requisition was logged in, sent to a buyer, researched, and placed, we took this segment of the job and asked: How can this be improved? Ideas were requested from everyone, the clerks as well as the buyers. A special effort was made to elicit the ideas of those who sat silently. We changed the data listed on the incoming log to make this log useful for later follow-up. We designed a form for the log. We set standards for the length of time desired from receipt of the requisition to log in, and from log in to placing the requisition on the buyer's desk. We made it mandatory to notify the requisitioner that the order had been placed. Thus we proceeded step by step.

The process took seven lunch periods spread over three weeks. Individual responsibilities were discussed, agreed to, and recorded. From the notes, I drafted an operating procedure for the department and had each person review it. We modified the draft in a group meeting. When we all agreed to it, it was published within the department.

The result? Processing time was shortened. Users of the function were kept better informed. Complaints were reduced significantly.

Example two: The employee relations function consisted of one supervisor and two support staff. When the company was very small, this group built a reputation of being responsive to everyone's requests. There were no formal procedures. The function operated at the direction of the president or vice-president and in the manner that either of them specified at the time. These two officers were very happy with the way the operation worked.

As the company grew, the responsiveness that had pleased management deteriorated. Several important actions were forgotten and not done. The supervisor, who gave the support staff instructions on almost every move, was overworked. The sheer number of details became overwhelming. Very few forms were used. Most actions were documented by memos placed in the files, which took a lot of the supervisor's time.

The supervisor and I spent an hour a day for a month going through each of the activities for which employee relations was responsible. We combined our ideas and experience and wrote departmental procedures. The method was the same as described for the purchasing function. We went through each activity step by step. We designed forms for a dozen or so frequent actions such as salary changes and address changes, and a requisition for hiring staff. The responsibilities of each of the two support staff members were defined. Performance standards were established for accuracy and timeliness.

The procedures, forms, and assignment of responsibility thus derived may not have been the best possible, but they were much better than what had existed.

Maintaining Procedures.   Procedures must be reviewed as conditions change. Growth of the organization is one such change. As soon as one person can no longer know the status of all activities and control the paper flow, simple procedures and a broad delegation of authority become necessary. With further growth, authority must be delegated more narrowly to more people, and responsibilities must be more clearly defined.

There are other changes that require a review of existing procedures. The company starts to do business with the government and a host of new regulations and paperwork requirements result. The company enters a new field, with customers and suppliers who are used to working in a different way, and it must adapt to their customs. Federal or state regulations impose new rules on the way the company may operate and require reports on compliance with these rules. It must change its operations to accommodate the rules and reports.

When the company contracts in size, existing procedures may be too complex for what becomes a simpler operation. Personal control may again be possible. The procedures should retrace the path they took as the organization grew. They, too, should shrink. There should be less complexity. With fewer people involved, the degree of specialization should diminish. With less activity, the manager to whom the operation reports will be closer to the actions and the problems. Thus fewer reports to management should be needed. This is probably the hardest lesson to implement, but it is also one of the more important. Complex procedures add to the overhead cost. Maintaining them when they are no longer needed can kill a company.

Enforcement. Procedures must be enforced. As people move into a department from some other part of the company or from another company, they often bring with them the methods they have been using. With their varied experiences, they may bring many incompatible methods. The organization needs *one* way to perform each function. As each new person joins the group, he or she must be made to follow the procedure that everyone else is using.

Responsibilities. An important principle for improving the efficiency of a single function is to delegate to the support staff as much responsibility as each person is willing and able to accept. Of these two words, the word "willing" is the more important. If willing, the support staff person can be trained to handle more demanding jobs, and responsibility can be added a little at a time. In the purchasing example given above, a clerk moved from being a clerk to the position of expediter. She later became a buyer.

When you establish job responsibilities, you are depending on the ability of each incumbent. In the example above, the clerk was able to assume progressively more of an expediter's job because she had the intelligence and the desire to do so. When a person leaves and is replaced, do not assume that the new person will fit smoothly into the shoes of the one who left. The replacement may not have the same ambition, or the same experience and talent, although he or she will have other abilities that can be utilized.

When the staff changes, the supervisor should look at the job assignments and see if a different mix of responsibilities would improve the effectiveness of the operation. If this is not done, after several staff changes the assigned responsibilities may no longer match the talents of the existing staff. In preparing the procedures, keep in mind that the responsibilities assigned must match the abilities of each staff person, and that both the abilities and the people will change with time.

Flow of Work

Determining the sequence of steps is part of establishing the procedures. But what of the other three aspects of work flow: the balance of work load among the staff, the physical layout of the operation, and the way the paperwork is transported from one work station to the next?

Work Load Balance. An expert can look at a procedure and at the number of steps assigned to each person and know immediately where the bottlenecks will be and whose work load will be too light. Most of us cannot do this. The present supervisor of the function, however, should have a pretty good feel for how much time it takes to perform any one step. The first approach to balancing the work load in a revised procedure is to have the supervisor review it from this point of view.

If there is an engineer on the task force familiar with work measurement techniques, the engineer may want to use time standards as an aid to balancing the work load. This will be very helpful if the process does not take too long. The author, however, is not an advocate of using this technique in the office. The accuracy attainable, considering the variation in work habits among different people, is not much better than the educated estimate of the present supervisor. Further, the implication that all staff members are like measureable, passive machines will negate the motivation and creativity that each person possesses.

When the assignments of the procedure steps to each person have been reviewed and revised to make the work load as even as you think possible, do not try to refine it further. Wait until the procedures are put into effect. After a reasonable shakedown period, take another look at work loads. There is nothing in the rules that says you can't revise a procedure once you see it in operation.

Layout and Work Transport.   Ideally the entire function is housed in one room or work area. This avoids the need for couriers or the company mail to handle work while it is still within the department. This consolidation of work area is sufficiently important that the expense of moving people and even removing walls can be justified. Productivity is enhanced and time saved by eliminating transportation steps. The function should also be located as close as possible to its users. It should also be close to any functions in the paper chain that either precede or follow it.

If the function is well laid out, each subsequent step in performing a job can be initiated by placing the paperwork in the in-basket at the neighboring desk. Next best is to get up and walk a few paces to the in-basket at the next work station. If possible, the room layout should allow work to flow from one end of the room to the other, or else around the room in a circle. Avoid layouts that require people to crisscross a room both to get work and to pass it on.

In some functions a backlog of incoming and outgoing work is inherent in the operation. These functions require ways to stack the work. A copying center is an example.

To make the input–output methods effective, look at available office equipment as well as layout techniques. The least effective method is to stack all incoming work in one huge pile and take the jobs from the top or bottom of the pile. It is better to use a rack with a series of horizontal slots, each of which can hold one job. If jobs are handled on a first-in, first-out basis, the work is inserted at one end of the rack and removed sequentially from the other. Pigeonholes in a wall are good, especially for output, where each slot can be labeled with the name of a department or location.

Other means include using one of more trays or racks, each representing the type of equipment the job will run on. In the copying center, for example, blueprint work would go to one rack, photocopy work to another, printing to a third, cutting and binding to a fourth, and so on. There are many alternatives, but just one concept should be selected and used.

When transportation of the work is necessary, decide between use of the company mail and using one of the staff as a courier. The decision involves a trade-off between cost and speed.

Forms

When writing the procedures, determine where new forms are needed, where existing forms need to be changed, and where existing forms should be eliminated.

If there are specialists in forms design at your company, use them. There is more to this subject than you may think. We listed some of the attributes of a good form earlier in this chapter. We will have more to say about forms design in the chapter on formal work measurement techniques.

Reports

A fertile field for improving productivity is the elimination of unnecessary reports. It costs time and money to make up a report. Some supervisors spend up to one-third of their time collecting data for a weekly or monthly report, and then writing and editing it.

Reports often date back to some time when the organization was going through a crisis, when some particular information was needed to solve a problem. A supervisor was asked to prepare a report on subject X. Importance and urgency were stressed. Nothing was said about its being a one-shot requirement. After the problem was solved, the need for the information disappeared—but no one thought to tell the supervisor, who continued to believe that the report was urgently needed. I have often seen this. From time to time, the supervisor should ask what is done with the reports he or she prepares.

You, the change agent, should question any report whose use is not immediately obvious. Recommend its elimination and show how much time this will make available for constructive work. You may also wish to suggest consolidating several reports into one. But redesign of the reporting structure is a major subject itself; the pattern of reports should not necessarily follow the logic observed by system analysts. Reports to management must match the thinking patterns of those who use them. Therefore those members of management who use the information must be consulted and their wishes followed.

MULTI-FUNCTION CHANGE

The most common form of a multi-function study today is the study of office systems automation. Because of its objective and its breadth, this is a special type of study, which will be discussed as a part of Chapter 7.

Other multi-function studies usually are concerned with the interface of two functions.

Sometimes this is a jurisdictional matter, such as whether the data processing function should purchase and maintain all the word processing equipment. These disputes are usually solved with very little study or analysis. If a study is made, it is confined to the issues raised by the parties in dispute. The parties present their points of view to a superior officer in the company who makes the decision. This decision is often somewhat arbitrary because there are usually good arguments on both sides.

The more difficult situation involves the interface of two functions: for example, that of the department secretary and the central word processing function; the legal department and the central records management function; word processing and central graphics; almost everybody and the copying center. In each case, the first party named needs help from the second party during the progress of the jobs they do. During a part of the time, the job is no longer under the first party's control. The first party remains responsible for getting the job done, but someone else has temporary control. This leads to concern, especially if the first party is under pressure to complete the job as soon as possible. This leads to the first party's wanting its own word processing, microfilm equipment, graphics, copy equipment, and so on.

In these cases, the statements of policy must clearly state the roles and jurisdiction of each department. Can the legal department have its own records function? Can every department have its own copier? The decisions usually involve matters of cost and specialized expertise. You, or the task force, must weigh the importance of these factors. If you opt for a change in policy, clearly define what the new rules are.

At the interface between functions, each function's procedures must specify:

1. The step at which a job moves to another department.
2. Who is the first department's contact with the second department.
3. The performance standards and turnaround times agreed to by the second department.
4. How the work moves from the one department to the other and back again.
5. How an emergency situation is handled.

If these points are clearly defined and the persons in charge of each are reasonable, the problems that may exist will be resolved. If the issue involves egos or ambitions, you need to bring this to the attention of higher management. Resolving ego problems is just as important a part of improving overall productivity as any change in procedure, but it is one that line management must handle.

COST JUSTIFICATION

There are three kinds of cost justification that can be used when you suggest changes to an operation. The first is to justify buying equipment that improves the staff's productivity. The second is to justify the change on grounds that it increases efficiency and so reduces time and costs. The third is to justify adding additional staff to reduce or eliminate backlogs, improve the quality of support being provided, or speed up the response time. We discuss each.

Buying Equipment

This is the easiest of the three cost justifications because it is purely quantitative and the results are self-evident. However, there are three alternate ways to do it. One is payout or payback; the second is cost avoidance; the third is alternative costing. They all reach the same conclusion. The method you use depends on which one your management prefers.

Assume there are now three secretaries using good-quality correcting typewriters. Assume that use of word processing equipment results in a 33% increase in typing productivity. This is reasonable. Assume further that a secretary and a word processing operator make the same salary, namely, $16,000 per year including payroll expenses and fringe benefits. Last, assume that both the typewriters and the word processing equipment have a useful life of five years.

Payout Method.   From the assumptions, the output of three word processing (w.p.) stations and three operators equals that of four typewriters and four secretaries. If the organization's work is expanding and it plans to add a fourth secretary, substituting three word processors (or converting the three present secretaries to word processing operators) will achieve the same 33% increase in work output. These are the alternatives:

```
A: 3 w.p. systems @ $11,000 each ..... $33,000
B: 1 add'l secretary + typewriter ........  17,000 1st year
                                and 16,000/year thereafter
            Payback period ............  2 years
```

In alternative A, the cost of the word processing equipment is a one-time expense. No additional salary cost is involved in this alternative because it does not add people. In alternative B, the additional equipment cost is only $1,000 for another typewriter, but there is a continuing annual salary cost of $16,000 for the additional secretary. The cost of the three word processing systems will offset the cost of an additional secretary and typewriter in two years. The pay-out (payback) period is two years.

Cost Avoidance.   Based on a five-year life for the word processing equipment:

Cost of 4th secretary × 5 years	$80,000
1 typewriter	1,000
TOTAL	$81,000
Cost of w.p. equipment	$33,000
Cost Avoidance	$48,000

Over the five-year life of the equipment, the organization has avoided spending $48,000 by buying the equipment rather than hiring the additional secretary.

Alternative Costing.   Again, over the five-year life of the equipment:

Plan A

3 w.p. systems	$ 33,000	
3 operators × 5 years	240,000	
TOTAL		$273,000

Plan B

4 secretaries × 5 years	$320,000	
1 new typewriter	1,000	
TOTAL		$321,000

Savings over the life of the equipment	$ 48,000

These examples have been simplified by omitting salary increases for the secretaries and operators and ignoring the discounted value of future-year savings. These refinements can be added. But generally it is not an exact dollar savings figure that is desired; it is knowing whether one solution is more or less expensive than another. For this purpose, the simplified methods shown will suffice.

Increased Efficiency

An improvement in efficiency always sounds good, but there is only one way it can show up as a cost savings—if it reduces the time and work hours required to do a job and thus permits it to be done with fewer people.

Any estimate of the the number of work hours reduced by using a revised procedure will be subjective. You have no measurements and no way to make measurements until the new procedure is in effect. However, the supervisor of a function can usually make a pretty good guess of work hours required for each step of the revised procedure. This comes from experience—knowing the work hours required now and seeing what will be eliminated or changed. The supervisor of the function must implement the changes when they are approved, and he or she will be judged on whether the promised improvement is achieved. For this reason it is wise to get the function's supervisor to commit to an improvement, even if there are industrial engineers on the task force who might make a better estimate.

Take an example. Let us assume $10.00 per hour for the function's staff, including fringe benefits. If the proposed changes are estimated to save 300 work hours per month, the resulting cost saving should be:

$$300 \text{ hours/months} \times \$10.00/\text{hour} = \$ 3,000/\text{month}$$

However, savings come only in increments of one person. Unless you can find some way of having one person split his or her time with another operation, it will take a reduction of 173 work hours per month to save one person's salary, and of 346 work hours per month to save two people's salary, and so on. In the 300-hour example above, only one person can be transferred out unless you find some way of saving 46 more hours. If you can't, the savings become:

$$1 \text{ person} \times \$ 10.00/\text{hour} \times 173 \text{ hours/month} = \$1730/\text{month}$$

The other aspect of justifying efficiency involves listing the jobs not being done or not being done well because of lack of time or people. You show the activities that can be undertaken with the staff time made available. This is not a cost savings, but it may be a powerful argument as justification for a change.

Additional People

It is possible that the inefficiencies discovered are due to a lack of people rather than of poor procedures. Backlogs are too long. Or the existing staff, to keep the backlog down, cannot take the time to do an adequate job. You have examined the policies and procedures and suggested improvements. You have concluded that the time savings made available still will not be enough to let the existing staff do a proper job. The lack of staff is the real problem. You are therefore in the position of recommending an increase in staff.

Your justification must be based on the cost to the company of the inefficiencies that result from the present lack of staff. For example, lack of sufficient facility design staff results in a manufacturing area not being ready on schedule. What is the cost to the company of that delay? A shortage of purchasing personnel makes delivery of some equipment to you one week later than it should be, and there is no substitute work to do while waiting for delivery. What is one week of your time worth? These are the costs of inadequate staffing.

To justify an additional person, a series of such cases must be collected and totaled to estimate the cost of inadequate staffing. This cost is compared to the cost of the additional person. For example:

Cost of Delays Due to Inadequate Staffing (Jan.–Mar.)

case a	$ 3,400
case b	650
case c	80
case d, e, f, g, etc.	10,870
Total, 3 months	$15,000

Cost of Additional Person (inc'l fringe benefits)

Total, 3 months	$ 6,750

What of time saved? Is not that of value in itself? Yes, there is value in completing a job sooner, but one cannot quantify it. Not all managements will agree with this concept. Therefore it is better to translate time saved into what will be done with the time made available.

This chapter has described the activities you, as change agent, must cover when planning to change an office system. After you have decided what to change, you must sell the change to management, and then you, or a responsible supervisor, must implement it. But before we discuss these subjects, we will describe in detail the office system elements you should consider using to improve productivity. In the next eight chapters, we describe equipment and work techniques that may serve this purpose.

SUMMARY

Before making any type of change, it is important to understand the existing system or procedure. You need to determine: the philosophy of the operation, the policies and procedures being followed, the responsibilities of the people involved, the flow of work within the operation, the forms that are in use, the adequacy of equipment, the size and quality of staff, and the reports that are generated. Specific questions about each of these subjects are suggested in this chapter.

Some companies are tightly controlled companies, some go "by the book," and others are more open. Your approach to initiating change differs in each case. When the study is completed, prepare a report summarizing the present system and noting where your questions have uncovered possible areas for improvement.

If the proposed change affects only one department, look first at its objectives, which are often multiple and conflicting. See if the policies fit the primary objectives. Determine whether the procedures are simple, clear, and unambiguous. One way to simplify a procedure is to hold a brainstorming session. Procedures must be enforced. Newly hired employees or transfers must operate in the approved way. As the staff changes, reexamine the job assignments; people are not cast in a mold that fits a job description. Examine work flow for balance of the work between people and for physical layout. Forms should be looked at and redesigned if necessary. The necessity of reports should be questioned.

Jurisdictional disputes sometimes arise in multi-function situations. There may also be communication problems at the interface of two functions.

All changes must be justified. Three ways to justify equipment that improves productivity are shown: the payout method, cost avoidance, and alternative costing. Justifying a change to increase efficiency without reducing costs is more nebulous. You calculate the number of work hours saved and list the important new activities that can be handled with the time made available.

If the existing inefficiencies result from lack of staff rather than poor policies or procedures, costs will be increased. Justification for more staff is based on the present cost of the inefficiencies versus the cost of more help.

FOR FURTHER INFORMATION

Cecil, Paula B. Chapter 9, Office Automation Analysis and Feasibility Studies, in *Office Automation, Concepts & Applications*. Menlo Park, CA: Benjamin/Cummings Publishing Co., 1984.

Garon, Jacques T. In the Beginning the Feasibility Study, *Computerworld*, 16 (June 23, 1982): 25A; A Stitch in Time . . . Feasibility Study II, *Computerworld*, 16 (Sept. 29, 1982): 39A.

Lieberman, Mark A., and Selig, Gad. Chapter 6, How to Apply Needs and Requirements, in *Office Automation: A Manager's Guide for Improved Productivity*. New York: John Wiley & Sons, 1982.

Ruprecht, Mary M., and Wagoner, Kathleen P. Chapter 12, Office Support Systems Study, in *Managing Office Automation*. New York: John Wiley & Sons, 1984.

4
Office Elements

"I'm just not comfortable talking to a machine. It's not natural. And besides, they're so inflexible. If you get mixed up and are not quite sure what you said, or whether your grammar is right, you can't look back and see what you did."

Quite true. But use of dictation systems is the quickest and least expensive way to improve the professional person's own productivity. In this and the next chapter, we describe dictation systems and the other office elements that can enhance your effectiveness and the effectiveness of the support staff. We indicate what these systems do and how they work. Later, in Chapter 8, we discuss how to use them effectively.

DICTATION SYSTEMS[1]

Advantages of Dictation

A study by one of the leading consultants on office systems has measured the average time required for a manager or professional to create a document by writing longhand, dictating to a secretary who uses shorthand, or dictating into a dictation machine. The findings are shown in Table 4-1.

The secretary, too, is more effective when dictation is used. These findings are shown in Table 4-2.

When you combine these data, using machine dictation is almost five times faster than writing a document in longhand.

The point can be made more dramatically in terms of costs. This is shown in Table 4-3. The costs shown are only the salaries and associated fringe benefits of the originator and transcriber, using a salary of $28,000 per year for the originator and $14,000 per year for the secretary. Fringe benefits are assumed to be 35% of salaries. The input and transcription speeds for each method are taken from Tables 4-1 and 4-2.

It is clear that use of dictation equipment is an important way to improve productivity. Not all documents lend themselves to dictation, but most do. We

---

[1] Portions of this section on dictation systems are adapted from Davis, Reba, and Balderston, Jack, *Word Processing Supervision,* Indianapolis: Bobbs-Merrill Publishing Co., 1984, Chapter 6.

Table 4-1. Handwriting and Dictation Speeds.[a]

METHOD	AVERAGE SPEED
Longhand	10–12 words/min
Shorthand dictation	25–30 words/min
Machine dictation	80–120 words/min

[a]Ruprecht, Mary M., New Managerial Techniques for Productivity Measurement and Improvement, Talk to Syntopican XI, Association of Information Systems Professionals, June 1983. Reprinted by permission of Mary M Ruprecht, CMC; Mary M Ruprecht & Associates, Inc., Duluth MN 55811.

Table 4-2. Transcription Speeds.[a]

SOURCE	AVERAGE SPEED
Longhand	25–30 words/min
Shorthand	40–45 words/min
Machine	65–75 words/min

[a]Ruprecht, Mary M. Ibid.

have more to say in Chapter 8 about the types of documents that should be dictated and the types that should not.

There are three categories of dictation systems. These are:

1. Centralized dictation systems
2. Desktop recorders
3. Portable recorders

Table 4-3. Salary Costs for a 200-Word Letter.

	LONGHAND	SHORTHAND	MACHINE
Creation:			
avg. speed, words/min	12	30	80
cost:			
originator	$5.10	$2.10	$0.75
transcriber	N.A.	1.05	N.A.
TOTAL	$5.10	3.15	0.75
Transcription:			
avg. speed, words/min	30	45	70
cost:			
transcriber	$1.05	$0.70	$0.45
Total Salary, 200-word letter	$6.15	$3.85	$1.20

N.A. = not applicable.

Centralized Systems

In these systems, the equipment housing the magnetic media that captures your voice is centralized somewhere in the building. You access the system through a special desktop microphone which is connected by cable to the central unit. Or you may access the system through your telephone instrument by dialing the extension number of the dictation system and using the push buttons or rotary numbers on your telephone instrument to operate the system.

Endless Loop System. There are two types of centralized system. One is the endless loop tank. As the name indicates, this is a box containing a continuous loop of magnetic tape whose length varies with the equipment model. A typical system holds three hours of dictation.

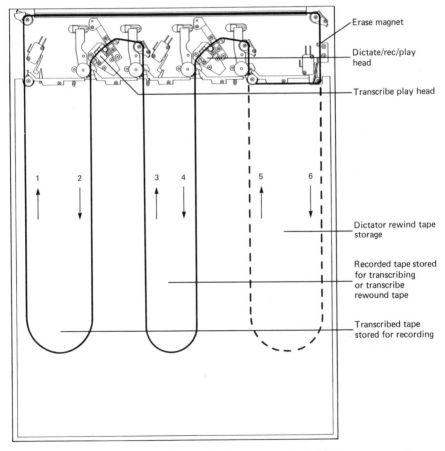

Figure 4-1. Diagram of endless loop dictation tank. Courtesy Dictaphone corporation.

Mounted inside a sealed box are an erase head to clear the tape of earlier dictation, a recording head, and a playback head. The recording and playback heads are placed far enough apart that much of the tape can accumulate between them. Thus transcription may take place many yards of tape later than the dictation or may occur within minutes of dictation and even while the dictator is still talking. A diagram of this system is shown in Figure 4-1.

Cassette Bank System. The central cassette bank is a recorder-transcriber holding a dozen or so tape cassettes. When accessed using the desktop microphone or the telephone, the equipment takes a cassette from a "waiting stack," places it in the record position, erases the prior dictation on the tape, records what you dictate, and then ejects the cassette onto a second "awaiting transcription" stack. The equipment can be programmed to eject the cassette when it is full, after each message, after a certain length of talk, after a certain number of messages, or after a preset length of time has elapsed after the first message. (See Figure 4-2.)

Tank and Bank Networks. Several endless loop tanks or tape cassette banks can be tied together in a network. When one person is dictating into a tank or bank, that unit is tied up for the duration of the dictation, and no one else can access it. Similarly, when one transcriber is taking dictation from an endless loop tank, no other transcriber can access that tank. Therefore several such units must exist in the central location, enough to handle the anticipated number of people wishing to use the equipment at the same time. The units are tied together in a network so that if the first unit is busy or full, the call is routed to the next available unit. The user does not know which particular unit holds his or her dictation.

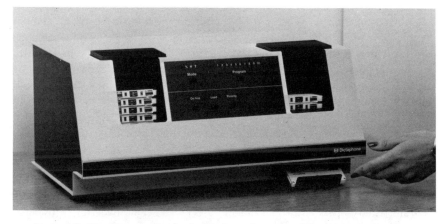

Figure 4-2. Cassette recording bank. Photograph courtesy Dictaphone corporation.

Control Consoles.   The major vendors of centralized dictation systems sell control consoles for these systems. These are terminals with appropriate software that allow the supervisor of the transcribing unit to monitor the status of all transcription work.

The console shows the status of every job. It can also show the size of the work backlog, the current assignment of each person who is transcribing tapes, the status of each tank or bank (whether in use or waiting, holding work for transcription or empty), and the existence and location of priority jobs. The control system also maintains operating statistics such as the quantity of work performed by each operator and by the whole staff, the length of each job, the time each is received and completed, and the resulting work turnaround time. The supervisor can program the console to show author, department, type of document, and other appropriate information about each job. For a large company with a lot of dictation flowing to a central transcription unit, this type of control is necessary.

Desktop Recorders

These are units that sit on the desk, in contrast to hand-held portable recorders. They do not look very different from the desk microphone units that access the centralized systems, but there is one very important distinction. In the desktop recorder, the recording head is part of the unit. Thus these desktop units are self-contained.

These recorders use a hand-held microphone, and most record onto removable tape cassettes. The commonly used controls, namely, "Record," "Pause," "Play Back," "Stop," "Rewind," and "Fast Forward," are operated at the microphone using buttons and slide switches. This makes it possible to dictate using only one hand, which both holds the microphone and operates the equipment.

Desktop units can also be used for transcribing dictation. Almost all allow a foot pedal control to be attached, which is essential for hand-free transcription. However, it is generally wise to have a separate unit for transcription, in order to avoid unplugging the recorder, carrying it to a secretary's desk, plugging it in, and attaching the foot pedal unit. More important, it permits you to dictate another document on a second cassette while the secretary is transcribing the first one. Having to share a unit when you have several things to dictate delays either your dictation or the secretary's transcription.

Portable Recorders

These are small self-contained, hand-held units that weigh from 6 to 12 ounces and are battery-operated. Some models use rechargeable batteries. Most provide for 115-volt ac as well as battery operation, and some can also use the 12-volt dc cigarette lighter in an automobile. The controls are slide switches and buttons that can be operated with the fingers of the hand that holds the unit. Many of the newer models use microcassettes or minicassettes instead of the standard-size cassettes. The difference is important, and is discussed in the next section of this chapter.

These units are not as rugged as desktop units. They may lack more exotic features such as cuing the start and end of each document, but they all possess the six critical controls noted earlier. They are very useful for carrying on trips or for take-home work, for recording meetings and lectures, and for people who like to pace the floor while dictating.

Cassettes

Tape cassettes are not all alike. Equipment made for use with one type of cassette will not work with the others. Some standard-size cassette transcription units come with adapters to accept the smaller cassettes, but generally you should standardize on one size of cassette and have all your equipment compatible with it.

Standard Cassettes.   The standard cassette is $2\frac{1}{2}$ in. $\times 4$ in. The magnetic tape travels from a spindle on one side of the cassette, past an erase head to eliminate prior dictation, and past a record/read head to the spindle on the other side. The erase and record heads are active when you are in the record mode. The read head operates (and the erase head doesn't) when you are in the playback mode. The tape has two tracks. One track is used as the tape travels in one direction; the other track is used after you flip the cassette over from side A to side B so that the tape travels in the other direction. Most standard cassettes used for dictation hold either 30 minutes or 45 minutes of talk on each track.

Within the standard cassette family there are two types of tape drive. Equipment that uses one is not compatible with equipment that uses the other.

The more common drive is the capstan drive. The capstan is a wheel, placed near the tape heads, that rolls against the tape, pulling it from one spindle, across the heads, and to the take-up spindle. It rotates at a constant speed, and therefore the tape travels at a constant speed. For most equipment, this speed is just under two inches per second.

The other tape drive is the spindle drive. The take-up spindle is the driving mechanism. It rotates at a constant speed of revolution, pulling the tape from the first spindle and across the heads. As the tape accumulates on this spindle, its effective diameter increases. Therefore the tape speed also increases. A spindle drive thus creates a variable tape speed across the heads.

Microcassettes. Microcassettes are about half the size of standard cassettes, $1\frac{1}{4}$ in. $\times 2$ in. In other respects they look and work just like the standard cassettes. Most hold 30 minutes of dictation on each side (i.e., on each track). This length of time is achieved on the smaller unit by reducing the tape speed to just under one inch per second. Equipment vendors using microcassettes have standardized on use of the capstan drive.

Minicassettes. Minicassettes are almost, but not quite, the same size as microcassettes; the difference is slight enough to fool the casual cassette buyer. Equipment designed to use minicassettes will not work with microcassettes, and vice versa. Most equipment using minicassettes uses a spindle drive.

Transcribers

The transcriber unit for an endless loop system is connected directly by cable to the transcription head in a central tank. It sits on the desk of the secretary or word processing operator.

In transcribers for cassette banks, as well as for desktop units, the cassettes are inserted into the transcriber unit. This requires that all cassettes be brought to the location of the transcriber.

All transcribers should be foot-pedal-operated with controls for "forward," "stop," and "backspace" on the foot pedal. This is essential for efficient transcription. The transcriber's hands must be free to work the typewriter or word processor keyboard. On–off switches, speed controls, tone controls, and other extras that are used infrequently may be on the desk console, but not the three controls that are in constant use.

Transcribers come with earphones. Most of these fit into the ear like the earphones you get in the coach section of airplanes and are just as uncomfortable. More comfortable earphones, like stereo equipment phones that fit over the ears, can be used. They are available from office supply houses or audio shops. A few extra dollars spent on comfort here will pay off handsomely in productivity.

As noted earlier, some transcription units designed to use standard cassettes have adapters to hold microcassettes or minicassettes. Performance with an adapter is not always reliable. When a dictator has spent a lot of time and effort in dictating a tape, it is a shame to have the tape break in an adapter, or wrap around its capstan or spindle. It is better if each type of cassette is transcribed on a unit specifically made for that cassette.

Need for Standardization

The earlier discussion has made clear the importance of standardizing on one type of cassette. There will be an unnecessarily large outlay for transcribers if all three types of cassette are in use in your organization. Transcription will also take longer because one type of transcriber must be unplugged and another type located and plugged in.

It is also necessary to restrict the brands of recorder and transcriber that the organization uses. A cassette recorded on a spindle drive machine may not transcribe well on a capstan drive transcriber, and vice versa.

On some brands of recorder, especially the less expensive hobby models that the professional may have at home, the record head may not track on the tape in exactly the same place as the read head of the transcriber. Voice quality will deteriorate if the recorder and transcriber track differently. Voice ghosts will result if prior dictation is not fully erased. In the worst case, the transcriber may not pick up any voice signal at all. The brands of recording equipment that the staff members are allowed to use should be specified based on tests using transcribers selected by the company.

Advantages of Each Type of Dictation System

The *centralized systems* are less expensive when a lot of dictation equipment is required. Since the people doing the transcribing are working full time on this task, the turnaround time for the work is short and predictable. Two to four hours is typical. Full-time supervision of the unit assures that priority or unusual jobs get proper attention. Central systems are also good for salespeople or others who call in from outside the building to dictate sales orders or to leave a request for information. The machines are left on 24 hours a day to accept dictation. This helps the dictator who is three time zones away from the transcriber or the person who wishes to record information during the weekend or at night.

There are three advantages of *endless loop* systems over the cassette banks:

1. The tape in a loop tank is never handled; it stays clean and undamaged.
2. There is no danger of tapes being lost.
3. Turnaround can be almost immediate on rush jobs because there is no waiting for cassette transport.

There are disadvantages too:

1. Only one dictator and transcriber can access a tank at one time.
2. Transcription must generally be in the same sequence as that in which the dictation was placed on the tape loop.
3. If service is needed on the tank unit, the waiting dictation is inaccessible until the unit is repaired.

Advantages of the *cassette bank* system are:

1. It is easy to take dictation out of sequence, an especially important consideration in handling priority and rush work.
2. The total length of tape available in all the cassettes is much greater than the length of an endless loop.
3. Several transcribers can work concurrently on different cassettes from a single cassette bank.

The primary disadvantages are:

1. The cassettes must be handled and moved.
2. There is always the danger of cassettes being damaged or lost.

The *desktop recorder* is better for long documents or creative writing. If you are interrupted in the middle of dictation, the central system will cut you off after a preset period of silence. When you return, the next part of your document will be on another cassette or on another loop. The portable desk unit is yours alone. You can dictate a few paragraphs, turn it off, and do something else. When you return, you pick up the dictation where you left off on the tape. You can rewind the tape to hear where you were and continue. To the transcriber, there will not even be a pause. You can replay portions, erase,and talk over. You have greater flexibility.

The disadvantage of the desktop unit is the need to transport the cassettes to a secretary or to a central transcription unit. This takes time. Also, if you place a series of short notes or letters on a single cassette tape, transcription of the first note cannot start until you finish the last note and release the cassette.

The *portable recorder* is more versatile than desktop units since it can be carried around, will fit into a briefcase, and can be used on trips. It has the same advantages over centralized systems as mentioned for the desktop units.

The portable recorder also has the same disadvantages as the desk units. In addition, it is not built as ruggedly as the desk units. Battery life is only from 2 to 10 hours, depending on the model. Rechargeable batteries are a useful feature, but their life before needing to be recharged is often not as long as that of regular batteries. This can be important if you are taping a lecture and are not able to reach a wall outlet to recharge when the batteries run out. AC adapters are useful but, again, you may not be near a wall outlet when you need one. The controls are much easier to work on some portable units than on others.

In buying desktop and portable recorders, pay particular attention to compatibility with the transcriber you have.

ELECTRIC AND ELECTRONIC TYPEWRITERS

The electric typewriter is the workhorse of the present-day office. With the "lift off" or correcting feature, the newer typewriters have made it possible to correct simple typographical errors without redoing an entire page.

New in the last few years is the electronic typewriter. The distinction is not always clear-cut. The feature that we use to distinguish the two is memory. The electronic typewriter has a small amount of memory, whereas the electric typewriter doesn't have memory.

Memory is the ability to store and recall keystrokes. If the electronic typewriter has a one-page memory, it can store about 2,000 characters. Memory can reside on a magnetic disk or tape, or in an electronic chip. The form in which the characters are stored does not matter. The important concept is that what you type is stored within the machine.

This memory is used to print a copy of a document at rapid speed. Once a page is assembled in memory, the secretary presses the "print" key. The machine then prints at speeds up to 130 words per minute, three times faster than most secretaries type on a standard electric. After pressing the "print" key, the secretary need not do anything else at the typewriter until it has finished printing and the paper must be removed. She or he is free to do other work while the machine prints.

More important is the ability to correct and edit a page before printing it. If a typing mistake is made, the typist backspaces over it. This erases from memory the characters backed over. There is no "white out" or "lift off" tape needed. When the text is printed, it is as if the mistake never happened. If an error is found after the text is printed, the secretary scrolls through the memory to locate the error, deletes it, and types in the correct material. If an author wants to change a word, the secretary scrolls through memory to the word and replaces it with a new word.

To do this, most electronic typewriters have a "window" display, typically 12 to 20 characters in size. While the secretary is typing, this window shows the most recent characters entered into memory. During correction or editing, the window shows the position within the stored text that will be accessed if a key is pressed to erase or enter a new character.

Memory size varies from a couple of lines to 16 pages, depending on the model. If you need a memory larger than this, you are entering the area of word processors.

Editing Features

Electronic typewriters contain microcircuits. This technology is used to add other features that enhance typing productivity. We mention a few of the more important features found on some electronic typewriter models.

Automatic Centering.   One keystroke places the heading centrally between the margins.

Decimal Alignment.   When one is typing a column of numbers, this tab key moves the digits to the left of the tab position so that the decimal point, or the "unit" number if there is no decimal, is always at the tab position.

Word Wrap.   During typing, the first word that exceeds the right margin setting is automatically placed on the next line. The typist continues typing without pause and without having to look or to listen for a line-end signal, or to press a carriage return key.

String Search.   The machine searches the text in its memory for whatever string of characters the typist designates. It positions the input key at this string so that a correction or change can be made to it. The string is usually a word or words, and is shown in the "window." If the string cannot be found in memory, a message or a light indicates this.

Phrase Memory.   Short phrases or blocks of text can be stored in the memory and recalled with one keystroke. A signature block or address can be stored in this manner. Technical and hard-to-spell words can be stored.

Some electronic typewriters also can store formats, allow more than one pitch setting or line spacing within a document, print bold characters, and print white on black.

Not all electronic typewriters have all of these features. The more features, of course, the higher the price. Electronic typewriters cost between $1,200 and $3,000, depending on features.

Automatic centering, word wrap, and decimal alignment (if you do a lot of statistical typing) alone can increase typing productivity by 10% to 20%. With a typing improvement of only 10%, a $3,000 electronic typewriter can pay back its cost in two years.

WORD PROCESSORS

Electronic typewriters represent the initial stage of word processing. They are the bottom of the line of high technology text-manipulation systems. The term word processors is usually reserved for more powerful equipment than the electronic typewriters just described. We define the difference between electronic typewriters and word processors as the absence or presence of a video screen.

The video screen and other enhancements that we are about to describe give all the advantages of the electronic typewriter and a lot more. One study in which the author participated showed a productivity increase of 30% using word processing equipment instead of electric typewriters for the input of text. The figures were 5.25 pages per hour for the word processor and four pages per hour for the standard electric typewriter.[2]

This is not the principal advantage of word processing equipment, however. It is most useful in the revision process. This same study showed the word pro-

---

[2]Smith, Janine, and Balderston, Jack. Measuring the Productivity of a Word Processing Center, *The Office*, 96, 5, 102 (Nov. 1982).

cessing operator handled ten pages per hour of revision work while the secretary, who must type each page over in full, handled four.

In terms of cost per page the differences are not as dramatic, since the word processing equipment is considerably more expensive than a typewriter. But revisions done on a word processor still hold a factor of two advantage over revisions done on a regular electric typewriter. The data are shown in Table 4-4.

The study by Mary Ruprecht shows an even greater advantage for word processors. She finds an average of 375 lines per day produced on a standard electric typewriter versus 2000 lines per day for a stand alone word processor and up to 3000 lines per day for shared logic systems.[3] The difference between stand alone and shared logic systems is covered later in this chapter.

Ease of Original Input

Word processors do all of the things an electronic typewriter does and more. There are no mechanical keys or moving print balls that can hold down the typist's speed; the electronic systems in the machine work faster than anyone can type. The typist watches a screen and so can see errors, misalignments,

Table 4-4. Comparative Costs, Word Processing and Typewriter.[a]

COST ELEMENT	WORD PROCESSING	TYPEWRITER
Per Person, Per Hour		
Salaries	8.40	8.40
Fringe Benefits at 38%	3.19	3.19
Supplies	1.18	1.00
Equipment Depreciation and Maintenance	2.55	.25
Supervision	2.27	1.20
Sub-Total	$17.59	$14.04
Utilization Factor (reciprocal 85%)	3.10	2.48
Total, without overheads	$20.69	$16.52
COST PER PAGE, ORIGINAL INPUT		
Pages per hour	5.25	4.0
Cost per page	$ 3.94	$ 4.13
COST PER PAGE, REVISIONS		
Pages per hour	10.3	4.0
Cost per page	$ 2.01	$ 4.13

[a]Reprinted with permission from *The Office*. November, 1982.

[3]Ruprecht, Mary M. New Managerial Techniques for Productivity Measurement and Improvement, Talk to Syntopican XI, Association of Information Systems Professionals, June 1983.

problems with the page layout, and so on, while typing. Other features that we describe later add to the ease with which various formats can be established.

Ease of Revision

More than ease of original input, however, the reason for the increased productivity of word processors is the ease with which revisions can be made. You can scroll through a document, watching it on the screen, making corrections and revisions as you go. You can add a word here, delete one there, change a spelling error, invert two sentences, and so on, with the touch of a few keys. Nothing need be printed until the typist is completely satisfied with the text. If changes are still wanted after the document has been printed, the text is pulled back to the screen, changed, and sent back to the printer. While the printer is printing, the typist can do something else.

This book was written using a word processor. Its many revisions could not have been made as fast or as inexpensively in any other way.

Here is a scenario that is not at all farfetched: You, the professional, have a letter ready to send. As you are about to sign it, you spot a typographical error. You circle the mistake in pencil and take it back to your secretary. She inserts the disk containing the letter into her word processing equipment and brings the offending page from memory to the screen. The elapsed time thus far is 10 seconds. She scrolls through the document to the mistake (5 seconds), inserts or deletes a character to make the correction (3 seconds), checks the new version on the screen (5 seconds), pushes the print button (1 second), and a corrected original comes off the printer (40 seconds). Total time is one minute.

You decide that the letter would be clearer if you moved paragraph three ahead of paragraph two. A couple of sentences should be deleted and some words added in several places. Before you are through, the margin looks like a colony of ants has been holding its annual jamboree there. Your secretary again brings the text from memory to the screen, scrolls through it to mark with a special function key the start and end of paragraph three, marks its new location in front of paragraph two, presses another key, and, presto, the paragraphs are inverted. She makes the other changes in a similar manner. Total time, including printing, is eight minutes.

Now the words are correct, but you do not like the way the page looks. Perhaps some underlining, bold printing, and indenting of key phrases will make the message stand out more clearly. Again, your secretary uses function keys to underline, use bold print, and indent the words or lines. This time it may take three or four minutes.

In less than a quarter of an hour you have completely revised a letter three times and had it printed and ready to go out.

Terminology

This is as good a place as any to note a difference in terminology between the secretarial and word processing fields. In word processing, the person at the keyboard is a "word processing operator" or "word processing specialist" rather than a "typist" or "secretary." This person does not "type"; she or he "inputs" or "keyboards." What you input are "keystrokes." These keystrokes are stored by the word processing equipment. We will use this terminology throughout the rest of this book.

Ergonomics

Ergonomics is the study of people's interaction with their work environment. It has particular relevance to word processing because operators are asked to spend a full workday looking at a video screen, and to sit relatively motionless in one position. Unlike the secretary, they do not have other things to do to break the monotony of typing. Their jobs do not involve walking in and out of a boss's office, going to a copy machine, taking papers to other parts of the building, and so on. They are essentially full-time machine operators. It is important that the working conditions make their jobs as untiring as possible. Tired operators make errors. Tired operators work more slowly. To achieve the high productivity promised by word processing systems, you need proper working conditions for the operators.

There are many studies under way on how to reduce fatigue for those who sit at a video terminal. In several of these, the emphasis is on operator comfort, although it is not clear that comfort equates to less fatigue. Equipment and furniture designers are changing their products to make them more "ergonomic." There is no consensus yet on the best working conditions, but the following principles are accepted by many of those studying this subject.

Equipment. The word processing equipment should be designed in the following way:

1. The keyboard and screen should be separated so that the operator can move each to her or his position of maximum comfort.
2. The screen should be tiltable and rotatable to an angle that minimizes glare.
3. The angle of the keyboard should be adjustable, and the keyboard height should be low enough that the operator may rest her or his wrists on the work surface or on the keyboard itself.

Furniture. The following principles apply to the furniture:

1. Both the work surfaces and the chair seats should be easily adjustable for height while the operator is sitting at the word processing station.
2. That part of the work surface holding the keyboard and that part holding the screen should be adjustable to different heights. This will permit the operator to look down at the screen while keeping her or his arms almost parallel to the floor.
3. Adjustments should allow the operator to attain the sitting posture shown in Figure 4-3.

Working Conditions.   The following principles apply to the way operators spend their time on the job:

1. Operators should alter their posture frequently; any posture maintained too long causes muscle fatigue.
2. The eyes must be rested frequently. A 15-minute work break after the second, fourth, and sixth hour and a 5-minute break after the first, third, fifth, and seventh are minimum requirements.

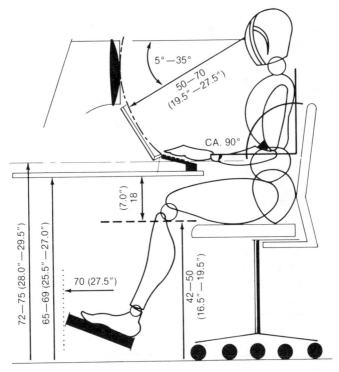

Figure 4-3. Ideal furniture and equipment heights and angles to minimize operator fatigue. Courtesy Ergotech, Inc., Newbury Park, CA.

Use of these principles increases operator productivity. In one study, a 25% difference in work output was found when the same operators used well-designed work stations versus stations that were "conventional."[4] In another study, a 10% to 15% increase in productivity was measured.[5] Even at 10%, work stations designed using ergonomic principles will pay for themselves in one year or less.

Equipment Configurations

Word processing equipment can be configured in:

1. Centralized systems
2. Organizationally decentralized systems
3. Functionally decentralized systems
4. Mixed systems

There are advantages and disadvantages to each. Which is best depends on the type of work being done in the office.

Centralized.   The word processing stations are placed in a single central location under the direction of one supervisor or manager.
The advantages of this configuration are:

1. The operators are all full time on the equipment, and thus they become more proficient than in other arrangements.
2. The operators can easily help each other.
3. The operators are more closely supervised than they are in other situations.
4. The workload is easy to schedule, and jobs are easy to assign.
5. Several operators can be put on one high-priority task.
6. Expensive specialized equipment such as optical character readers or laser printers can be justified because many stations will use them.
7. Operator training is easier than it is with other configurations.

The disadvantages are:

1. The interaction between the operator and the author of the work is less close than it is in other patterns.

---

[4] Study by Marvin J. Dainhoff, Laurie Fraser and B. J. Taylor. Quoted in Channer, Stephen D., The Case For Furniture Befitting the Human Condition, *Modern Office Procedures,* **28,**6 (June 1983): 58.
[5] Study by T. J. Stringer. Quoted in Lauder, Rani, The Ergonomics of Furniture Adjustability, *The Ergonomics Newsletter,* **2,**1 (Jan.–Feb. 1983): 4.

2. The distance from the authors to the center may slow communication and document handling.
3. A large room is necessary.

Organizationally Decentralized. The word processing stations are placed near the users under the organizational control of the departments in which they are located. There is no central function.

The advantages of this configuration are:

1. There is close and rapid interaction with authors to obtain clarification and instructions.
2. There is faster response time for the department's top-priority work than with the centralized configuration.
3. Operators learn the special terminology used by the department in which they work.
4. Operators learn the handwriting and dictation habits of members of their department.
5. Confidential work remains within the originating department.
6. Different equipment can be acquired, each system optimized for a department's needs.

The disadvantages are:

1. More stations and more equipment are usually required than are needed with the centralized arrangement.
2. Operators are more susceptible to interruptions.
3. Help from other operators who know the equipment or the particular application is harder to obtain.
4. There is no supervisor who understands the word processing operation, knows what productivity to expect, knows the needs of operators, and can train operators. This usually results in lower productivity than is possible with a centralized system.
5. The equipment brings noise to what may be a quiet area.
6. It is difficult to get help from another department's operators when one department's high-priority or lengthy jobs are in danger of missing deadlines.

Functionally Decentralized. Here the stations are placed in the departments where the users reside, but the responsibility for supervising the operators and for maintaining the equipment in operating condition is retained by one word processing supervisor.

This arrangement retains the six advantages noted for the organizationally decentralized system and adds three others:

1. Knowledgeable supervision of all operators raises their productivity.
2. Work from overloaded operators can be reassigned easily to underloaded operators.
3. Salaries of operators stationed in different departments will be comparable, and will reflect their relative performance.

The first five disadvatnages noted for the organizationally decentralized function still apply, but the sixth one does not. There is one new disadvantage, however:

1. There is no direct relationship between the operator and the department manager whose work the operator is doing.

Mixed Configuration. This arrangement tries to match the advantages of both centralized and decentralized systems. In this configuration, decentralized stations are established for major user departments, which handle their small jobs and rush jobs locally. A word processing center is also established, which takes the longer jobs and those that require more sophisticated equipment or operator knowledge than the locally handled ones.

In a mixed configuration, the decentralized stations should be functionally, not organizationally, decentralized. The supervisor of the center should supervise all the word processing operators and be responsible for all equipment.

Which Configuration Is Best? If much of the company's work consists of long documents such as specifications, contract proposals, and long reports, a centralized or mixed configuration works best. The need to spread a job among several operators is extremely important in this instance. So is meeting deadlines.

If the workload is mainly correspondence, form letters, forms to fill in, and accounting tables, and the departments all have different needs, the organizationally decentralized concept is better. Coordination of work between operators is less necessary. Local control is more important.

If you have a mixed situation, the mixed configuration will fit best.

Equipment Categories

There are three types of word processing equipment:

1. Stand alone systems
2. Shared logic systems
3. Distributed logic systems

Stand Alone Systems. These units are self-contained. A central processing unit (CPU) and memory are part of each individual desktop unit. The units

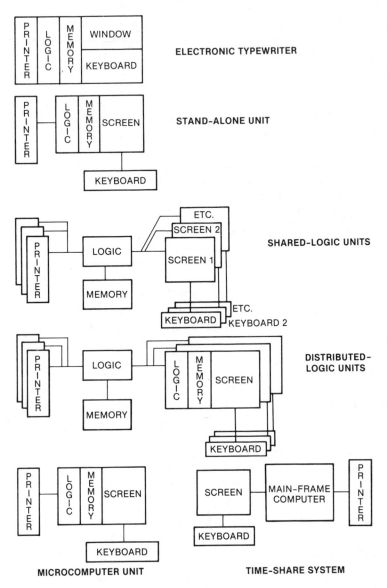

Figure 4-4. Word processor equipment categories. Reprinted with permission from Reba Davis and Jack Balderston, *Word Processing Supervision,* c 1984, The Bobbs-Merrill Company, Inc.

are independent of each other, although many stand alone models can be tied together in a network that allows each to communicate with the others. They may share use of peripheral equipment such as printers and optical character readers (OCR). The latter arrangement is sometimes called a shared resource system.

The advantages of stand alone units are:

1. They are independent. If one unit fails, the others are still operating.
2. If bought in small numbers, they are less expensive than shared or distributed systems.

Their disadvantages are:

1. Limited processing ability: The CPU capacity is limited. The full set of operating instructions must reside in each unit's CPU, and may use a good part of its information-handling capacity.
2. Limited memory: Internal storage capacity is limited by the capacity of the CPU. The hard or floppy disks they use are also limited in capacity.
3. Noncompatability: Work done on units of one make or model cannot be read or edited on other makes or models.

Shared Logic Systems.   The units share a separate CPU and, usually, separate large-capacity memory disks.

The advantages of shared logic systems over stand alone units are:

1. A larger memory capacity is available to each station.
2. More complex programs can be used because the separate CPU has a larger capacity.
3. The shared logic system is less expensive when many stations are attached to one CPU. The system cost is largely in the CPU and central memory. Additional dumb (no CPU or disk drives) terminals can be added at one-fifth the cost of a stand alone unit.
4. Several stations can access the same document simultaneously.
5. Many different peripherals can be used by each station because each is accessed through the CPU. This permits any station to use several printer types, an OCR, a communications line, and so on.

The disadvantage, and it is a major one, is:

1. When the CPU is down, all stations are dead.

Distributed Logic Systems.   This is a marriage of stand alone and shared systems. Distributed logic systems are essentially stand alone units with limited internal memory and processing power that are attached to a central CPU and memory bank. Small programs can be run at each station without using the central CPU. When you have a complex program, or need to access the large central data base, that ability is instantly available.

The concept is excellent. How it fits a particular company's needs depends on what capacities each vendor has built into his stations and central unit. The individual stations are more expensive than the dumb terminals of a distributed logic system because they need their own CPU's and disk drives.

Equipment Features

Editing Features. In the section on electronic typewriters, we described the features of *automatic centering, decimal alignment, word wrap, string search,* and *phrase memory.* The word processing equipment has these features plus many others. We will not define all the features that are available; that is too long a list. The ones below are the more common and useful ones. Knowing what these capabilities are and what the jargon means will give you an understanding of the types of revisions word processing can do easily. You should also know, however, that not all equipment models have all of these features.

Stored Formats. Margin settings, tabs, indents, and so on, are stored as part of the document. Each time a document is retrieved from memory, the machine will be set at that document's particular format. If you change settings within a document, this change will also be remembered.

Automatic Underlining. You define the start and end of what you want underlined using only one or two keystrokes.

Automatic Pagination. The equipment knows what page of the document you are on and prints the correct page number.

Automatic Repagination. If you add or delete large blocks of text, the equipment correctly renumbers all pages.

Automatic Headers or Footers. You input the text of a header or footer and designate where you want it. The equipment places this text at the desired location on each page. As you add and delete text, the header or footer stays at the correct location. Some equipment will place a header at the top left corner of even pages and top right corner of odd pages and incorporate the correct page numbers.

Automatic Footnote Location.   When you use a footnote, it will always appear at the bottom of the page on which it is referenced, even when insertions or deletions change the reference location.

Block Move and Block Copy.   You define a block of text and move it intact to a new location in the document (block move) or copy it to another location (block copy). This feature is used to invert paragraphs or sentences, and to copy formulas or legal phrases that occur often in a document. It is also useful in conjunction with *phrase memory.*

Global Search and Replace. This is a more powerful version of string search. Global search locates a string of characters or words at every place they appear in a document. Replace allows you to replace this string with another string or set of words. The replacement may cover every appearance of the string automatically. Alternately, you may request the equipment to show you each string location so you you can make individual decisions on whether or not to replace. This is useful for changing someone's name in a form letter while leaving the text the same.

Sort   (also called *list processing*). With one or two keystrokes, you sort a column of words (e.g., names) into alphabetical sequence, or numbers into numerical sequence in either ascending or descending order.

Column Move.   This is similar to block move except that the block being defined is a column of numbers. It is useful in statistical work.

Automatic Hyphenation.   During text input or repagination, this feature locates words at the right margin whose ending falls outside a ''hot zone'' several characters wide (whose size can be defined by the operator). It either requests a hyphenation decision by the operator or hyphenates automatically based on rules stored in its program.

Math.   This feature adds, subtracts, multiplies, and divides numbers. It may also calculate percentages.

Justification.   This feature justifies lines at the right margin, making an even right margin as is done in books and newspapers, rather than ragged right margin as in most typed copy (see Figure 4-5). Justification may be interword (spaces are added between words to justify the line) or intercharacter (spaces are added in one-eighth or one-sixteenth of a character width between the individual characters).

Ragged Right

The text on the left side of this figure is typed in the normal ragged right fashion as is used by most companies for reports and for memos and other correspondence. That on the right side is the same text printed out justified at the right margin as is done in newspaper columns and books. In this case, the justification is done by adding spaces between words. In some word processing systems, the spaces are added between each character. This gives a more even appearance to each line.

Right Justified

The text on the left side of this figure is typed in the normal ragged right fashion as is used by most companies for reports and for memos and other correspondence. That on the right side is the same text printed out justified at the right margin as is done in newspaper columns and books. In this case, the justification is done by adding spaces between words. In some word processing systems, the spaces are added between each character. This gives a more even appearance to each line.

Figure 4-5. Ragged right and justified copy.

Spelling Checker.   This is a dictionary of several thousand words that the equipment uses to check the words that have been input. When it discovers a word not in its dictionary, it highlights this word on the screen. The operator can correct or accept the word. It is useful for finding typographical errors.

The above editing features, and others that are available on many models, save the operator considerable amounts of time in laying out and keying a document. It is these features that result in a 30% improvement in productivity for the original input of a document, and a factor of three or more improvement for revisions to the document.

Keyboard.   The keyboard of the word processor is the standard typewriter "qwerty" keyboard, with other keys added. Use of the familiar keyboard reduces the training time needed for a typist to use the equipment.

Keys that are often added are these:

Cursor Keys.   There are four keys with arrows pointing up, down, left, and right that move a mark on the screen up a line, down a line, or one character to the left or right. This mark, the cursor, shows the operator where she or he is in the text. The directional cursor keys are most conveniently grouped in a diamond pattern so that the direction of cursor movement is related to the location of its key.

Ten-Key Pad.   These are the ten keys familiar on an adding machine or calculator. With the number keys are instruction keys to add, subtract, multiply, divide, and total. The number keys are also on the top row of the standard keyboard, but many people find the ten-key pad easier to use when inputting arithmetic tables.

Insert. This is a special function key that instructs the word processor to insert at the location of the cursor whatever is input next. This insert may be characters from the keyboard or may be a block of text retrieved from the memory.

Delete. Another special function key, this instructs the word processor to delete at the position of the cursor whatever you do next. This key, when held down, may backspace over one or more characters. Used in conjunction with *word, line, sentence,* or *paragraph* keys, it will delete the length of text specified.

Control, Code, or *Command.* These are alternate names for a key that is used in conjunction with other keys to initiate the other special functions that the equipment can perform. Usually one of the letters on the keyboard follows use of this key. *Control, M,* for example, might mean "move" the specified text. *Control, F* might mean "file" the document, and so on. Most of the special editing features of word processors are accessed through a *code* key.

Format. This key initiates a program to let you format or reformat a document. For example, this key followed by "L" followed by the digits "one" and "zero" might set the left margin to space 10.

Other Features of Keys. There can be other special function keys that are labeled with a particular feature. Some equipment models use many special function keys. Other models use the *code* plus a letter sequence to perform the same functions.

Some models label special function keys with numbers. Numbered keys are often *multi-function.* Each key means one operation when you are in the text input mode, another when you are formatting, a third when instructing the printer, and so forth. On the bottom line on the screen, just above each key, the equipment specifies that key's function in the mode you are in.

Numbered keys may also be *programmable* by the user. This means that a series of commands that you often use can be assigned as a string to one key. Pressing that key activates the series of steps. One example might be to sort a list of names of frequent customers and print address labels for each.

A *help* key is sometimes available. Pressing it at any stage brings to the screen an explanation of the function you are trying to perform and instructions on what to do next.

An *escape* or *undo* key is also found on some models. This reverses the last step in case you find you gave the wrong command.

The Screen. Some word processors come with full-page screens. These show 54 lines of text. Most of the equipment comes with a half-page screen that shows about 24 lines at a time. All have an 80-character line width. In addition to the text lines, there is always a status line at the top or bottom that tells you where you are in the document, and often a format ruler as well.

The equipment allows you to scroll horizontally or vertically. Perhaps you have set the right margin at space 100 to handle a wide table. When you input to the right of the eightieth character, the screen will move the existing text to the left, opening up the spaces between 80 and 100. Vertical scrolling scans the document line by line so that you can see the other part of the partial page, or the top of the next page or the bottom of the prior page.

Screens use different phosphors to create the character images. Some are green on black, some amber on black, some black on white, and some white on black. Experts are debating which of these is easiest on the eyes, but there is no agreement yet.

The biggest problem for people who look at the screen for many hours a day is glare. The screen should have a rough or coated surface to cut down reflections, or use a filter in front. The operator should also be able to tilt the screen or rotate it to a position having minimum glare. It is best if the screen and keyboard units are separate. The operator can then place both the screen and the keyboard at the height and distance of maximum comfort.

Figure 4-6. Word processor showing screen, disk drives, and keyboard. The CPU is in the case beneath the screen. Photo courtesy NBI Inc.

Control Unit and Memory. The word processor is a computer. Like all other computers, it has a central processing unit (CPU). If the word processor is a stand alone unit, this CPU resides inside the case. If the word processor is part of a shared logic system, the CPU is in a large separate box, connected by cable to the word processor terminal.

The CPU controls the unit's operation. You type an "a." The CPU translates this into the ASCII or EBCDIC code for "a" (the specific "0" and "1" combination that defines an "a"). It stores this in a random access memory (RAM) chip. It also keeps track of the location of the "a" within the chip. At the operator's command, or when the chip starts to fill up, the equipment will move the input to an external memory, usually a magnetic disk.

The CPU also contains the "program" that you are operating. The word processing program takes the commands that you input at the keyboard, translates them to machine language, and executes the desired function. You push *delete, word,* and the CPU finds the location of each character in that word and eliminates each from memory. The operation is not quite this simple, but this is a useful way to visualize how it works.

There is internal memory, the chip or RAM, and there is external memory, the disk. The larger the internal memory, the more work can be held there and the more complex can be the programs that are run. If the RAM is small, some complex operation like alphabetizing a list of names will be very slow as the word processor has to pull some names from the disk, work on them, put them back on the disk, pull out others, work on them, merge the lists, and so on. For simple word processing, a RAM of 64,000 bytes (64 KB or 64,000 characters) is sufficient. For a complex program, you need a RAM of 250 KB.

The size of the external memory, the disks, does not limit the total amount of information you can store. You can have as many removable disks (floppy disks) as you need. You insert each into the word processor as you need the information stored on it.

Disk capacity, however, determines how much information can be worked on at one time. If you are only writing short letters, disk memory size can be small because no letter is likely to exceed a dozen pages. One page is about 2,000 characters or 2 KB. Thus 48 KB of space on a disk (24 KB for the stored letter plus another 24 KB to provide temporary storage while you are editing) takes care of that 12-page letter. But what if you have the employee personnel files on disk, and you want to sort through to find all the people whose anniversary is next month, and you want this listed by department? If the entire file is not on one disk, this sorting operation will be very lengthy and difficult.

Removable floppy disks are available in capacities ranging from about 125,000 up to 1,000,000 characters. Fixed or "hard" disks have capacities up to 10 million characters. The upper limits are being raised by new disk designs each year.

Some floppy disks are 8 inches, some 5 inches, and some 3 to 3½ inches in

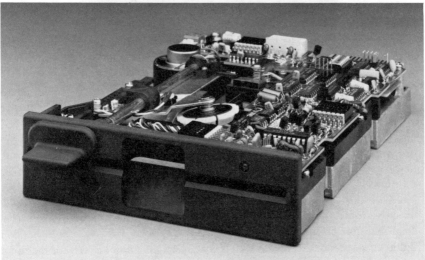

Figure 4-7. Floppy disk (top) and hard disk (bottom). Top photo courtesy 3M Corporation; bottom photo courtesy Pegasus, a division of Great Lakes Computer Peripherals, Inc.

diameter. The size does not necessarily represent the capacity. Some 3-inch disks can pack 1 million characters while their larger brothers have only one-quarter that capacity. Some disks are double-sided, others single-sided. Some are single-density, some double, some quadruple. This terminology refers to the number of tracks on the disk and the packing density of characters onto each track. As you might guess, each word processor is designed to use one type of disk and can use only that type.

All stand alone word processors have two disk drives. This means you have two access ports and can fit two disks into the unit at the same time. This is important when you need to read material from one disk to another, such as when you are archiving information or when you are making a back-up copy of your disk. Having back-up copies is imperative because disks can go bad or be damaged, in which case you need the duplicate. In the writing of this book, each chapter had its own disk. Any disk that was worked on during the day was copied at the end of that day. If something happened to the working disk— and it did several times—the back-up was always up to date through the previous day, and only the current day's work was lost.

If you have a hard disk in a stand alone unit, there will be a port for a floppy disk as well. This is for back-up or for archiving material you are no longer working with frequently. You can back up on the floppy disk only that part of the hard disk you have used that day, thus avoiding having to copy 10 million characters every evening.

Shared logic systems have hard disk memories in the central unit, and each station accesses the memory through a cable connection. The keyboard and screen do not know or care if the control and memory unit are sitting on the same desk or are 50 feet away. The huge central memories also need back-ups. The back-up disks may be other hard disks that are removable, may be high-density floppy disks, or may be magnetic tape.

Equipment Peripherals

Besides the keyboard, screen, CPU, and memory, there are three primary attachments to the word processor. These are a printer, a character reader, and a communications link.

Printers.   The word processor, unlike the typewriter, does not automatically print out what is entered through the keyboard. The word processor stores the contents in memory. To see it on paper you must attach a printer.

A word processor printer, however, is more than just a machine to drive a printing element. Some printers have a buffer memory that will store a page or more of text awaiting printing. Some have communications ability so that you can tie a word processor to a printer using a telephone line and print a document in San Francisco that you created in New York.

Each vendor's word processing CPU handles the code commands differently. The underline command uses one code in one model of equipment, a different code in another model. One model underlines character by character; another underlines the entire string at one time. Because of these differences, the printer's electronics must understand what the CPU commands mean. So the printer must be matched to the make and model of word processor you select. This is very important.

There are five types of printer available:

Figure 4-8. Daisy wheel (top) and thimble (bottom) print elements. Photos courtesy of Qume Corporation, A Subsidiary of ITT Corporation, and of NEC Information Systems.

1. The character printer
2. The dot matrix
3. The ink jet
4. The laser
5. The line printer

The character printer is the most common type in office use.

The *character* printer prints one fully formed character at a time, just as the typewriter key does. The type quality is as good as that from the best office typewriters. Most character printers use a daisy wheel print element. This is a wheel with one or two characters mounted on each spoke. To print a letter, the appropriate spoke is hit from behind, and the character hits ribbon and paper. It is fast, allowing print speeds up to 55 characters per second.

A modification to the daisy wheel is the thimble printer. The wheel is bent 90 degrees and rotates horizontally instead of vertically. Some printers also use the "golf ball" typing element.

The character printer is sometimes called a *letter-quality* printer. This is a misnomer because other types of printer also produce output whose quality is suitable for correspondence.

The *dot matrix* printer is the type most often used with personal computers. It is less expensive and faster than the character printer. In this type, a vertical bar of small pins, often nine pins long, travels horizontally. The outline of each character is formed by having the appropriate pin strike the ribbon and paper at the position necessary to form the character. Each character is a series of dots, commonly in a 7×9 matrix. Printers with a 7×9 matrix are considered to be draft-quality printers. (See Figure 4-9.)

Dot matrix printers with dot densities of 12×18 or higher are starting to

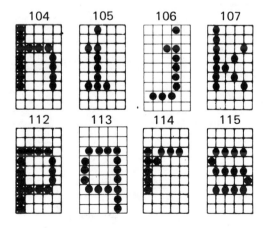

Figure 4-9. Dot matrix letters. Courtesy Epson America, Inc.

appear on the market. At these densities it is hard to tell a character formed by a dot pattern from the fully formed character of the daisy wheel printer. Because the traveling bar of pins is inherently faster than a wheel that must be rotated and also is simpler in concept, these high-density dot matrix printers may become the standard of tomorrow.

Ink jet printers squirt a small jet of ink onto the paper in a pattern similar to the dot matrix. There is no ribbon and no contact with the paper by any part of the printer. These are even faster than dot matrix units, having print speeds up to 300 characters per second, and are virtually silent. (See Figure 4-10.)

Laser printers use a laser beam to paint an image of each letter directly onto the paper. This image is fused onto the paper in a manner similar to that used by copy machines. Very high quality, equal to book print quality, can be attained. Type styles and sizes can be programmed at the printer and changed easily within the document. This is a very versatile technique, competitive with photocomposition. At present it is expensive and suitable only for very high-volume operations.

Line printers print an entire line at one time by handling all the character spaces simultaneously. Extremely high speeds are possible but quality is generally poor. These printers are often used with mainframe computers.

Sheet and Envelope Feeders. The printer will print a page unattended while the word processing operator is working on the next document. But this

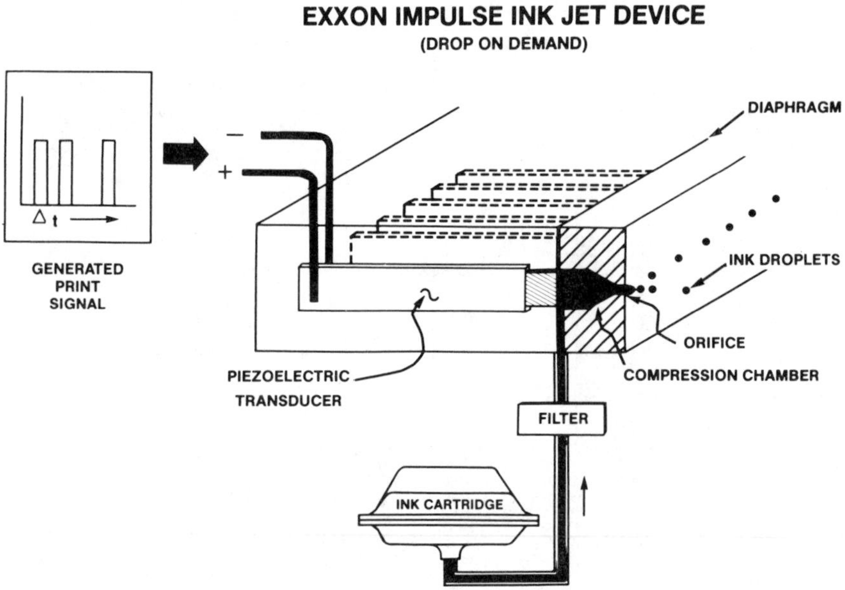

EXXON IMPULSE INK JET DEVICE
(DROP ON DEMAND)

Figure 4-10. Schematic diagram of an ink jet printer. Courtesy Exxon Office Systems Company.

advantage is lost if the operator must get up and go to the printer after each page is printed to remove the finished sheet of paper and insert a fresh one. If continuous form paper is not acceptable for output such as correspondence, a sheet feeder becomes a necessary attachment to the printer.

The sheet feeder feeds cut paper into the printer from one or two trays, and it stacks the finished pages. The two-tray feeder holds letterheads and plain sheets, or regular size and legal size sheets. Some feeders have a third tray for envelopes. The sheet feeder must be matched to the printer because it must accept commands through the printer regarding which tray the next page comes from. (See Figure 4-11.)

Optical Character Recognition. Optical character recognition (OCR) is a way to read typed documents directly into a computer or word processor memory without having to re-key the document.

The OCR scans a piece of paper with a series of very thin light beams. If the light sees white paper, there is a strong reflection. If it sees black, such as from part of a character, there is less reflection. A beam scans the page, and the reflectance pattern of each character is compared to the pattern of each letter

Figure 4-11. Dual sheet and envelope feeder mounted on printer. Photo courtesy ZIYAD (R), Inc.

and number stored in the OCR's memory. When the OCR makes a match, the ASCII or EBCDIC symbol for that character is sent to the word processing disk. Thus a typed or printed page is quickly transferred from paper to disk. (See Figure 4-12.)

It is not quite that easy. The pattern recognition built into the OCR's memory must match the type style on the document. An OCR programmed to recognize Letter Gothic will not read Courier or Prestige Elite. The OCR must also know the way in which the word processor stores characters on its disks. Thus a double match is required. One match is to the type style and the other to the word processor's command program. Some OCR's can be programmed to accept more than one type style and to handle more than one model of word processing equipment.

There are some other problems. Because OCR's read the difference between black and white, they are very sensitive to dust, dirt, and smudges. A small

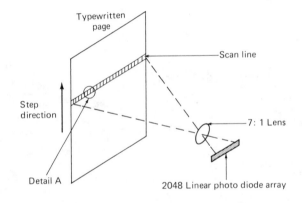

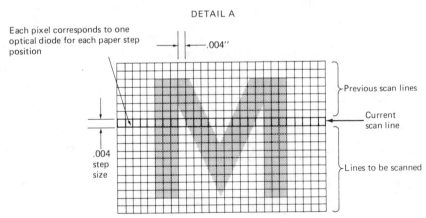

Figure 4-12. Diagram of OCR scan system. Courtesy Dest Corporation.

dust speck may be read as a period. They are also sensitive to paper alignment. If the line creeps up out of the scanner beam, it may not see the tail of a "y" and may read it as a "v," or it may not recognize a character at all. All OCR's insert a symbol in the text where they cannot interpret a character. Every page that has been scanned must be proofread carefully for errors.

Communications.   Most word processors have communications as an avilable option. This allows text to be sent to or received from another word processor of the same model, and sometimes other makes and models. Most communications options allow communications to IBM mainframes. Most can also act as sending and receiving terminals for telex and TWX.

SUMMARY

Use of machine dictation is five times as fast a way to input text as is writing longhand. It also represents a five-fold savings in cost to the organization.

Three categories of dictation equipment have been described: centralized systems, desktop recorders, and portable recorders. There are two forms of central systems: the endless loop tank and the cassette, either of which can be tied into a network of several units so that multiple users can access the system at the same time. Centralized systems are the least expensive approach when there are many users and are appropriate for dictation of short and routine documents. Desktop units are best for long documents and creative writing. Portable units are good for trips.

There are three types of tape cassette, which are not interchangeable. Standard cassettes are about 2½ in. × 4 in.; microcassettes and minicassettes are both about 1¼ in. × 2 in., and use a tape speed half that of standard cassettes. There are differences between the types that make them noncompatible.

Electronic typewriters, which are typewriters with a limited memory, are at the low end of the word processing spectrum. Features found on some units that enhance productivity include: one-keystroke centering, decimal alignment, word wrap, character string search, and phrase memory.

Word processors add a video screen, a larger memory, and additional features to the electronic typewriter. With word processors, the time and cost of typing a page are less than with a standard correcting typewriter. The cost of revising a page is less than half that with a typewriter.

Ergonomics involves adapting work stations to humans. Work surfaces and chairs with adjustable heights, tiltable and rotatable screens, and movable keyboards help to reduce fatigue and enhance productivity by 10% to 25%. Work breaks each hour are important.

Word processing systems can be configured as centralized, organizationally decentralized, functionally decentralized or mixed. The advantages and disadvantages of each have been described. Which configuration is better depends on the type of work in the company. If each department's needs are different or the work consists of simple correspondence or forms, the organizationally decentralized concept is best. If there are a lot of long documents and high-priority work, the centralized or mixed concept is best.

The advantages and disadvantages of the three types of word processing equipment have been described: stand alone systems, shared logic systems, and distributed logic systems.

In addition to the time-saving advantages also found with electronic type-writers, word processors may feature: stored formats, one-keystroke underlining, automatic pagination and repagination, automatic headers and footers, automatic footnote location, block move and copy, global search and replace, automatic hyphenation, justification, sorting, math, and spelling check.

Features of the keyboard and screen have been described in this chapter, as has the operation of the central processing unit and memory storage disks.

There are several types of printers available: character printers such as daisy wheel or thimble printers, dot matrix printers, ink jet printers, and laser printers. Other peripheral equipment that supports word processors includes optical character readers and communications options.

FOR FURTHER INFORMATION

Dictation Systems

Kupsh, Joyce, Anderson, Donna, and Meyer, Lois. *Machine Dictation and Transcription*. New York: John Wiley & Sons, 1978.

Word Processing

Bergerud, Marly, and Gonzalez, Jean. *Word/Information Processing: Concepts of Office Automation*, 2nd ed. New York: John Wiley & Sons, 1984.

Davis, Reba, and Balderston, Jack. *Word Processing Supervision*. Indianapolis: Bobbs-Merrill Publ., 1984.

Glatzer, Hal. *Introduction to Word Processing*. Berkeley, CA: Sybex, 1981.

Goldfield, Randy J. *Implementing Word Processing*. New York: The Free Press (Macmillion, Inc.), 1983.

Ergonomics

Springer, T. J., *Ergonomics: The Real Issues, Office Administration and Automation*, XLV, 5 (May, 1984).

5
More Office Elements

"My Apple is really useful here in the office. I used to spend a lot of time just waiting for a terminal to be free so I could get on the large computer. Now I can do my analyses right here at my desk. I don't understand why the company won't buy them for us. I had to buy this with my own money and bring it in from home."

"I know what you mean. I've got an IBM personal computer that I bought for my job. I didn't pay for it though. A certain amount of creative financing with the expense accounts got me this one."

"What about my DEC professional? For my type of work, it's the best. I paid for this one and programmed it at home. I still carry it home in the car on weekends. I wish I could have one in the office and one at home."

Personal computers, also known as PC's or small business computers, have invaded the office by the hundreds of thousands. Many of them have arrived by bootlegged means. Legitimate or not, they are a very promising way by which to improve office efficiency and for the professional to increase his or her own personal effectiveness.

Other office elements whose functions affect office productivity are data processing, telecommunications, reprographics, mail, and files management. This chapter discusses these elements, and their integration with each other and with the functions covered in Chapter 4.

PERSONAL COMPUTERS

The personal computer (PC), or small business computer, is becoming powerful enough to handle many functions in the office. Its use can:

1. Speed up the professional's analytical calculations.
2. Improve decisions by permitting more alternatives to be considered.
3. Search data bases outside the company for reference information.
4. Aid the secretary and the professional in maintaining schedules, appointments, tickler files, and other aspects of "desk management."
5. Help the office staff maintain records, lists, inventories, and indexes that are easily accessible, simple to search through, and always up to date.

6. Aid the secretary by being used as a word processor.
7. Speed up information flow by acting as an electronic mail station.

The PC should not be considered a competitor to a large central computer or a local minicomputer. It is an assistant to the mainframe, taking some of the computing work load and doing it efficiently away from the host machine. It is like a paraprofessional helping a professional. Those computing needs that do not require the power or capacity of the expensive mainframe are done much more conveniently on individual PC's.

Analytical Support

The professional should consider the PC as a personal tool, much like the office calculator and the telephone. Each PC should have programs that are specific to the professional's particular job. Your PC should have programs that handle the types of calculations and tasks that you perform.

If you are an engineer, there are programs for the PC that work the formulas you frequently use. If you now do your calculations manually, this is a major time saver. If you now use the mainframe, you no longer need to worry about its being "down" or tied up with higher-priority work. Having the programs you use available on your own PC provides more flexibility in the way you use your time.

If you are in charge of a program or project, you are concerned with cost control. Each month you get long tab runs from your financial group, in which are buried, for example, data on purchases charged to your project. With a PC, you no longer need to leaf through the runs, copy off the few figures you need, and add them manually. You use your PC to call up the monthly report from the main data base, and you select the segment you want, namely, payments on purchase orders. You sort through this segment using your project number, purchase order numbers, dates, or item names. You get on your screen only the items you are looking for. To get a total cost for what is shown, you push the PC's "total" key. This is faster than manual methods and less prone to error. It is also more current, for the data base will be updated daily as invoices are paid, accounts credited, and so forth.

If you are an accountant, your PC will have a series of accounting programs, statistical analysis programs, spreadsheets, and the ability to prepare tables, graphs, and reports in the format that you habitually use. As you enter data into accounts payable, a program calculates your cash needs by day or week. Another program ages all accounts due and highlights those that require attention. A discounted cash flow analysis requires that you enter only the amount, the discount rate, and the time. If your manager likes to see results in graphical form, a program draws bar charts, pie charts, or line charts directly from the tabular data calculated by the PC. All these tasks can also be done on the main-

Figure 5-1. IBM personal computer. Photo courtesy IBM Systems Products Division.

frame, but the PC's allow the professionals to have special programs that cover their respective functions and to have access to these programs at all times.

If you are in marketing, you do a multitude of studies on demographic trends, market penetration, territorial sales, and so on. You are manipulating large quantities of data. There are undoubtedly more questions to which you want answers than there has been any way to get them, at least with limited staff and time. The PC gives you the chance to ask a question at 9 o'clock and have the answer by 9:15.

Use of a PC will generally speed up the professional's analytical work. It is slower than a mainframe for very complex calculations; you may want to keep doing them on the central computer. But for many professionals and many tasks, the PC is more effective. We have given only a small sample of the many analytical programs that a PC can handle. For each profession, there is a different set. The PC hardware can handle thousands of problems. All that is required is different sets of software packages. We have further comments on software availability later in this section.

Decision Support

All professionals are asked to make judgments. PC programs allow "what if" questions to be asked on any subject that can be stated as a formula. The formula can be as simple as a profit and loss calculation or as complex as a model of the national economy. "If I raise the price of one product line by 3%, what is the effect on sales and profits?" "If the price of a material drops by 5 cents per pound, can I drop my finished goods price below my competitor's and still maintain my profit margin?"

A model can be prepared of a production flow process, a chemical reaction, a market, a decision tree, and so on. For each model one variable can be changed, and the program will calculate the effect on all other parameters. The calculation is performed in a matter of seconds or minutes. Many alternative strategies can be tried out to help the professional reach a better decision.

Information Searches

The PC gives you access to a world of information outside your company. Using a telephone line connection, you can access the Dow Jones Retrieval Service or the text of the *New York Times*. You can search the business literature of the past ten years to see what articles have been written on any subject. You can find out how to clean up chemical spills, what patents have been filed on a subject, or anything else that is outside your normal range of reading. (See Table 5-1).

With the PC, you can search the engineering and scientific literature for references to any subject; the *Engineering Index* and *Chemical Abstracts* are available to you on the screen. You can get the full text of all legal decisions handed down by the federal and state courts. You don't even have to look page by page through a magazine or set of documents to find what you need. You can select those that match your needs exactly by using key words to define the subject you want. You can also limit the search to stay within a specified range of dates.

Desk Management

This term is used to cover the self-help functions often handled by accessories on a desk. Examples are an appointment calendar, a ticker file, a telephone directory, a personnel roster, an address list, a file index.

A PC can be used by itself for analytical support, decision support, and information searches. For desk management, however, the PC must be tied into a network. For useful desk management, the secretary should have a terminal tied to the manager or professional's PC so that she or he can both write and read entries on that PC. To make it cost-effective to have telephone lists, rosters, organization charts, and announcements accessible through a PC screen, most of the staff must be on the network.

Department Records

Inventory lists, file indexes, status reports, follow-up ticker lists, schedules, and many other paraprofessional and clerical operations performed within the de-

Table 5-1. Data Bases Available through Personal Computers.[a]

ABI/INFORM (business management and administration)
AGRICOLA (agricultural library)
AIRLINE SCHEDULES
BOOKS IN PRINT
CHEMICAL ABSTRACTS
COMPUTER AND CONTROL ABSTRACTS
DOW JONES AND S&P INDEXES
ELECTRICAL AND ELECTRONIC ABSTRACTS
ENGINEERING INDEX
ERIC (education database)
FEDERAL and STATE NEWS (UPI)
HARVARD BUSINESS REVIEW
HOTEL and RESTAURANT GUIDE
INTERNATIONAL PHARMACEUTICAL ABSTRACTS
INTERNATIONAL SOFTWARE DATABASE
MAGAZINE INDEX (over 400 U.S. magazines)
MANAGEMENT CONTENTS
MATHEMATICAL REVIEWS
MEDLINE and MEDLARS (medical topics)
MICROCOMPUTER INDEX
MOVIE and TV REVIEWS
NEWSSEARCH (index of the *New York Times, Washington Post, Wall Street Journal,*
   Los Angeles Times, and *Christian Science Monitor*)
NTIS (government published technical reports)
PAIS (public service information service)
PATDATA (all patents registered since 1975)
PHYSICS ABSTRACTS
PSYCHOLOGY ABSTRACTS and PSYCH INFO
SOCIAL SCIENCE CITATION INDEX
SPORTS NEWS
STANDARD & POOR'S NEWS
STOCK and BOND PRICES

[a]Partial list of data bases available through BRS/AFTER DARK (1200 Route 7, Latham, NY 12110), KNOWL-EDGE INDEX (DIALOG Information Services, 3460 Hillview Ave., Palo Alto, CA 94304), and THE SOURCE (SM) (1616 Anderson Rd., McLean, VA 22102).

partment may be handled by PC programs. In some cases, the expense of input to a PC program will not be worthwhile. But if the information is to be transmitted, copied onto another report, or manipulated in some way, it usually pays to automate the function.

Secretarial Word Processing

All PC's can run word processing programs. Some programs are easier to learn and use than others. PC's have fewer special function keys and fewer features than dedicated word processing equipment, and most PC's are slower in executing editing functions. For a secretary who types most of the time, the dedicated word processor will be more effective. It may be preferable to have a secretary who is mostly an administrative assistant be part of the PC network. This is a decision the manager must make.

As more PC functions are placed on word processors and as better word processing programs are made available for PC's, this dilemma will disappear. You will have the best of both worlds. Until then, a choice is required.

Electronic Mail

Once a PC network is in place and most professionals and managers are on it, messages can be sent from screen to screen, bypassing the paper copy step. This process is electronic mail, a subject that is discussed further in Chapter 7.

Standardization

One problem involving office use of PC's was illustrated by the imaginary conversation at the start of this chapter. What do you do about a mix of models? Should you standardize on one model, or on a few?

The problem is that a program written to run on one model will not run on another without being modified. This is true even if both models use the same operating system, such as CP/M (Control Program for Microprocessors) or MS-DOS (Microsoft–Disk Operating System). Information generated in the format used by one model cannot be read directly by another model. You can end up with a computer tower of Babel.

This is the same issue one faces with standardizing on word processors, typewriters, copy machines, dictation equipment, and so on, but it is more complex and potentially more expensive than standardizing in those cases.

It probably is not too important which PC model or models the company accepts, provided they meet the following criteria:

1. The PC is able to communicate with the computer mainframe in which the company's data reside.
2. Many software programs are being written for the equipment, not only by the hardware vendor but also by the major independent software houses.
3. Upgrades to the equipment capabilities are anticipated from the vendor.

Mainframe Compatibility.   The first of the above criteria is very important. If you need accounting information, production statistics, inventory numbers, and so forth, that are kept in the mainframe system, you should be able to bring those data instantly to the screen as you do your work. This mainframe compatibility should be required for all PC's throughout the organization. If there is any exception, it should be only for those few individuals whose jobs really are isolated from the rest of the working staff and who need a special application that is available only through some other equipment model.

Software Availability.   Software programs for PC's that are commercially available now number in the thousands, with the number still growing by leaps and bounds. You can buy a program to do almost any business function. More software programs are available for some PC's, however, than for others; so it is important that you know what software you want before you decide on the PC hardware. Be sure that the software package comes configured for the particular model you are considering. You may be told that a program runs on any CP/M or on any MS-DOS equipment, but that does not necessarily mean that it comes configured for the particular PC you are considering. (See Table 5-2.)

There is so much software available commercially at very low prices, that it is both foolish and expensive to spend time creating a program. Only when you are sure there is no suitable program available should you do your own. Simi-

Table 5-2. Software Programs for PC's, a Partial List.

Word processing	Business graphics
General accounting	Project planning
General ledger	Scheduling
Accounts payable	Project tracking
Accounts receivable	Project control
Payroll	Business marketing
Financial analysis	Interactive training tool
Inventory control	Electronic mail
Job costing	TWX, telex terminal
Cash flow analysis	Desk calendar organizer
Time billing	Telephone directory
Property management	Personnel list and data
Spreadsheet analysis	Statistical analyses
Testing "What if . . ." hypotheses	Quantitative decison making
Tax planning	File indexes
Income tax preparation	Data base systems
Amortization calculations	Household finance
Learning programming	Household inventory
Order entry	Games
Mailing list management	Interactive books
Address file update	Spelling checker
Forms design	Thesaurus
Retail management	Library cataloging
Legal office management	Metric conversion
Medical office management	Learning computers
School administration	Communications
Real estate analysis	Stock market analysis
Time management	Literature searching
Writing composition	Speed reading
Computer program languages	Photocomposition

larly, the temptation to customize a software package should be avoided. You and your staff will spend the bulk of your time creating or modifying programs rather than using them. It takes a month or two to become proficient on a packaged program. But it may take six months or more to customize a program and a year to create a program from scratch.

Homemade software will also contain "bugs" or errors. This is inevitable with any program. You cannot anticipate all the wrong commands an operator may use and assure that one of them does not jam the equipment. You will be debugging for a long time. On purchased software, the package supplier brings out corrected copies, usually at no cost to you. Using purchased software, you can also get updates and modifications at a relatively low cost.

Because there are so many PC models and because the capabilities of each are being modified and improved at least once each year, many companies have chosen to standardize on one or two of the better-known brands. This strategy optimizes the needs of the staff as a whole. It looks to the future as well as to today. However, because of this standard some professionals may not get the combination of hardware and software that is best for their current needs. Nonetheless, if the standard hardware is adequate, stay with it. New software will be coming, and your equipment will always be compatible with the other PC's and the PC network.

Within the above limitations, the PC is a major means of increasing the professional person's productivity. Many of the "clerical" activities that are performed by professionals (see Chapter 2) can be automated through use of the PC.

DATA PROCESSING

Data processing has been a major part of the office for over two decades, and it has taken over much of the routine paperwork. It does the accounting and prepares checks. It takes raw numbers from the manufacturing area and creates status reports on production. It may issue production orders. It takes stockroom withdrawal slips and creates inventory status reports. It may print restocking orders. It maintains the personnel files, remembering your birthday, when your next review is due, and your salary history since you joined the company. It saves a lot of clerical work and time.

Uses

The power of data processing is the ability to manipulate vast amounts of data rapidly. The data are numbers, any kind of numbers: sales, production, inventory, accounting, salaries, dates, employee I.D.'s, and so on. To handle payroll, employees are given numbers. To make personnel records easier to handle, departments and job classifications are given numbers. Any information that you want to sort and select is handled best by use of numbers.

Data processing uses this power to create useful information from a jumble of raw data. We distinguish between information and data as follows. Data are individual facts or statistics, any one of which has no significance in itself. Information is data that have been processed and summarized in a form from which something can be learned, or a decision can be made. The ability to create useful information from data is essential to the operation of every business. Its importance cannot be overemphasized.

For example, you pour into the computer ten thousand numbers that represent a day's sales on each of 1000 products in a dozen territories by 100 salespeople. The computer program digests from this the sales by product, by person, and by territory. It compares them to last week's sales and last month's and last year's. It calculates sales commissions. It shows what is still in inventory. It hightlights any shortages. All this is information necessary to make decisions about production, distribution, credit, financing, and so forth.

Data processing creates and manipulates information. This is not, as some data processing managers would have you believe, the same thing as managing information. The activities involved in managing were listed in Chapter 2. Managing involves planning, directing, and controlling. Corporate executives, not data processing experts, plan (decide) what information is needed, direct its acquisition and its form, and control what parts of it are seen by whom and also what use is made of it. Data processing is a vital function, and its managers have a very important role in the corporation, but they are not information managers.

Regimentation

Data processing is a regimented discipline. Because of the cost of programming and the cost of mainframes, most business programs are written as single-purpose inflexible programs. The report formats are built in, the time of the month a report is run is preestablished, and the form in which the input must be provided is fixed.

Each report is designed to serve several people. It shows what each person wanted to see at the time the program was written. If this turns out not to be what is really needed, or if staff changes bring in new managers who want different information or another format, that is generally too bad. The long list of other things to program and the cost of reprograming usually prevents a change. Therefore, you must learn how to read the reports that exist and how to find the information you want in them. Rarely can you customize a data processing report to show only what you want to see and to show it in the form in which you want to see it.

One result of this is a degree of inflexibility shown by many people who have a strong data processing background. Those who are inflexible make poor change agents. They are usually not the people to put in charge of automating an office function. Inflexible people and those not truly oriented to providing service should not manage a word processing group, nor should they supervise any other aspect of office support.

Networks

Besides operating the mainframes, minicomputers, and programming applications, the data processing function is also involved with networks.

Networks tie computers, word processors, and PC's to each other. Networks within a company building or group of buildings are local area networks, often abbreviated LAN's. LAN's are a very complicated subject.

There are PBX, broadband, and baseband networks. A PBX (Private Branch Exchange) network uses the existing telephone system. With a digital switching unit (DBX) the telephone wiring can be used as both a voice and a data network. A *broadband* network uses coaxial cable, and different frequency bands to send simultaneous messages along the cable. Cable television is a broadband network. A *baseband* network also uses cable, but transmits only one message at a time. Ethernet is a baseband network. There are pros and cons for each and a considerable difference in cost.

There are star, ring, and bus networks—these designations refer to the layout of the stations on the network. In a *star* network, there is a central control or switching station, and all others branch out from it. A message originating at one station goes to the switching station and is routed from there to its destination. In a *ring* network, all stations join hands in a circle, and the message is passed from station to station until it reaches its destination. In the *bus* network all stations branch from a single cable. It differs from the ring in that the ends are not joined. The message is inserted onto the bus, travels along it, and is extracted by the proper receiving station. (See Figure 5-2.)

There are also different techniques to access the networks and to allocate messages to the channel. No one of these is compatible with the others.

If you are planning a local area network, involve the data processing experts in the selection. If you already have one, see them to learn the uses and the limitations of the equipment you have.

TELECOMMUNICATIONS

Both voice and data communications come under this heading. Local data networks were discussed above. In this section we restrict the discussion to voice communications.

We tend to take the telephone for granted, not giving it much thought until

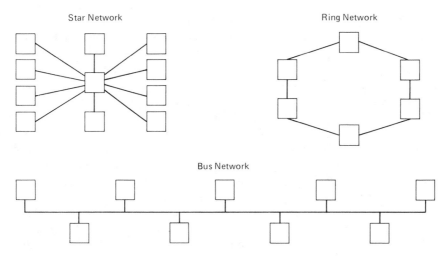

Figure 5-2. Three network topographies.

we are unable to reach somebody and become frustrated. The telephone can be a big time saver, or a big time waster.

Equipment

Until recently, all telephone equipment belonged to one of the common carriers. You leased your desk instrument. If you had a company switchboard, you leased it too. You paid for access to the telephone company switching network, which was probably located in a building at some distance from you. You also paid for all the calls you made over the cables and lines that the telephone companies had installed to your building and across the nation.

Today you can own the desk set and your company switching system. You can use the cable, microwave, and satellite links of companies other than the common carriers. Technology is replacing analog voice switching and transmission with digital switching and transmission. Voice networks are becoming the same as data networks.

Costs

You should know about costs of telephone systems leased from the common carriers. Rates are regulated by the states and vary from state to state, but the concept is the same throughout the nation. First, you pay a separate charge for every feature on your system. You can get a list of charges for each option, but this list is neither easy to get nor easy to read and understand.

On a desk instrument, there is a base monthly charge for the set. There is an additional monthly charge for each option you add: the intercom line, the buzzer, each button on a multi-button set, the light behind each button, push-button calling, the "hold" feature, Call Forwarding, Call Waiting, and so on. Business rates are higher than residential rates. A fixed monthly charge of $50 for a five-button phone is not unusual. This fixed cost does not include message units and long distance charges. If you purchase the system, you have a high one-time outlay, but you avoid the monthly equipment charges.

Charges for local and long distance calls do not differ significantly between business service and the residential service you pay for at home. These rates are being overhauled at the time this is written (early 1984), and this statement may no longer be true as you read this.

Use of WATS (Wide Area Telephone Service) lines reduces long distance rates. For each outside line that you designate, you guarantee that you will use a certain number of long distance hours per month for which you pay a flat cost. For use above the guaranteed minimum, you pay a long distance rate that is somewhat lower than regular long distance rates. Thus WATS time is not "free" to a user except when the company fails to use its guaranteed minimum.

There are companies that compete with AT&T for long distance service. In some locations and for some patterns of long distance calling, their rates are lower. The rates for each competing company are different, and it takes a thorough analysis to determine which is the least expensive system.

The telephone is a major business expense, which can constitute as much as 10% of a business's total overhead cost. Often one of the least controlled costs, it is also one that each person can influence significantly by placing calls through the minimum cost route (e.g., WATS) and by reducing the length of each conversation.

Telephone Tag

The most frustrating aspect of telephone calling is the unanswered phone at the other end. Almost as annoying is reaching a secretary or an answering service that promises to have the person call back but cannot tell you when to expect the call. This starts a game of telephone tag. The person calls back, but you are out or tied up; someone takes a message at your end. Later you call, and the other person is out. This game can go on for days. It can prevent you from finishing a job. It also costs a lot of your time and runs up the telephone bill.

Estimates suggest that only 20% of all telephone calls get through on the initial try. What can be done to reduce this source of waste?

An unanswered phone is inexcusable. If callers are trying to reach you, their time should not be wasted by having to call repeatedly. They should be told when to expect to find you in. They may want to call someone else if you will not be available soon.

There are several ways to assure that any incoming call is picked up. One is to "call forward" to a secretary. If the secretary is frequently away from her desk, "call forward" to a message operator. Use of a dedicated message operator is generally less expensive and more reliable than using a busy secretary. In either case, the professional must remember to tell the secretary or operator the time at which he or she will return. You must also remember to call for accumulated messages. A light at the telephone can be used to inform you that a message waits, as is done at many hotels.

Another method is to have callers leave messages on a tape recorder. This concept is good, but many people dislike talking to a recording machine. When someone calls, that person expects to reach you, and to take a minute or two saying "hello" and "how are you" and making other small talk. This gives the caller time to gather his or her thoughts. The person confronted with a recorder is generally not ready to leave a concise message about what he or she wants. A variation of the recorder is "voice mail," which has certain advantages. It is discussed in Chapter 8.

REPROGRAPHICS

The term reprographics covers all forms of copying and printing. It used to be that "copying" meant use of photocopiers or xerography equipment. Some years ago, these were short-run, slow machines with relatively poor copy quality and a relatively high cost per copy. Their advantage was convenience and ease of use. A user could make the copies without help. "Printing" was done on offset equipment that was high-volume, fast (after set-up), high-quality, and had a relatively low cost per copy. Printing equipment required special training to use.

Today the line between copying and printing has blurred. There are fast copiers that handle high volumes with excellent quality and require little operator training. (See Figure 5-3.)

Traditional Photocopiers[1]

Traditionally, copying is thought of in two categories:

1. Centralized high-volume copiers
2. Convenience copiers

Central Copiers. High-volume, long-document copying is done on a central copier. This copier should be fast, and should have an automatic feeder on

---

[1]This section is adapted from Davis, Reba, and Balderston, Jack, *Word Processing Supervision,* Indianapolis: Bobbs-Merrill Publishing Co., 1984, Chapter 14.

Figure 5-3. High-volume copying machine. Photo courtesy Xerox Corporation.

the input side and sorter bins or a collator on the output side. It should be able to staple or bind the documents.

The central copier should have all possible features that your organization can use. *Reducation capability* is important, generally to reduce 10 × 14 in. paper and 11 × 17 in. paper to 8½ × 11 in. If you have a photo lab or graphics unit with a variable focal length reduction camera, that camera can take care of other reduction sizes, and the two standard reduction modes will be adequate on the copier. If you do not have such a camera, and you prepare lots of drawings and charts, consider a copier that has a fully variable reduction capability. *Two-sided copying* is important to reduce the amount and cost of paper used and reduce the bulk of large reports. Controls to *vary image darkness* allow you to copy from poor originals and to make good overhead transparencies.

A large central copier is less expensive to use on a per-copy basis than is a convenience copier. On a leased central copier that turns out 100,000 pages per month, it costs between four cents and six cents to copy one page. This cost includes the equipment lease, paper, toner, and salary of the machine operator. A large part of the central copy costs are fixed costs (i.e., the operator's salary and the equipment's minimum monthly lease). Therefore, the more that is sent to the central copier, the less expensive will be the cost per copy.

Convenience Copiers.   The one and two copies required of a letter or document draft are done on convenience copiers. These are slower, have fewer features, are easier for the user to operate, and are far less expensive than central copiers. In a large office, convenience copiers are located so that one is readily accessible to all secretaries and staff.

Since convenience copiers are do-it-yourself machines, the user has instant turnaround time. If you want a copy of a page in order to write notes on it for retyping, or to send it to another person, this immediate availability is important. Many professionals do their own copying so they can make marginal notes on a page while their thoughts are still fresh. However, it costs about ten cents a page to copy a page on a convenience copier, including the time of the user.

The Mix of Copy Machines. As professionals and secretaries become used to making their own copies, they tend to request more features on the convenience copiers. They want to make more of their copies on the nearby machines, even when the number of copies is large and the need is not urgent. So they ask for faster convenience copiers with features such as collators and feeders.

For lower overall cost, the organization wants as much work as possible routed to the central copier. The central machine's role is mainly for large jobs where its speed enables a lot of work to be done rapidly. The large machine is not efficient on small jobs that require more time to set up than to run. In general, it is more efficient to do jobs where each page must be handled individually on a convenience copier and do production runs on the central machine.

To assure that this happens, the organization should avoid placing collators and input feeders on convenience copiers. Multi-page documents are rarely the type of work that you need to have copied instantly. To provide a reasonable response time from the central copy room, the standard for work turnaround time should be two hours (except for several-hundred-page documents). This is sufficient for all but emergency cases.

Laser Printers

This equipment stands at the interface between copiers and printers. Laser printers use laser beams to paint the image of each character (actually a very tight dot pattern) on the paper. Since the laser beam is computer-controlled, the beam can be made to imitate any type style available. The result is typeset-quality characters. (See Figure 5-4.)

Laser printers can use word processing disks as input, but not all disks can be read by all printing systems. Disks from the equipment of two major vendors can be used as input today; those from other vendors will undoubtedly be usable in the future. Some laser printers mix copying with printing. A page placed on the ground-glass screen is copied in the same way as by conventional copiers. The copied pages can be collated together with printed pages in one document.

Ra

Figure 5-4. An 8 point character formed on a Xerox laser printer, shown actual size and enlarged approximately ten times. Courtesy the Xerox Corporation.

Laser printers can be very fast, one-half to two pages per second. They are also quite expensive. But for very large volumes where the choice lies between a conventional print shop and a laser printer, the laser printer may be the better and less expensive option.

Less expensive laser printers are available that are smaller, slower and have fewer features than the ones just described. They fit on a desk top, range in price from $3,000 and $10,000, and operate at speeds of eight to twelve pages per minute, much slower than the full featured machines. They will not provide the print quality shown in figure 5-4 since the dot resolution pattern is less dense. Their print quality, however, is better than dot matrix printers.

Their role is similar to that of the convenience copier. A convenience copier does not have the speeds, options, or quality of a more expensive central copier, but it is simple to operate and inexpensive enough that several may be placed near users. It allows the professional staff to handle their small, simple copying jobs. Desk top laser printers fit this same description. They may be used as high quality printers for office PC's and word processors, making one or two original sets of a letter or report for direct distribution without further duplicating. They will not be useful, however, for multiple copies and long documents. They are quieter than dot matrix printers, which will be an important consideration in some office locations.

Phototypesetting

This process produces print-quality type on a photographic positive film. It uses the same type styles used by printing presses. The output looks exactly like that in a book or newspaper. The film is usually a strip as wide as the width of a page and many yards long, and is cut into page-size lengths. Each of these becomes a master from which a plate is made. The plates are put on a press, and the document is printed in the conventional way.

The character image is formed in much the same way as in the laser printer. It may be painted by an optical beam, or a laser beam that is computer-controlled. In some equipment, it is formed by a set of masks cut in the shape of each character. The input to a phototypesetter can be a word processing disk. Because this technology is older than the laser printer, input is accepted from the equipment of more vendors than is the case today with laser printers. Codes are inserted at the phototypesetter to specify type styles and formats. The equipment's computer reads the text from the word processing disk, reads the codes that define type style and size, and creates the appropriate set of character images.

One advantage of typeset output is the smaller space required for a printed document in contrast to a typed document. Print, including phototypeset print, uses proportionally spaced characters and a smaller type size. As a result, there are more characters per line and more lines per inch. About twice as much text can fit a printed page as on a typewritten or word processor output page. It is also easier to read, as is evident in Figure 5-5, where the same text is shown in 12 pitch prestige elite and typeset.

MICROGRAPHICS

Micrographics is the use of microfilm and microfiche.

Microfilm is a very fine-grain film, usually 16 millimeters in width. Each page of a document is photographed, and each page image occupies one frame. Microfilm comes in 200-foot rolls, each contained in a cartridge. Each cartridge holds the images of approximately 5000 pages, about the same quantity as two file drawers.

Microfiche are 4 in. × 6 in. sheets of film. On each of these the photographic images of 288 pages can be stored. Some microfiche can pack even more pages.

Both film and fiche require special optical readers. Some readers include a printer. At the press of a button, a photographic copy is made of the page you have on the screen.

Advantages and Disadvantages. The advantage of microfilm or fiche is the ability to replace an entire file cabinet of paper copies with about two rolls of film or about two inches of fiche. For documents referred to only rarely, this is a very cost-effective means of storage. The need for the special reader is the main disadvantage. Some people find that microfilm readers cause eyestrain and do not like to use them. Good-quality readers are important if you have a micrographics program.

We will return to micrographics in the discussion of file management later in this chapter.

MAIL

Slow mail deliveries, both mail within a company and the U.S. mail, can hold up work and reduce productivity. What can be done about it?

This partial page is typed in 12 pitch using a prestige elite type style. It is reproduced full size within the 4 1/2 inch by 7 inch text margins of this page. A full 8 1/2 x 11 inch page with top and bottom margins of an inch and a half, and left and right margins of an inch and a quarter would contain about 3000 characters. Spaces are counted as characters and four lines are assumed blank due to paragraph breaks.

The bottom part of this figure shows this same text typeset in the type style and size used in this book, namely Times Roman and 10 point. The smaller type size and use of proportionally spaced letters condenses the text to about half the space used by the typed version. On an 8 1/2 x 11 inch page with the margins as above, about 5500 characters would fit.

(same text as above, typeset)

This partial page is typed in 12 pitch using a prestige elite type style. It is reproduced full size within the 4½ inch by 7 inch text margins of this page. A full 8½ x 11 inch page with top and bottom margins of an inch and a half, and left and right margins of an inch and a quarter would contain about 300 characters. Spaces are counted as characters and four lines are assumed blank due to paragraph breaks.

The bottom part of this figure shows this same text typeset in the type style and size used in this book, namely Times Roman and 10 point. The smaller type size and use of proportionally spaced letters condenses the text to about half the space used by the typed version. On an 8½ x 11 inch page with the margins as above, about 5500 characters would fit.

Figure 5-5. Text compression with phototypesetting.

Figure 5-6. Microfiche (upper left), Microfilm with cartridge (right), and aperture card (lower left). Photo courtesy 3M Office Systems Division.

Company Mail

One to three hours should be the standard for the elapsed time from pickup from an out-basket to placement in the addressee's in-basket, provided you are both in the same building or adjacent buildings. This implies a minimum of four full mail runs through the buildings each day.

Sorting.   Some mail operations collect all outgoing mail, bring it to a central mail room, sort it there, and then distribute it on the subsequent mail run. This procedure is efficient, but it is also slow. The cart arrives at the sorting room at the end of one mail run. As there is not time to sort the accumulated mail before the next mail run starts, the sorted mail goes out on the second subsequent run. If there are four runs a day, this means that an envelope placed in your out tray at 9 A.M. cannot be delivered to the addressee until about 2 P.M.

One alternative for larger organizations is to sort en route. The mail cart has slots or folders for each mail station. As the mail clerk picks up from the out trays, she or he places each envelope in the addressee's slot. Those addressees whose stations come later on the same run will get their company mail almost immediately. At the latest, the company mail will be delivered on the next run. Mail must go to the central mail room to be sorted only if there are parallel mail runs and the envelope goes to the other run. The process is faster if the company uses an internal ZIP code with the ZIP numbers assigned in the same sequence as that in which the mail is delivered. The clerk can locate the correct slot or folder rapidly.

Mail Boxes.   Another alternative exists for very small companies. This is a series of mail boxes or cubbyholes located in one wall of the mail room. One mail box is assigned to each group or department. The department secretaries or other designated persons get the mail from these boxes and bring the outgoing mail to the mail room.

U.S. Mail

You cannot do anything about the operation of the postal system, but you can know:

1. The exact times at which incoming mail is sorted and delivered.
2. The exact times at which outgoing mail is sorted and dispatched.
3. What alternative mail carriers are available.

Incoming Mail.   Find out from your local postmaster at what time incoming mail is sorted and at what times the post office generally completes this job. Usually sorting is done in the morning. It may be completed quite early, say 9 A.M., or it may continue until 10 or 11 A.M. If you have a courier pick up the mail, or if a company clerk picks it up from a post office box, it is best to arrive just after the sorting is completed. On certain days, such as Monday, and at certain times of the year sorting takes longer. You should allow for this.

P.O. Box.   Use of a post office box can save a day's time in receiving mail. One company at which the author worked had deliveries both to the street address and to a P.O. box. Mail delivered to the box often arrived at the company's mail room a day earlier. The day of delivery depends on whether the mail carrier leaves the post office to make the rounds before or after the sorting is completed.

Outgoing Mail.   Find out from the postmaster when and where outgoing mail is sorted. Sometimes this is done at the distribution center rather than at the local post office. What is the latest time a letter can reach the local post office and be sure to go out that same evening? The usual time is 5 or 6 P.M. Is there an earlier cutoff time for letters headed for the airport rather than for local distribution? Is there a later pickup time at another nearby post office? If you know the answers to these questions, you can time delivery of your correspondence to be sure it leaves the day it is mailed.

Private Couriers. There are package and mail courier services. These pick up from your office late in the afternoon and deliver directly to an address in major U.S. cities the next morning. Know the pickup times for each major courier in your area. Know the cities in which each promises next-day delivery. These services cost about $25 to $30 for a small package and $10 to $15 for a two-ounce envelope, but there are times when this cost is worthwhile. Local couriers will also handle pickup and delivery from and to the post office and hand deliver within four hours in your community.

FILES MANAGEMENT

Files management, or records management as it is more properly called, is one of the more important and neglected of office functions. A lot of time can be wasted searching the files for a document whose date and title are only vaguely remembered, or for a document created yesterday that has mysteriously vanished in the bowels of the file cabinet. If a really critical document cannot be found at all, or is found one day after a lawsuit is settled, this can be a major catastrophe for the company.

In many companies, even today, the secretaries or the managers each design their own filing system. Some file by subject, with a fine breakdown within each category. Others file by subject but with no structure within the subject field. Some file by author, some by recipient, some by date. When the manager and secretary leave the organization, their successors may not be able to locate what is in the files. When they do, it is a slow and inefficient process.

The important records of a company are sufficiently critical that a good method is essential for indexing and locating the documents needed.

Computer-Aided Filing and Retrieval

Micrographics and computer-assisted retrieval (CAR) provide the best answer today. Microfilm is the least expensive way to file documents for archival storage. It is also tamper-proof. Words cannot be changed on a film image, nor can a page be "lost." Documents should be filmed in duplicate and the second copy stored in a vault away from the building. In case of fire or other catastrophe, one copy of all the vital records will survive. If the working copy becomes scratched or is tampered with, it can be replaced with another copy made from the duplicate.

Files are only as good as the index that allows you to find what is in them. Through CAR, a master index is prepared of the company's critical documents which is kept in a computer. The computer's ability to search through long lists of index terms and use them to select the document you request is the key to a good retrieval system.

A good CAR system indexes each document by author, title, recipient(s), date, subject, sponsor, contract or program number, and all the key words.

Key Words. Key words are those that describe the content of a document. Suppose you make the following statement: "I'm looking for a letter written about last August that describes the *legal* implications of the *contract* we had with one of the local *hardware* suppliers—I don't remember which *company*. It had something to do with the *cost* of *maintenance* parts." That's a pretty vague statement from which to start a manual search through a file cabinet. The key words in the statement are those in italics. These each describe one of the key parts of the request.

Boolean Logic. Key word searches require use and understanding of Boolean logic. This is a scheme using the relationships between subjects (or words) to define the set of objects (or documents) you want. Here are the relationships:

- *A and B*. The document must contain *both* words A and B.
- *A not B*. The document must contain key word A *but not* key word B. For example, you want all documents written on automation except those dealing with word processing.
- *A or B*. The document must contain *either* the word A *or* the word B.
- *Greater than A* (used with numbers or dates). You only want documents *later than* date A.
- *Less than A*. This is like the preceding relationship, except that it provides all documents *before* the date specified.
- *Greater than A less than B*. This combines the above two concepts to create a range of dates. You want only documents *between* dates A and B.
- *A within x words of B*. Some systems allow *word proximity* searching. This will locate all documents that have word A located within x words of B. It is used to locate phrases such as *office* of the *future*. But beware—in this example it would also find anything else where the two words were that close, such as "In this office, there's no future."

A search combining some of these concepts might be for all documents on office automation, except for word processing and electronic typewriters, written after 1975. This is *(A and B) not C not D greater than E*.

Boolean logic searches can also be done on personnel records. You can get a list of people whose salaries are greater than $50,000 a year and who are not managers or higher *(greater than $50,000 and less than Manager)*; salespeople in Michigan outside of Chicago (Michigan *and not* Chicago). This search technique can also be used to locate one document, or a set of documents, within the records of accounts payable, purchase orders, engineering drawings, and any other collection of like files. It is a very useful program.

Finding the document is easy using key words and Boolean logic in a CAR search. Let us return to the perplexed person who is worried about the hardware contract. You enter the computer with a request to find all documents that have been indexed with: *contract* or *legal;* and *hardware* or *maintenance;* and *company;* and *cost.* The computer will sort through its key word file and list those documents that were indexed using this combination. Cost–company–hardware–contract would qualify for the search. So would cost–company–maintenance–legal and cost–company–hardware–legal. If you wanted to narrow the search further, you could also enter as a date limitation: *from June to November.* This brackets the "about last August" part of the statement.

In this example, three documents might meet the search criteria. CAR will show, on the computer screen, the rest of the index including author, date written, document title, and so on. Generally this will be enough to let you determine which of the three documents is the one you want. CAR also knows where the documents are filed. It shows the roll and frame number for microfilm, card number for microfiche, box or cabinet number for hard copy. CAR works most effectively when tied directly to a microfilm reader-printer. If the documents are on microfilm, you can insert the designated film cartridge in the reader-printer, and the computer will dial up the right frame number. The document image comes immediately to the screen. A similar method is available for microfiche.

The above scenario can be executed in less time than it takes to read it.

You need a way of getting the documents to the person in charge of records

Figure 5-7. Kodak KAR-4000 automated electronic filing system. Photo courtesy Eastman Kodak Co.

management. If you have a word processing center or a copying center, it can route a log of its work to the records manager as a check on what should be received. There is no foolproof method. The cooperation of the secretarial staff is essential. So are periodic reminders from top management.

Manual Filing

If your organization does not have computer-aided retrieval, it may have a standard filing structure imposed throughout the company. Almost any standardized system is better than none. Through its use others will be able to find documents when you and your secretary have moved to other and better positions.

Subject filing is still the most useful method. This is not surprising; it comes closest to a key word system, which is the most thorough method. You can try to create a key word manual file by cross references, but it soon gets unwieldly and is really not practical.

Some secretaries have adopted the practice of filing several copies of everything. One copy is filed by subject (the organization's standard, or hers, or yours). One is chronological by the date written or received. One is a working file kept in a folder or tray for as long as its subject is active. This practice is a boon for copy machine vendors. If the company has no standards, or you have doubts that you can find a document using the standard system, this is not as bad a concept as it sounds. The least efficient system is one in which you cannot find the document at all.

A personal file for active subjects is a good concept. You can file them in any way that fits your thinking. They are not the official records of the company, and there must be other copies filed in the "proper" way. If to you the heading "George" matches a topic about which you are fighting with someone named George, a personal file so labeled is fine.

The problem with personal files is that they are rarely purged. They are kept for years, long after the subjects are obsolete. You tend to look to them, rather than to the official files for material. Perhaps yours are so extensive that you and your secretary neglect to keep up the official files. This behavior can be fatal; do not allow it to happen. Resolve that you will dispose of personal files as each project is completed. Limit yourself to one file cabinet drawer, or to the credenza behind your desk. This forces you to throw away the documents that you longer need.

If you have a PC, and a Boolean logic search program is available for it, consider using the PC to imitate a CAR system. Working with your secretary—who must, of course, be a part of this project—set up a set of key words and index your personal files and recent official files to these words. Your company sooner or later will use CAR, and you will have a jump on the rest of the staff.

Records Management

A complete records management program includes:

1. Files management
2. Defining archives and retention schedules
3. Protection of vital records
4. Use of micrographics or other storage means
5. Forms management
6. Correspondence control

Files management is discussed above, and micrographics was covered earlier in this chapter. Here are brief comments on the other functions.

There must be agreement on what documents are to be kept and for how long. Certain documents are required by law to be kept for specified lengths of time. For others you have a choice. It isn't necessary that every piece of paper be in the archives; so a decision is needed on what should be part of the records system. Some files in the system may be centralized, some kept off site, and some located in specific using departments. Retention schedules must be established for each type of document that is part of the records system. Polices and procedures must also exist to assure that the retention schedules are followed, and that documents are destroyed at the proper time.

Records protection covers possibilities of fire, theft, and alteration. Use of a vault with controlled access takes care of anything except a catastrophe. Off-site storage of a duplicate set of the vital records—those essential to keeping the organization in business—protects against the latter possibility.

Micrographics is generally used only for records management; hence it is usually performed by the records group. Control of the vault and of off-site storage is also part of the group's function.

Forms and their proper design were discussed in earlier chapters. A good records manager is trained in forms design. Forms also have a habit of appearing from nowhere, designed by a staff member to handle a specific need of the moment. The number of forms may get out of hand, with more than one serving essentially the same purpose. To assure that forms are used where appropriate, are designed properly, and do not duplicate each other, control over their creation and distribution is often established within the records management function.

A complete archiving function must contain incoming correspondence as well as documents originated by the organization. In larger organizations, there is also the problem of routing incoming mail that is addressed to the company but shows nobody's name. Some organizations also want assurance that certain incoming documents are seen by the legal department, or by the public relations people. These are some of the reasons for establishing control over correspondence.

Nothing short of a comprehensive records program is really adequate, considering the high cost of mistakes in our regulated environment.

THE INTEGRATED OFFICE

All the office elements described in this and the previous chapter can make the professional's life easier and more productive, or make it miserable and unproductive. We have shown ways in which each element can operate to enhance office productivity and also be of help to the professional. We cannot leave this subject, however, without a few words about the integration of these support functions.

The trend is toward a combination of many of these elements into one integrated office support function. Use of dictation systems makes the input to word processors faster and more accurate. Electronic typewriters may substitute for word processors where usage is low, and text may be interchanged between them. PC's or small business computers may perform some of the word processing and computing tasks as well as help the professional do the routine parts of his or her job. Reprographics can use word processors for their input and telecommunications for their output. Micrographics and files management may use computer assistance for searching and word processors or PC's for indexing. Telecommunications and networks tie the automated equipment together. Of all the functions we have covered in these two chapters, only the mail seems not to be a direct input or output of one of the other functions. But even here, electronic mail is on the horizon using telecommunications networks or PC terminals. Each of these support activities interrelates with the others.

This technological marriage of so many of the office support functions has a major implication for how these support services should be organized. Traditionally, each has grown up separately, with responsibilities scattered throughout the organization chart. Data processing often reports to the controller. Word processing may be decentralized to each using department or report to an administrative group or to the data processing department. Mail and micrographics usually is part of an administrative service function or, in a small company, is run from the executive office. Telecommunications, until quite recently, was not a function at all. Its responsibility still is often split between data processing for networks and a chief telephone operator for voice communications.

This historic hodgepodge must not survive. To achieve the advantages that can derive from the technical interaction of these office systems, the functions themselves must be organizationally integrated. One person should be placed in charge of all office support functions with responsibility to tie them together as the need becomes apparent and the cost can be justified. This technological and organizational integration will be a major factor in achieving the potential efficiencies suggested by the Booz·Allen & Hamilton survey cited in Chapters 1 and 2.

SUMMARY

Continuing our list of office elements, the personal computer (PC) does not replace the company mainframe or minicomputer but is a personal tool the professional can use to speed up analytical calculations, improve decision making, search for reference information, and aid in desk management. The office staff will use it to keep and search records, lists, and inventories; as an occasional word processor; and as an electronic mail station. Standardization on a PC model that can communicate with the company's mainframe and run many commercial software programs is important.

The power of data processing is the ability to manipulate vast amounts of information rapidly and to create useful, sorted, summarized information from a jumble of raw numbers. Networks tie together the PC's, word processors, and computers. There are PBX, broadband, and baseband networks, each incompatible with the others.

Telephone systems may be analog or digital systems. Digital voice signals may use the same networks that data use. Telephone costs are a major overhead expense, and some suggestions for reducing these costs have been provided in this chapter. Telephone message taking is important because telephone tag is a major waste of time. The Call Forwarding feature which routes calls to a secretary or message center solves this problem.

High-volume central copiers are for major copying jobs and convenience copiers for one or two copy runs, since their cost per page is about double that of the large machines. Laser printers are almost equal to offset printers in quality. Phototypesetting from a word processor is another method of high-volume printing.

Microfilm or microfiche can replace a file cabinet full of paper with two rolls of film or two inches of fiche. It is an economical form of storage.

Sorting of company mail while it is in transit can save hours in delivery time. Knowing the sorting times of the local post office can get both an incoming letter and an outgoing one delivered a full day earlier. Private couriers promise next-day delivery in major U.S. cities.

Vital documents need a filing and retrieval method that assures their immediate availability. Use of microfilm coupled with key word indexing and computer-aided retrieval achieves this; Boolean logic searching finds a document when only its general content is known. Subject indexing is best for manual files. A good records management program is vital to an organization. Its elements include files management, defining what documents to retain and their retention schedules, records protection, micrographics, forms control, and correspondence control.

All the elements described in this and the previous chapter should be combined into an integrated administrative support organization. As this happens, the improved efficiency factors suggested by Booz·Allen & Hamilton will be easier to achieve.

FOR FURTHER INFORMATION

Personal Computers

Books on personal computers are reaching bookshelves at the rate of several a week. Thus any list shown here will be out of date by the time the reader looks at it. Check with a good bookstore or computer center for a recomendation pertinent to your particular interests. The books below will get you started.

Fluegelman, Andrew, and Hewes, Jeremy Joan. *Writing in the Computer Age: Word Processing Skills for Every Writer.* Garden City, New York: Anchor Books, 1983 (using PC's for writing).

McGlynn, Daniel R. *Simplified Guide to Small Computers for Business.* New York: John Wiley & Sons, 1983.

McWilliams Peter C. *The Personal Computer Book,* 3rd ed. New York: Ballantine Books, 1983 (revised frequently).

Data Processing

Gessford, John Evans. *Modern Information Systems.* Reading, MA: Addison-Wesley, 1980.

Kanter, Jerome. *Training Your Computer.* Englewood Cliffs, NJ: Prentice-Hall, 1981.

Telecommunications

Green, James H. Chapter 8, Binding the Office with Communications, and Chapter 9, Communication Networks, in *Automating Your Office.* New York: McGraw-Hill, 1984.

Kaufman, Robert J. *Cost Effective Telecommunications Management: Turning Telephone Costs into Profits.* Boston: CBI Publ., 1983.

Reprographics

Hanson, Richard E. *The Manager's Guide to Copying and Duplicating.* New York: McGraw-Hill, 1980.

Hanson, Richard E. Copiers: The Boom in User Friendliness, *Office Administration and Automation,* December, 1983.

Micrographics

National Micrographics Association, Ellen T. Meyer, ed. *An Introduction to Micrographics*. Silver Springs, MD: NMA, 1980.

Files and Records Management

Maedke, Wilmer O., Robek, Mary F., and Brown, Gerald F. *Information and Records Management*, 2nd ed. Encino, CA: Glencoe Publ., 1981.

Thomas, Violet S., Schubert, Dexter R., and Lee, Jo Ann. *Records Management Systems and Administration*. New York: John Wiley & Sons, 1983.

6
Techniques for Work Measurement

We have discussed each of the more important elements of the office paper-work system. The reader is now familiar with the function of each of these systems and how each can help in the quest for improved effectiveness and higher office productivity. But, as in all things, each element can be done well or poorly. How do we know if our procedures are good or bad? How can we measure productivity so that we know when the procedures have been improved? What work measurement techniques exist that are more useful than the brainstorming approach described in Chapter 3? When is the use of such techniques appropriate?

In the present chapter we present the classic work measurement approaches, using office procedures as our examples. We show how they can be used to measure work output and to improve present methods. We comment on their usefulness and their limitations. We start, however, by discussing the difference between productivity, efficiency, and effectiveness and deciding which of these we want to measure. Some authors have defined these terms in other ways; so be careful in carrying a set of definitions across from one author to another.

PRODUCTIVITY, EFFICIENCY, AND EFFECTIVENESS

Up to this point we have written about improving the productivity and effectiveness of office operations, using the words almost interchangeably. They are not the same. There is a very important difference between productivity, efficiency, and effectiveness. So let us first define each.

Productivity

Productivity is a measure of quantity produced. A copy center turns out 100,000 pages. A purchasing group writes 500 purchase orders. A word processing group turns out 120,000 lines of text. But we also need a unit of time. The production quantity can be infinite, given enough time.

So we specify how much product is produced over some length of time. The productivity was 100,000 pages last month, 500 P.O.'s for the month, 120,000 lines during the month. The time used can be per hour, per day, per week, month, or year. You use whatever makes sense in the specific case. Is the information part of a monthly report? Monthly rates will be the most meaningful. Are we comparing last year to this year? An annual rate is the most understandable unit. Are we discussing hourly rates? Use hourly quantities. Always specify the unit of time being used.

Productivity, then, is a measure of output per unit of time.

Efficiency

Efficiency is a measure of output in relation to input. It is often expressed as a percentage. It is a technical term, useful in engineering and manufacturing. A solar energy converter is 20% efficient if 20% of the sun's energy striking the panels is converted to heat. A manufacturing process for electronic chips is 80% efficient if 80% of the parts produced are good and only 20% are rejects. These are absolute values of efficiency that can be mesured accurately.

It is more difficult to apply this concept to office functions. If a copier is fed 100 sheets of paper to get 96 good copies, it has a wastage factor of 4%. Its copying efficiency is 96%. If the word processing equipment is "down" an average of five hours a month, its "uptime" is 97% (168 out of 173 hours). This availability or "uptime" is a measure of efficiency. But we generally do not use the word "efficiency" to describe these situations.

We say that Mr. A is "efficient," whereas Mr. B is not. What do we mean? We may mean that Mr. A is more effective (definition to come). Or we may mean that Mr. A is more productive than Mr. B. A puts out more work in a week than B. These terms are often interchanged in normal conversation. In the sense of measuring output divided by input, we cannot apply the term efficiency to one person. We cannot measure the amount of energy or the amount of thought that a person puts in. These are the real measures of a person's input. We can only measure the amount of time put in. That gives productivity, not efficiency.

We say that a procedure is "inefficient." By this we mean that there are unnecessary steps involved, or that the number of people in the process is too great, or simply that it takes too long. The number of work hours or the elapsed time on the input side is higher that we think it should be. We do not use "efficiency" as a quantitative measure. We cannot say that this procedure is 80% efficient, as the engineer can with the solar converter. In discussing people and procedures, we use the words "efficient" and "inefficient" in a relative sense.

The concept of efficiency is useful for comparing two activities. If one production line manufactures 100 widgets (output) at a cost for materials and labor of $1,000 (input), it is more efficient than a line that makes 100 widgets at a cost of $1,100. One can also express this in terms of work hours. If material costs are the same, a process that takes 100 work hours to make a product is more efficient than one that takes 110 work hours. (Note that we use work hours. Elapsed hours would measure productivity, not efficiency.)

The same is true of office work. A procedure that takes 10 work hours is more efficient than one that takes 15 work hours.

If we want to improve a procedure, or see if one method is better than another, use of efficiency as a comparative measure is quite adequate. "The procedure recommended takes 30% fewer work hours than the existing procedure." "It takes Ms. A 15 work hours to do this job and Mr. B 20 hours on the same job. Ms. A is more efficient than Mr. B." This is the way in which the term efficiency should be used.

Efficiency measures output per unit of input.

Effectiveness

Effectiveness measures output against the purpose of an activity. This is often a qualitative rather than a quantitative measure. It is often, too, a subjective measure. If the objective was accomplished, the job you did was effective.

Note that this says nothing about your productivity or efficiency. You may have taken far too long and used too many work hours in accomplishing the job. You were effective but not productive or efficient. Similarly, you can be productive and efficient but not effective if you fail to meet the objective.

An objective of the purchasing group is to buy at the lowest possible price. If the group does so, it is effective. If it doesn't, it isn't. How do you measure this? You spot-check prices from different local vendors on a sample of items that were purchased. You determine what percentage of the buys were placed at the lowest available price. If the lowest price was obtained on 90 buys out of 100, the purchasing group was effective in meeting this objective 90% of the time. Another objective of the purchasing group is always to obtain delivery by the requested date. If 95 out of 100 items arrive on or before the date re-

Table 6-1. Productivity, Efficiency, and Effectiveness.

Productivity: Output per unit of time.
Examples: pages per day
widgits per month
P.O.'s per month

Efficiency: Output per unit of input.
Examples: widgits per work hour
P.O.'s per work hour
80% acceptable parts

Effectiveness: Whether output meets its objective.
Examples: purchase orders all at lowest price
annual budget met
work turnaround time met

quested, the purchasing group is effective on this objective 95% of the time. Are values of 90% and 95% good or bad? That is for higher management to decide.

There can be multiple objectives, as in the above example. You may be effective in meeting one objective and fail miserably to meet another. Multiple objectives are the usual situation.

A copy center may have three objectives: (1) two-hour turnaround, (2) high-quality output, and (3) low cost. Each of these objectives competes with the other two.

For example, take a day when there is an unusually large backlog of work. If you elect to meet the turnaround time, quality may suffer. You cut corners in order to meet the schedule. You do not take time to check the input pages for very light originals that require special attention, or perhaps you don't check the output for misaligned pages. If you decide to meet the turnaround time and also to hold quality high by bringing in extra help, the costs will increase. In each case you have been effective in meeting two objectives and failed to meet the third. When you discuss effectiveness, always note which of the objectives is being considered.

Optimizing and Suboptimizing

What are we trying to optimize? Productivity? Efficiency? Or effectiveness?

The answer in every case should be "effectiveness." The office functions exist to support the money-making side of the enterprise. They are effective only if they maximize the objectives of the activity they support. This is a very important concept. To be sure it is understood, we will dwell on it at some length.

In support of manufacturing, the office functions are effective if they keep production high, costs low, and schedules intact. They are also effective if they minimize the amount of time the production supervisors must take away from production planning and production problems to handle their office paperwork. In support of sales, the early confirmation of an order is important because it gives the customer confidence. To be effective, the office system should minimize the time necessary to record the order, determine if the item is available in inventory, set the shipping schedule, and notify the customer and the salesperson.

An effective system may not be, and generally will not be, the most efficient one for the office. In being effective, you aim to optimize what the profit-oriented groups in the company—manufacturing, sales, engineering—are doing. You do this at the expense of optimizing your own operation. In the above examples, you keep production rolling on schedule and at cost even if this requires a buyer to spend five times the usual amount of time to track down an order and expedite its delivery. You confirm a sale within a half day of receipt, even if this disrupts your other activities. You anticipate the problems of the production supervisor and do as much as you can to take the paperwork burdens off this person's shoulders. You optimize other individuals' costs and time, not your own.

Here is another example, using purchasing. The most productive and most efficient buyer collects all the orders going to one supplier until he or she has several that can be handled with one telephone call and one purchase order. For the same dollar value of orders (output), the number of orders placed and the cost of placing them (input) is lower. The purchasing system is more efficient. But it may not be effective. One of the orders being held may be for a critical part that is delaying a shipment, or may involve a warehouse restocking order for parts that will run out the day after tomorrow. Purchasing will be efficient, but the functions it supports will suffer. This is not effective operation.

This illustrates the problem of suboptimization. Each individual function tends to optimize its own efficiency. In this way it looks good on the record. If it accomplishes more output with less manpower and lower cost than does a similar group in another organization, its manager expects congratulations and a raise for his or her efficiency. But this efficient function may not be effective. Management statistics generally measure efficiency, not effectiveness, because the output and input data are easy to collect. Lack of effectiveness is discovered only through user complaints. Management must put the primary emphasis on meeting each support function's objectives—on effectiveness, not on efficiency. So must the manager of each such function.

Companies that conduct surveys to compare themselves to other organizations, and which reward their staff in part on the results, measure and pay for efficiency, not effectiveness. They are asking for suboptimization. Don't fall into this trap.

The key to being effective is knowing your objectives as defined by higher management. These are not always easy to determine. As we noted earlier, there are usually multiple objectives, and they are often contradictory. Both the manager and the users of each operation should know the hierarchy of objectives. If two are in conflict, which one should be met? Higher management must spell this out if they expect to have an effective support operation.

Work measurement techniques do not measure effectiveness. They measure either productivity or efficiency. It is very important to remember this. For the remainder of this chapter we will describe techniques that apply only to the measurement of productivity and efficiency.

MEASURING AND IMPROVING THE WORK PROCESS

The following techniques are generally used to determine how the present processes operate and to measure input to the work process, namely, time and work hours.

Preparing the Staff

You must have the cooperation of the people whose work you measure. If you don't, you will not get accurate data. People are very ingenious. If they feel that your investigation may result in a work speedup, they will sabotage your efforts. They will work more slowly than usual, or make the work appear more complex or difficult than it really is. They act in this way so that after you have made your measurements and suggested job improvements, they will be back to the pace that actually exists.

If a supervisor feels that your report will be critical of his or her procedures, you will encounter a very defensive and uncooperative individual. This behavior occurs any time you or others disrupt the established and accepted routine.

To gain the staff's acceptance, you must convince each person that he or she has something to gain from the process of measurement and the subsequent changes. The purpose of measuring a process is to improve it. The improvement will generally take one or more of the following forms:

1. A reduction of unnecessary steps
2. Improved work handling and work transfer steps
3. Better forms
4. Better definition of responsibilities
5. More responsibility for each person

The unstated fear in everyone's mind is that the changes will result in some workers' being laid off, or in the job's being restructured to so great an extent that the person's present skills cannot handle it.

Before starting an investigation, you must convince the staff that the advantages listed above will apply to each one of them, and that what they fear will not happen. If you cannot provide these assurances, your chances of getting valid data are poor. So are your chances of making a successful change to an improved system.

Charting the Work Process

Systems analysts have developed techniques for charting office processes which have been in use for several decades. These methods are simple for those trained in their use, but not for the uninitiated. There are two types of work charts. The *process chart* is a listing of all actions involving the paper flow; it measures the time involved for each step and the distances the paper must move. The *flow chart* is an overview of the process, and serves to show which steps occur in parallel and the relationship between steps.

In preparing these charts, standard symbols are used to designate different types of steps. These make it easier to spot unnecessary routing (transportation)

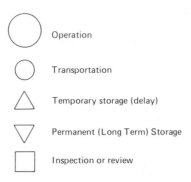

Figure 6-1. Common process chart symbols.

or holdups (storage) in the process. The symbols in common use are shown in Figure 6-1.

Process Chart. The process is broken down into its smallest individual actions. Special emphasis is given to movement of the paperwork from one location to another, such as from the incoming mailbox to the control desk in-basket, from a file cabinet to a desk, from the desk to the out-basket, from the out-basket of the control desk to the in-basket at the typing station, and so on. Emphasis is also placed on temporary storage or delay points, such as waiting in an in-basket or in an outgoing mailbox. The time for each step is measured and entered. So is any significant distance that the paperwork must travel. Figure 6-2 shows a typical process chart.

The separate columns for transportation, inspection, temporary storage (delay), and long-term or permanent storage highlight these activities. These are nonproductive steps. The first column shows the operations performed. These are the productive steps, though not necessarily as effective or efficient as they might be.

In preparing a process chart, pay particular attention to the temporary storage steps. It is easy to overlook them. A document is placed by the secretary on the buyer's desk. You may chart this as ''to buyer's desk'' with the next action being ''buyer calls vendors.'' That would be wrong. Ninety-nine times in 100, the document is placed in the buyer's in-basket. It may be hours or even days before the buyer takes action. The other step often overlooked is transportation within the department. Out-basket to in-basket is transportation, even if one is within arm's length of the other.

Flow Chart. Flow charts are the ones most people are familiar with. They show the flow of work in a horizontal direction on the chart. Parallel steps are shown above and below each other. The emphasis is on the operational steps;

FLOW PROGRESS CHART

PAGE____OF______

ANALYST	DATE
SUBJECT AND QUANTITY	

STEPS	PERSONS & DEPT. CONTACTED

SUMMARY AND KEY UNITS	No.	TIME	DIST.	SPACE
○ = Operation				
□ = Inspection				
⇨ = Transportation				
D = Delay				
▽ = Storage				
TOTALS				

STEP	SYMBOL	TIME	DIST.	SPACE	STEPS	Elim-inate	Com-bine	Im-prove	CHANGE Sequ	CHANGE Place	CHANGE Per-son
1	○ □ ⇨ D ▽										
2	○ □ ⇨ D ▽										
3	○ □ ⇨ D ▽										
4	○ □ ⇨ D ▽										
5	○ □ ⇨ D ▽										
6	○ □ ⇨ D ▽										
7	○ □ ⇨ D ▽										
8	○ □ ⇨ D ▽										
9	○ □ ⇨ D ▽										
10	○ □ ⇨ D ▽										
11	○ □ ⇨ D ▽										
12	○ □ ⇨ D ▽										
13	○ □ ⇨ D ▽										
14	○ □ ⇨ D ▽										
15	○ □ ⇨ D ▽										
16	○ □ ⇨ D ▽										
17	○ □ ⇨ D ▽										
18	○ □ ⇨ D ▽										
19	○ □ ⇨ D ▽										
20	○ □ ⇨ D ▽										

Figure 6-2. Process chart.

delay steps are usually omitted. The station at which an operation is performed is identified by its function or by the title of the person performing that step. Sometimes, the nature of the step is identified. The amount of information depends on the complexity of the process and the readability of the resulting form. If the step cannot be described on the form, it should be identified with a code, and an identifying page should be attached. Figure 6-3 shows a simple flow chart.

To many managers, particularly those with engineering backgrounds or advanced business degrees, flow charts are the easiest way to understand a process. The entire operation is shown on one sheet of paper. The codes are easy to read and understand. Consider using flow charts to describe both the ''before'' and the ''after'' situations.

Gathering Data.   The investigator can construct the process chart and the flow chart together if the operation is simple. Otherwise the process chart is done first and the flow chart made from it.

There are three ways to gather the data:

1. By interviewing those performing the operation.
2. By reading the written procedures.
3. By observation.

All three approaches are necessary. The workers are so familiar with what they do that it is easy for them to omit mentioning a step they do almost ab-

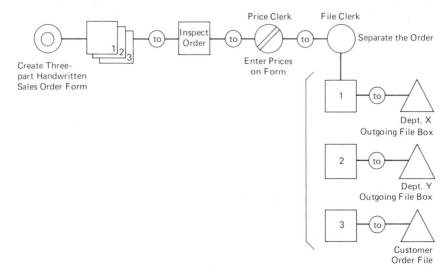

Figure 6-3. Flow chart. From Randall, Clarence B., and Burgly, Sally W., *Systems & Procedures for Business Data Processing,* 2nd ed., South-Western Publishing Co., p. 172. Reprinted with permission.

sentmindedly. Your observation of how the job is done and your reading of the procedures provides a check on what you are told.

The written procedures may not describe the procedure you observe. If you find this situation, always consult the supervisor of the function. Find out if the procedure is obsolete, or if the performer is not doing the job correctly. This discussion with the supervisor should be held privately to avoid embarrassing either the worker or the supervisor and to avoid any feeling that you are censuring the worker. If censure is appropriate, that is the supervisor's job.

You could determine the length of time required for each step by standing near the workers and timing a series of jobs being done. However, you would have to observe a large number of jobs to get an average for each step because no two jobs will take exactly the same time. This approach is very time-consuming. Instead, after you have finished the process chart, ask the workers and the supervisor for the length of time spent on each step. Use two or three casual observations as a check on their estimates. This procedure is usually sufficiently accurate for the purpose.

Distances can be estimated by pacing. Distances are important when a worker must leave his or her desk to walk to another place either to get or leave a document. Such movement not only takes time; it disrupts a routine. It may lead to conversation with fellow workers along the path or to an unscheduled rest break. Distances involved when a courier picks up a document are not significant to the study. However, the time that the courier keeps the document is very significant.

Forms for both process charts and flow charts may be obtained from engineering catalogs. When you have completed the charts, make clarifying notes to yourself. These will remind you of what each action does, or will explain the reason for an unusual step. Total the times for all the steps and compare this sum to the total duration of the process. Review and adjust the step times until they and the total duration are roughly in balance.

Be warned that preparing these charts is not nearly so easy as it looks. The untrained observer will miss steps or neglect to note steps that appear inconsequential but may turn out later to be a key to improvement.

Work Layout

This is a diagram or floor plan of the area in which the work is performed. The location of each desk, in-basket, out-basket, file, copy machine, or other object involved in the work flow is shown. The name (or a letter or number code) of each person who takes an action at one of these locations is also shown. The flow of work or paper from the time it arrives in the area until it leaves is shown by dotted lines and arrows. A typical work layout might look like that in the left side of Figure 6-4.

A floor layout is made using linear graph paper or any paper with ruled squares. You are not looking for architectural accuracy; so the scale you use is not important. It should be some quantity easy to measure and use, such as two feet per quarter-inch square. Measure the outside dimensions of the room and draw them on the paper. Add the columns, doors, windows, and any permanent fixtures. Note the location of electrical and telephone outlets. This is the basic room. Make several copies of this layout; you will use one copy to draw the existing furniture layout and the others for drawing improvements.

Draw the present location of desks, chairs, file cabinets, work tables, and so on. Use the process chart to draw arrows for each transportation step. Number them as in Figure 6-4.

Using the Charts

Look first at the process chart with a view to reducing the delay and transportation steps so that a greater proportion of the steps involve operations. Combine steps where possible. This eliminates both transportation and temporary storage delays.

Rearrange the work layout to reduce transportation distances. Move people, desks, files, and copy machines so that the paper flow moves in as straight a line as possible. Make the steps occur at adjacent desks if possible. Put files near the start or end of the process. After the work layout is simplified, it may resemble the right side of Figure 6-4.

As you gather the data and as you look at the charts, ask yourself the following questions:

1. What is the purpose of this step? Is it necessary?
2. Is this the best place to do the step?
3. Where else could the step be done?
4. Is this the right sequence for the step?
5. Can it be batched with another step?
6. Is the right person doing the job?
7. Is the work load for each person balanced?
8. Can the job be made easier or involve more responsibility?

Asking yourself these questions is the start of improving the operation. When you have made changes that permit a "yes" answer to all questions (except the last one, which should be "no"), you have improved the process as much as you can.

The key actions to take are:

- Eliminate: delays, movement, repetition.
- Simplify: actions, knowledge needed.
- Combine: steps, locations where performed.
- Reduce: number of different people involved.

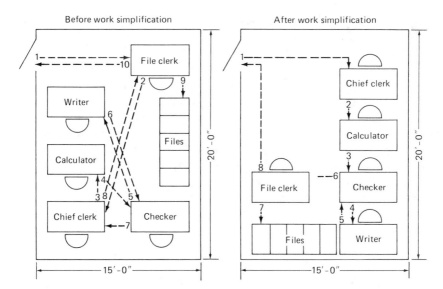

Figure 6-4. Work layout, before and after. From Stallard, John J., Smith, E. Ray, and Reese, Donald, *The Electronic Office A Guide for Managers*, Dow Jones-Irwin, 1983, p. 26. Reprinted with permission.

As you go along, prepare new process charts. Compare them to the original. Estimate new times for each step, and estimate the new total time. Try out your concepts on the function's supervisor because this person may see problems that you don't. Because the supervisor is the one who must implement any improvement, his or her involvement in the study from the outset is important.

MEASURING ACTIVITIES

In previous sections of this chapter we discussed work processes that could be charted. This topic covered tasks that are repetitive, that are done in the same way each time, and whose times can be measured. Many office functions are not repetitive; for them we cannot prepare a process chart. The functions performed by most office professionals fall into this category.

Variations of Some Office Tasks

In an accounting department, there are many functions to be performed. For some, each iteration of the task takes about the same amount of time or input; for example:

- Processing incoming invoices.
- Processing payroll checks.
- Processing outgoing invoices.

These functions cover accounts payable, payroll, and accounts receivable, respectively. But what about posting to the general ledger and subledgers? What about the preparation and modification of budgets? What about the pricing of orders or contract proposals? What about determining reasons for cost variances? In each of these cases, some jobs will be simple and quick and others long and complex. In these functions, each iteration is a different problem. You cannot prepare a standard process chart. You cannot observe a few cases and determine a standard number of work hours for each of them.

In the purchasing function, the following tasks take about the same amount of input for each iteration:

- Logging and typing of purchase orders.
- Expediting purchase orders.
- Processing receiving reports.

These tasks are relatively independent of the nature of the item bought or received. But what of placing a purchase order? It make take only five minutes to place an order for a screwdriver if you use a blanket purchase order with a local hardware supplier. It may take days or weeks to select a vendor and negotiate one order for a complicated machine tool or a quality control instrument. The amount of input (work hours) is not necessarily related to the dollar amount. It may take days to find a machine shop able to make a critical $10 part and only a couple of hours to buy $10,000 worth of typewriters.

What of the secretary's job? Its output is especially difficult to measure. Let's start with typing. You can count pages typed, but all the pages are not equal. Some pages are 10 lines long, others 50. Some pages have tables that take four to ten times as long to format and type as does straight text. Some are rough drafts in which a few typographical errors do not matter. Other pages are final copy where all errors must be corrected.

The secretary also answers the telephone, takes and delivers messages, takes and transcribes dictation, makes copies, files and retrieves, and does a multitude of other tasks. How do you measure a secretary's output? Some typing standards have been developed for different types of document. Standards have also been developed for transcribing dictation, making copies, and so on. You can compare each person against these standards for each particular part of the job. But these are an approximate measure at best.

The time that a buyer must take on each job depends on the nature of the buy. The work required of a budget analyst changes with every job looked at. As we noted above, the job of a secretary is equally varied. One can prepare a process chart for typing, although a standard time cannot be assigned to type a page. But one cannot draw up a process chart for a secretary's whole day or for that of the buyer or budget analyst.

To measure the efficiency or productivity of these jobs, you prepare, instead, an activity chart.

Activity Chart

An *activity chart* lists the duties or activities that a person performs. It shows the amount of time spent on each activity. It provides information on *what* the person is doing. In contrast to the process chart, it says nothing about *how* the person is doing it.

List of Activities.   To prepare the activity chart, each worker is asked to list the activities or duties that he or she performs. This list is reviewed with the supervisor, who adds duties that the worker neglected to include, or eliminates some that the worker should not be doing. When the content of the list is agreed to, the worker is asked to show the amount of time spent on each activity over several days or weeks.

Nonproductive Activities.   The chart must also show work time that does not contribute directly to the assigned job activities. We use the term nonproductive activity in this sense. There is no implication of slacking off in our use of the term.

Work breaks are scheduled for coffee time, rest rooms, stretching the muscles, and so on. These work breaks can be considered as fatigue time. The amount of fatigue time allowed should depend on the nature of the job. Workers who sit all day in front of a video display terminal (VDT) get eye fatigue. They also get fatigue in the muscles of the arms, back, and neck. Studies recommend work breaks for VDT operators that together remove one full hour from the eight-hour work day (see the ergonomics section of Chapter 4). Not all office jobs require this much fatigue time, but all jobs need some. Federal and state laws require certain rest breaks.

There is also personal time. This is time devoted to social conversation or grooming. Social conversation, in limited amounts, serves an important purpose. It is the way fellow workers get to know and to trust each other. A well-knit, cooperative work group will never be formed without a social element's being involved.

The final nonproductive activity, in our sense of this term, is meetings or training. The amount of time devoted to them depends on the supervisor or manager.

Activity Chart Form.   A simple form for gathering the data is shown in Figute 6-5. It requires the worker to draw a vertical line down the time axis in

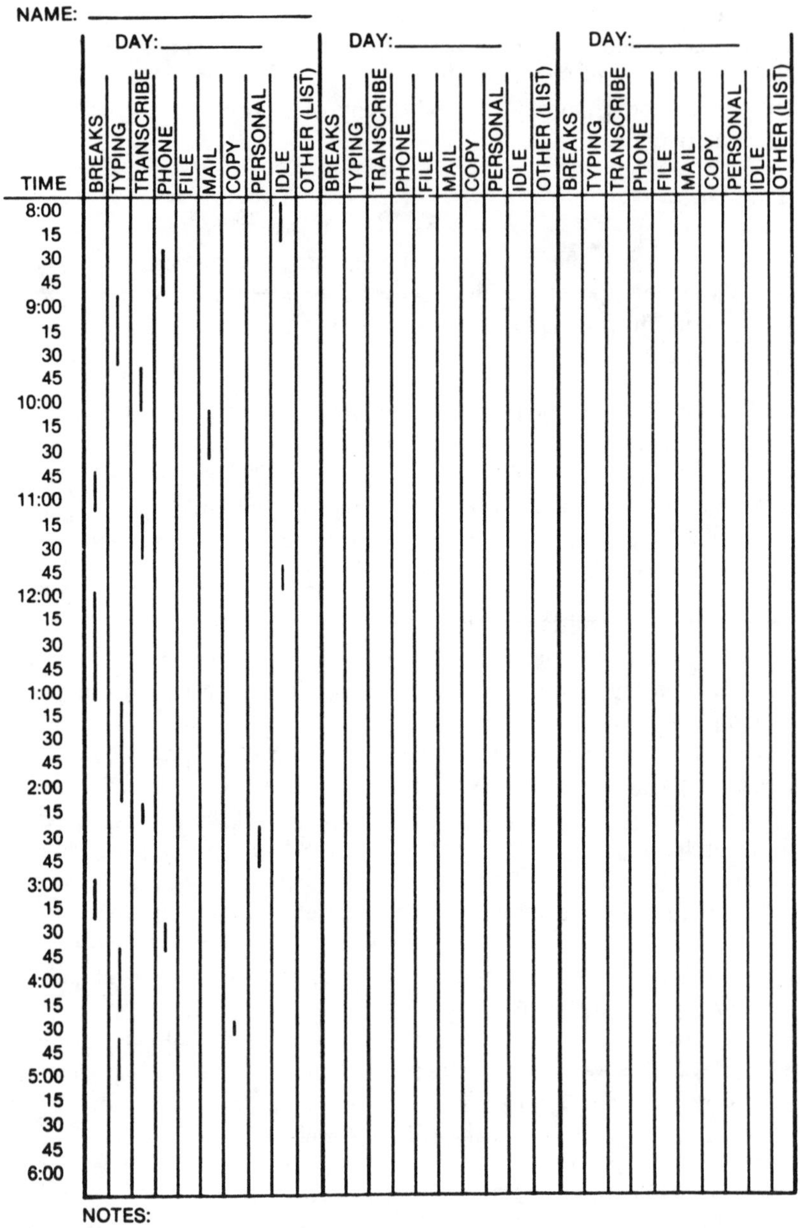

NAME: _____

| | DAY: _____ | DAY: _____ | DAY: _____ |

Column headers (for each DAY): BREAKS, TYPING, TRANSCRIBE, PHONE, FILE, MAIL, COPY, PERSONAL, IDLE, OTHER (LIST)

TIME
8:00
15
30
45
9:00
15
30
45
10:00
15
30
45
11:00
15
30
45
12:00
15
30
45
1:00
15
30
45
2:00
15
30
45
3:00
15
30
45
4:00
15
30
45
5:00
15
30
45
6:00

NOTES:

Figure 6-5. Activity chart, secretarial position. From Reba Davis and Jack Balderston, *Word Processing Supervision*, c 1984, The Bobbs-Merrill Company, Inc. Reprinted with permission.

whichever activity column he or she is working. The time devoted to each activity is easily determined by using a ruler to measure the lengths of the lines. From these totals a table is prepared showing the amount of time—or percentage of the work week—devoted to each activity, including the nonproductive activities.

The activity chart gives a measure of work input, either elapsed hours or work hours, for each activity. If you can also measure the amount of output— discussed later in this chapter—the two measures let you calculate productivity and efficiency. You can use these measures to compare people. When you see whose efficiency is highest, you can study how that person performs the tasks. Perhaps that person does the job in a different way; if so, this provides a clue on how to restructure the task. Preparing an activity chart may not be as elegant a method as drawing a process chart and analyzing its steps, but it can be almost as effective. It is usually faster and less expensive than a process chart.

COST CONSIDERATIONS

The preparation of any of the charts we have described takes the time of the analyst and the time of the worker. It can cost a lot of money to perform one of these investigations. How much investigation is worthwhile?

We suggested in Chapter 3 a brainstorming approach to improving a process or procedure. This requires minimal cost and time. If the concepts of process charts, flow charts, and activity charts seem overwhelming, you might try the brainstorming approach first. If that yields no useful results, then try the more formal methods.

Is the cost worth the benefit? This question must always be uppermost in your mind. Make an approximate estimate of your time, and that of the people you will interview and who will fill out forms for you. Price this out using average salary rates. Can you anticipate sufficient improvement to pay back this cost in about six months time? If not, try brainstorming. We suggest a six-month payback because one usually underestimates the cost of doing the study and overestimates the savings that will occur.

FORMS DESIGN

Use of a well-designed form can significantly increase productivity and efficiency. A poorly designed form can decrease them. There is an art to designing a useful form.

The following are the attributes of a good form:

1. Its title makes its purpose clear.
2. It has a short, coded identification number.

3. The line spacing permits use of a typewriter without readjusting the platen for each entry.
4. The spaces for entering information are long enough for what is needed, and high enough to allow uncramped handwriting.
5. Information is listed in the approximate sequence in which it will be used.
6. Captions and instructions are clear and complete.
7. Layout permits the user to eyeball vertically or horizontally instead of zig-zagging around the form.
8. Boldface, shading, or color is used to separate sections handled by different people.
9. Sections not to be filled in by the originator are blanked out, crosshatched, or otherwise clearly identified.
10. Enough copies are provided; copy routing and filing instructions are indicated.
11. Paper margins allow binding.
12. If it is mailed, the addressee block is placed so that window envelopes can be used.

If a process currently uses forms, check each one against this list. If a form flunks several of the criteria, it is worth redesigning because a bad form is a source of inefficiency. If you are proposing a new form for an activity, use these criteria in designing it. Check out a proposed form for both content and format with all who will use it.

MEASURING OUTPUT

Productivity is output per unit of time. Efficiency is output per unit of input, usually work hours. The process chart describes the input process and measures elapsed time and work hours. The activity chart measures work hours devoted by certain people to designated activities. We have covered input. We now need to define and measure output.

Taking the Measurements

The unit of output is different for every job. For the buyer, it is the number of purchase orders placed, or negotiations completed. For the maintenance crew, it is the number of repairs made. For the budget analyst, it is the number of analyses made. For the word processing operator, it is the number of pages or lines keyboarded. For the copy room operator, it is the number of pages copied. For the secretary, it is the number of pages typed, calls made or answered, messages taken or delivered, errands run, documents filed or retrieved.

Once you have decided what it is you want to measure, measuring output is merely a matter of counting. You ask the worker to keep a running count of each job completed. If you use prenumbered forms, such as purchase orders, it is easy to note the numbers in use at the start and end of the day and subtract one from the other. Do not forget to subtract any discarded or unused numbers. Counts of output should cover ten days or more if there is a large variation in the times required for each iteration. Spread these days throughout the week and month because some work has a cyclical pattern and may be heavier near the end of the month or on Mondays.

Using Output Measures

Productivity is output per unit of time. You can show the number of purchase orders issued per day, pages typed or copied per day, and so on. It is useful to tell management just how much work is being done, but productivity data are not of much help in improving the office functions except in one instance. If you have *too much* of something—too many reports, too much paper, too much time on the telephone—or *too little* of something—not enough documentation, not enough use of the central copier—you can use the concept of productivity to measure relative improvement.

It is more helpful in improving a function to measure its efficiency, output per work hour. Efficiency data are generally used to provide a comparative measure before and after you change a process or procedure. Efficiency may also be used to compare individuals doing the same job. The absolute value of output per work hour may not have any real meaning. The number of purchase orders per work hour tells you nothing unless you know for what types of purchases the organization writes P.O.'s, and for what it uses blanket orders or nonconfirming orders. Absolute values should not be used to compare different organizations. But relative values before and after a change give a true value of the degree of improvement achieved.

ESTABLISHING STANDARDS

Measures of output can be used to establish standards. A standard is the desired productivity or efficiency. It is established by management with the concurrence of those in charge of each operation and provides one of the goals for that operation. Often corporate budgets, work force levels, and profit projections are based on the output standards that have been established.

In a few cases—very few—there are industry-wide efficiency standards for an office function. Some have been established using engineering time and motion studies. From these studies, engineers have decided how many work hours it should take to perform a function. In over 90% of the cases however, standards are set using the firm's own work history.

Historic standards are set from the efficiency rate—output per work hour—of a fully trained, conscientious hard worker. Do not use the super performer or "workaholic." Use the good, steady performer. Her or his output becomes your standard.

When you have set a standard, stick to it. Change it only if either the procedures or the equipment being used is changed. If these changes improve output—and why would you make them if they didn't?—the standard needs to be brought up to date too.

What if the output of all the workers exceeds the standard? It is a poor standard. You probably did a poor job in establishing it. But stick to it for at least one year and preferably longer. Exceeding the standard is a motivating experience for the staff. If it doesn't cost you anything—that is, you are not paying piecework—this morale booster is a big help to the function's supervisor. Raising the standard so that many on the staff no longer meet it may result in lower overall output.

SUMMARY

Classic work measurement techniques have a limited application to office systems. They may be used to measure productivity or efficiency. They cannot measure effectiveness. Of the three, it is effectiveness that is most important.

We define productivity as output per unit of time; efficiency as output per unit of input, usually expressed as work hours; and effectiveness as output in relation to the function's objective. Managers of office functions tend to optimize their own efficiency, often at the expense of the effectiveness of the enterprise. All support functions should aim to optimize the company's productive activities, not their own. They, and higher management, need to guard against suboptimization.

Before the work of a function is measured, the staff of that function must be motivated to help; otherwise inaccurate data will result. The anticipated advantages are a reduced number of procedure steps, a better definition of responsibilities, and greater responsibility for many of the staff.

Process charts show each step of a procedure, with emphasis on the nonoperational steps of transportation and delay. Flow charts emphasize the relationships between steps. Activity charts are prepared for jobs that are not repetitive, such as the jobs of most professionals. Data are gathered by interview with the workers, by reading the procedures, and by observation. A work flow chart is made to show the paper flow. Improvements come from reducing the transportation and delay steps to a minimum, often by combining steps. A list of questions is provided in this chapter to help find other ways to improve a work process.

Work measurement costs time and money. One should always ask if the benefit is worth the cost. If a six-month cost payback is not foreseen, the brainstorming approach of Chapter 2 is suggested.

Use of well-designed forms improves efficiency. Twelve attributes of a good form are listed. Existing forms should be checked against this list. If they fail to meet several of the criteria, the forms should be redesigned.

Output is different for every job in every function. The key is determining what to measure. The measure itself is usually a simple count of items produced. When counting units of output, stagger the times of measurement throughout the week and month because some activities have cyclical patterns. Use output to calculate efficiency, that is, output units per work hour. Using efficiency, compare before and after a change to show the degree of improvement.

FOR FURTHER INFORMATION

Productivity

Schleh, Edward C. *How to Boost Your Return on Management.* New York: McGraw-Hill, 1984.

Work Measurement

Hammill, B. J. *Work Measurement in the Office, An MTM Systems Handbook.* New York: International Publications Service, 1973.
Nance, Harold, and Nolan, Robert E. *Office Work Measurement,* rev. ed. Melborne, FL.: Krieger Publ. Co., 1983.
Thursland, Arthur L. *Work Measurement: A Guidebook to Word Processing Management,* 2nd ed. Willow Grove, PA: Association of Information Systems Professionals, 1981.

Forms Design

Kaiser, Julius B. *Forms Design and Control.* New York: AMACOM, 1968.

7
Is Automation For You?

The office of the future! Computers perform all the dull and routine work. Information is available instantly. No more errors are made. People are free to use their heads rather than their hands. Are these promises real? Can we afford them? Should we automate the office?

The computerization of many office systems is certainly upon us. It will save a lot of drudgery. It will save time. It may even save money, though this is less likely. It will allow you, as a professional or manager, to make better decisions. This last point is where the real advantage of office systems automation lies.

Can you afford it? That question must be answered element by element. Today many elements that we describe are too expensive for any but the largest companies to use. But costs are falling, and falling fast. Technology is finding cheaper ways to package more powerful computer tools, and what is expensive today will not be tomorrow. The history of the pocket calculator and that of the office computer prove this.

In this chapter we look at each of the main office elements to provide the reader with an idea of what automating each involves and what advantage may be expected if this is done.

The evolution toward the electronic (automated) office is shown in Figure 7-1. As each of us moves toward the inner circle, we are further along some of the spokes than others. Eventually we will all be in the center, but this is decades away for most of us. In the meantime, approach each element as its need and usefulness become apparent, and as the cost becomes affordable.

VALUE OF INFORMATION, CONVENIENCE, AND TIME

Most of the recent technological innovations have not saved the office money. Perhaps the last major one to do so was the typewriter. It is moot whether the high-speed computer saves money in the accounting function over use of punched cards. The telephone is certainly more expensive to use than the mails. The copy machine costs more to use than carbon paper.

No one of us would dream of eliminating the computer, the telephone, or the copier. Why? They provide other things we consider important. The com-

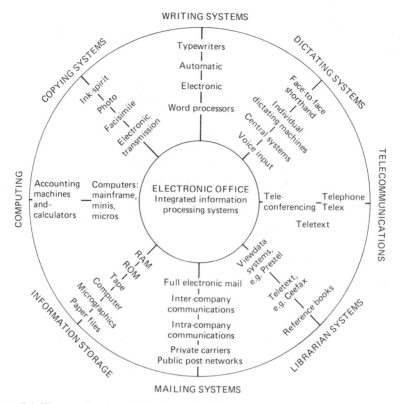

Figure 7-1. The evolution toward the electronic office. From Birchall, D. W., and Hammond, V. J., *The Electronic Office*, London, U.K.: Hutchinson Publishing Group. Reprinted with permission.

puter, once it is programmed and the data are entered, prepares the report we want. But it can also provide *more information* from these same data at virtually no additional cost. The telephone allows us to transmit information and make decisions immediately; it *saves time*. The copier is a less messy approach to duplicating a page. It permits more copies to be made, a lot more than we really need. It provides *convenience*.

Information, time, and convenience are worth money. We will pay to obtain them. Office systems automation promises to provide all of them. The real justification lies here, not in saving money.

Information

Business subsists on information. All decisions require it. Many managers feel that the more information they have, the better their decisions will be. The better the decisions, the more profit for the company. Therefore, more information will result in higher profits. Thus it pays to get additional information. That is their logic.

Clearly there is a point beyond which more information is a hindrance, not a help. Information has to be read and digested. One can be overpowered by too much information. Knowing what data to get, and when to stop gathering data is one of the attributes of the superior manager. It separates this person from the data hound who wants just a little more before making up his or her mind.

One can oversubscribe to the principal that more information is good. But more of the right information can make the difference between an outstanding decision and one that is merely adequate. In a competitive world, this is very important.

Using the power of the computer to select the appropriate information from a mass of available data provides more significant information and provides it fast. The ability to model "what if" situations—to change the variables in an engineering, production, inventory, sales, or financing decision—allows the manager to see which alternative improves overall performance or overall profit. It also shows how each change will affect the other elements in the equation. It allows the manager to see the effect of different decisions without actually implementing any of them.

Whether the right information is obtained and whether this leads to better decisions depends on the ability of the manager. But the tools to work with can be provided through automation of the office elements.

Convenience

This is a very subjective issue. What is convenience worth? In part the answer depends on the health of the company. If you are fighting off a bankruptcy filing and haven't seen figures in the profit column for years, convenience has zero value. But if you are healthy with a net profit of 20% or more of sales, you will pay for convenience.

Convenience affects your feeling of being in control. You don't have to scrounge for information; you have it at your fingertips. Equipment and supplies are handy to the place where you work, not three floors up in the building; this lets you do your job faster. But convenience is more than speed. There is an intangible something that makes your morale higher. You have confidence in your organization. It cares about you. It has done something to make your life easier, so you care more about it. One cannot put a value on this feeling, but it is real, and it is important.

Time

Time is money—a cliché, but a true one. Being first to the marketplace with a product can mean dominating that market. Being first to file a patent gives you a monopoly on the product. In the office functions, the sooner a problem is uncovered, the sooner it can be addressed, and the sooner it will be solved. Also, the sooner it is discovered, the less damage will occur before it is fixed.

Having data that are up to date for the day or the hour saves money. You need not allow for contingencies that may occur before you can learn that you have a problem. If seven days can elapse before the weekly report tells you of a large withdrawal or shipment from inventory, you must keep a supply of your stock on hand large enough to cover this possibility. If you have daily or hourly reports, you can take action to restock six days sooner. Therefore the inventory level can be lower.

If sales in one territory have fallen off and you have daily sales reports, you can investigate sooner and make adjustments sooner. If a project is going over budget and you have daily reports on cost status, you can react a month sooner than if you must wait for a monthly report. If the current real-time status of all purchase orders or maintenance requests is available through the computer in your office, you can spot problems daily or even hourly. You do not have to call a meeting or require written status reports to know where things stand.

What is the value of being able to write a message to someone in another building or city, have it delivered in minutes, and know the exact time at which it was read? What is the value of avoiding telephone tag? On more mundane office matters, what is the value of your secretary's keeping your appointment list current without having to enter your office and interrupt your meeting or your train of thought? What is the value of a log of incoming messages or phone calls that is always current to the minute? What is the value of an electronic tickler file that updates itself when you take some action on a subject?

These examples all indicate how time may be saved through automated systems. You cannot put a hard dollar amount on these time savings, but they do have value.

AREAS TO AUTOMATE

In whatever area you choose to start office automation, you will have trouble justifying the first use. This warning needs to be stated at the outset. Automation involves major initial expenditures for equipment. No single use will justify the cost in dollar terms alone. But once you have the first equipment, the cost of adding new features and new applications is much lower. It takes several applications really to justify the expenditure. On the first application, you are betting on the future. Your management must have faith that the payoff will be there when you take the first bold step.

Realize also that to take advantage of most automated systems requires that there be many users on the automated network. An electronic mail system is not useful if there are ony ten stations, and they are all on one floor in one building. But when the system expands to cover all floors in all buildings in all company locations, it will pay back its cost many-fold.

You have to start small in order to learn how to use these techniques and in order to find out which ones work for you. There is a pilot phase, just as in a production process. A pilot phase is not designed to make money. It is designed to learn and refine the process, determine operating costs, and decide whether to go ahead with full production. It is the same with office systems automation.

All of the office elements discussed in Chapters 4 and 5 can be automated except for dictation systems. Except for refinements in its control features, dictation is now about as automated as it will get. In the remainder of this chapter, we describe the automated version of these office elements and suggest guidelines for timing the move to each one.

Word Processing

Word processing is usually the entry point to automated office systems. The automated version of typing, word processing was described at length in Chapter 4. Features already available cover almost any text editing or text manipulation feature you are likely to want. Future enhancements lie in the use of word processing as an input to other functions such as printing, mail, and filing.

Any business can use electronic typewriters today. Their use improves typing efficiency by about 20%. They will pay for themselves in one to two years through increased productivity. To prove this:

1. Determine how much time each secretary or clerk now spends typing.
2. Convert this typing time to costs using an average salary and adding fringe benefits costs.
3. Divide by the anticipated improvement factor (here 1.20 for a 20% improvement) to determine the salary cost after converting to the new equipment.
4. Subtract the number in step 3 from the number in step 2 to determine the annual cost savings.
5. List the cost of the equipment.
6. Divide the annual cost savings into the cost of the equipment.

This gives the time, in years, required to pay back the cost of the new equipment.

Table 7-1 presents an example of such a calculation for a person who types 50% of the job time and who makes $275 per week plus 35% in fringe benefits.

Payback is generally one to two years for electronic typewriters that are in use most of the time. If the payback period is less than two years, we suggest that the change to the new equipment is justified. The electronic typewriter itself will last from five to ten years.

Stand alone video screen word processors of office quality cost $8,000 and

Table 7-1. Payback Calculation, Electronic Typewriters.

A. Annual Savings Through Typing Improvement
   50% of time typing @ $19,000/yr................ $8,700
   divide by improvement factor, 1.20.............. 7,250
   annual cost savings 1,450

B. Cost of Equipment $2,000

C. Payback
   ($2,000 divided by $1,450) .... 1.4 years

up, including a character printer. Large networks of shared logic or distributed logic terminals cost less than this per unit when there are four or more units.

To determine the payback period for word processors, assume a 50% improvement in input efficiency for the first input of a document and a factor of three improvement for revisions. The latter factor, of course, depends on how extensive the revisions are, and this, in turn, depends on your type of business. The 300% improvement is about average. Estimate your percentage of revision work, combine the improvement factors for original input and revision input in the proper proportions, and derive an overall improvement factor for word processing equipment. Mary Ruprecht, whom we have quoted before, suggests that this will be about a factor of two over the standard electric typewriter.[1]

Perform the same payback calculation described in the previous section. Table 7-2 presents an example using a typist who spends 80% of the job time typing. Once again, if the payback is two years or less, we suggest that the change to word processors is justified. Word processing equipment should last five years.

The choice between electronic typewriters and word processors depends on the anticipated usage for the equipment. If a secretary or clerk will use it for only a few hours a week, the more expensive word processor probably cannot be justified. Two elements should be involved in the choice. One is the cost

Table 7-2. Payback Calculation, Word Processors.

A. Annual Savings Through Typing Improvement
   80% of time typing @ $19,000/yr................ $15,200
   divide by improvement factor, 2.0.............. 7,600
   annual cost savings 7,600

B. Cost of Equipment .... $ 8,000

C. Payback
   ($8,000 divided by $7,600) .... 1.1 years

---

[1] Ruprecht, Mary M. New Managerial Techniques for Productivity Measurement and Improvement, Talk to Syntopican XI, Association of Information Systems Professionals, June 1983.

payback, calculated using the improvement factors, equipment costs, and amount of usage for each. The other is the set of features available on a word processor but not obtainable on an electronic typewriter. If one of these features is important to the particular operation, that operation should have a word processor.

Personal Computers

PC units at the low end of the cost scale, $3,000 or less including printer, are an important tool for those professionals and paraprofessionals who spend 20% of their time or more in calculating or writing.

A PC, with appropriate programs, cuts the calculation time by at least two-thirds over use of a desk calculator. It cuts the time to write a report by at least half over writing longhand, even for professionals who are poor typists. Determine how much time the professional or paraprofessional spends at these activities over a year, and do the cost justification calculation as described in the sections above. In Table 7-3 we present a sample calculation, assuming use of the PC only 15% of the time. It does not take much use to justify a $3,000 PC.

Remember the warnings on equipment standardization noted in Chapter 5. Also be sure that the professionals or managers for whom you buy the equipment will use the PC. Some won't.

More expensive PC's—and they can cost over $10,000 with graph plotters and multimegabyte memories—need more use to be justified. The alternative to buying them is often use of the company's main computer. Three factors must be weighed in making a decision between these two alternatives:

1. The availability of a better program on either the PC or the mainframe.
2. Availability of time on the mainframe at those hours or days when it will be needed.
3. Cost of using the mainframe versus cost of the PC.

Data Processing Terminal

The need for frequent access to the main computer may suggest placing a terminal permanently in a professional's office. Terminals are relatively inexpen-

Table 7-3. Payback Calculation, Personal Computers.

A. Professional Time and Cost Savings
15% of time using PC $6,000
divide by improvement factor, 1.60 3,750
annual cost savings 2,250

B. Cost of equipment $3,000

C. Payback
($3,000 divided by $2,250) .... 1.3 years

sive, $1,000 to $2,000 if purchased and under $100 per month if leased. But there is also the cost of running a cable connection to the office location, which may be greater than the cost of the terminal. Because people relocate their offices quite frequently, the cost of moving the terminal connection should also be considered.

The alternative is to set up terminal rooms in the building near user groups. Such rooms are probably needed anyway.

The personal terminal should not become a status symbol. Its justification is based on:

1. Frequency of use.
2. Proximity to a terminal room.
3. How often all units in the terminal room are unavailable.
4. The installed cost of the terminal versus the cost of wasted time of the professional.

The last point involves the same type of calculation as is made to determine payback. This is also a case where the intangible value of convenience must be considered.

Electronic Mail

The phrase "electronic mail" covers many alternate methods of transmitting messages electronically. It covers almost any method except postal mail, couriers, and carrier pigeons. The Western Union telegraph is electronic mail. Telex and TWX systems are electronic mail. So is facsimile. So are word processors communicating to each other. So are data processing computer systems that permit one terminal to transmit to another. So are communicating printer-copiers. Any of these methods will deliver a written message almost instantly from one location to another.

If you need written communication faster than can be handled by the U.S. mails, some form of electronic mail is appropriate for your business. Which of the forms is appropriate is a balance among:

1. Speed required
2. Amount of use
3. Cost

Telex. This is the least expensive method. Through this system, you can access any other telex station in the world. You dial that station number, and the connection is made. Directories are available of all stations on the telex or TWX (telex II) networks. The telex and TWX networks operate at a speed of 66 words per minute regardless of type of input or receiving station.

The equipment comes in several degrees of sophistication. You can input the message using equipment that looks like an electronic typewriter. This equipment is the least expensive, and costs about $1,500. It can send or receive, but not do both simultaneously. Video screen telex terminals cost from $2,500 to $5,000. You can edit on these terminals, store on a magnetic disk, and transmit at a later time. The more expensive units can send and receive at the same time.

Most word processors and some electronic typewriters and PC's have a communication option that lets them act as terminals for telex messages. If you already have this equipment, you need only add the option to have access to this form of messaging. Adding the communications option costs about $1,000 on electronic typewriters and $500 to $2,000 on word processors and PC's. It also requires an adapter (modem), which costs about $500, to connect the equipment to the telephone lines. It may require a dedicated telephone line, but so will most other electronic mail systems.

Facsimile. Facsimile transmission works directly with paper copies. It does not require someone to rekey the information to another form before it can be transmitted. Since much of the information one wants to transmit is already on paper, facsimile is an efficient way to handle it.

With most of the newer equipment models, there is no longer a problem of dissimilar models being unable to communicate with each other. Recent equipment adheres to one of three transmission standards, designated group I, group II, and group III. A group IV is being developed for equipment that will transmit both facsimile and word processing codes.

Group I equipment transmits at a speed of four to six minutes per page. Group II equipment has a speed of two to four minutes per page. Both use analog transmission, one FM and the other AM. Most equipment that can transmit or receive using group II standards can also transmit and receive using group I. Group III equipment uses digital transmission, which is inherently faster, with a rate of 20 seconds to a minute per page. Most models of group III equipment are designed also to send and receive group II or group I messages. They are therefore the most versatile.

Group I and II equipment models cost from $1,500 to $3,000. Digital group III equipment costs from $5,000 to $12,000. The range within these prices covers such options as automatic dialing, unattended operation, concurrent sending and receiving, larger-capacity paper trays, multiple paper sizes, automatic printing of day and time of receipt, and other features. The faster transmission speed of group III equipment reduces the long distance telephone charges (see below) so that it may be less expensive to use than the other equipment.

Figure 7-2 is a nomogram from which you can calculate the cost per page using either analog or digital equipment. You can use it to determine which is less expensive for your operating conditions. The cost of transmitting 500 pages a month is about $1.20 per page on either digital or analog equipment. At 1000 pages per month, using digital, the cost drops to about 70 cents per page. In general, businesses transmitting more than 500 pages per month will save money by using group III digital equipment.

There are many facsimile machines in use. Each one has a telephone number for its dedicated line. If you know the phone number for another machine, you can transmit to it. This network, therefore, can cover other organizations as well as other locations in your own company. The decision on whether to install facsimile depends on the quantity of paper you expect to send and whether it is worth that price to get immediate delivery.

Communicating Word Processors. Communications is an option on nearly all word processing equipment. It costs from $500 to $2,000.

Communicating by word processor is effective for documents that already exist on word processing disks or that will be placed on disks for later editing. It is not efficient to input a document only for the purpose of transmitting it. If the document exists in paper form, it is less expensive to use facsimile for transmission.

Identical equipment models can transmit to each other. Equipment of different models often cannot. This incompatibility has delayed use of word processors to transmit electronic mail. Unlike the facsimile vendors, word processing companies have been unable to standardize their communications. Therefore, communicating word processors are used mainly for transmitting documents within a company where equipment has been standardized. They are used infrequently for communicating to outside organizations.

Translation equipment that allows one model of equipment to talk to another is coming on the market. These translators work well on the standard keyboard characters. But translators do not handle all word processing codes, nor can a command that activates a function on one machine be sent to another machine that cannot perform that function. These problems will always limit the usefulness of code translators.

If you have word processors of the same model at other company locations, it is usually worth the cost to have the communications option on at least one machine in each separate building. You do not need it on all machines. You can bring the disk that contains the information to be transmitted to the machine that has the communications option.

For $2,000 or less you have the ability to transmit documents to executives at other locations for their review and comments while the documents are still in draft form. Editing can be done at the other locations. The drafts can be transmitted back and all comments consolidated by the originator. If this type of fast coordination is useful to you, the price of the communications option is small compared to the time saved and the convenience achieved.

Personal computers have the same communications abilities and limitations as word processors. Like models of equipment can communicate with each other. Equipment with the same operating system such as CP/M or MS-DOS can

EQUIPMENT

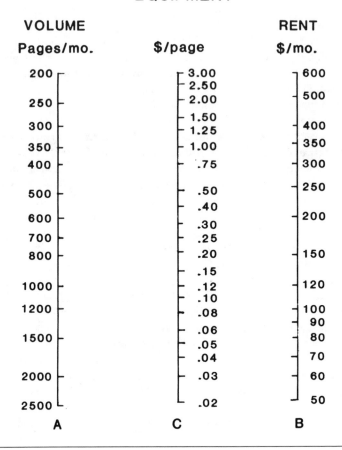

VOLUME	$/page	RENT
Pages/mo.		$/mo.

<table>
<tr><td>200</td><td>3.00
2.50
2.00</td><td>600
500</td></tr>
<tr><td>250</td><td></td><td></td></tr>
<tr><td>300</td><td>1.50
1.25</td><td>400</td></tr>
<tr><td>350</td><td>1.00</td><td>350</td></tr>
<tr><td>400</td><td>.75</td><td>300</td></tr>
<tr><td>500</td><td>.50
.40</td><td>250</td></tr>
<tr><td>600</td><td>.30</td><td>200</td></tr>
<tr><td>700</td><td>.25</td><td></td></tr>
<tr><td>800</td><td>.20
.15</td><td>150</td></tr>
<tr><td>1000</td><td>.12
.10</td><td>120</td></tr>
<tr><td>1200</td><td>.08</td><td>100
90</td></tr>
<tr><td>1500</td><td>.06
.05
.04</td><td>80
70</td></tr>
<tr><td>2000</td><td>.03</td><td>60</td></tr>
<tr><td>2500</td><td>.02</td><td>50</td></tr>
<tr><td>A</td><td>C</td><td>B</td></tr>
</table>

TO USE A NOMOGRAM

Determine a value for each of the outer lines in each figure.
Place a ruler across these values and read the value on the middle column.

For example, you are sending 500 pages per month (A). A machine renting for $350 per month (B) will cost $0.71 per page (C). At a 45 seconds per page transmission rate (D) and $0.40 per minute line rate (E), transmission costs are $0.30 per page (F). The total cost is $1.01 per page.

Figure 7-2. Facsimile cost nomograms. Reprinted with permission from *The Office*, May 1983.

TRANSMISSION

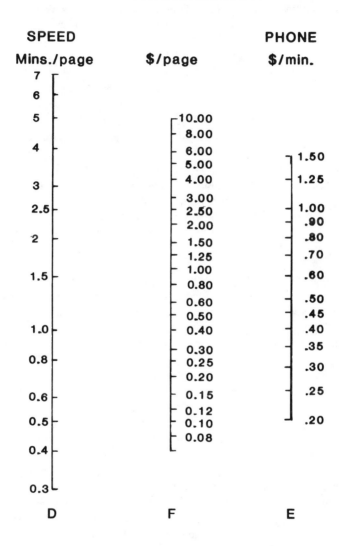

SPEED

Mins./page

PHONE

$/page $/min.

D   F   E

communicate only with loss of some codes. PC's with different operating systems cannot communicate directly. Translation equipment is available for some of the more popular PC models and has the same limitations in translating codes.

Data Processing Terminals.   The data processing network can be used for electronic mail. In this case, since all terminals use the central computer's processing unit, there is no problem with incompatible operating systems or with code translation. Whatever is written and formated at one terminal will be received in exactly that form at another.

The terminals form a network, with the computer at the hub. Anyone on the network can communicate to anyone else. Your organization's computer can also link to another computer and thus form an electronic mail path to other organizations. Because one manufacturer dominates the mainframe business, this intercomputer linkage is not so complex as linking word processors or PC's. This form of electronic mail, however, is not in widespread use. For reasons of security, few organizations wish to open up their main computers for others to access them.

Which Form of Electronic Mail?   Using telex is like sending a telegram. Because the message must be retyped, it's primary use is for short messages.

Facsimile now dominates intercompany electronic mail and will do so for some time. It provides paper copies of documents, still the most common form of electronic mail. It is the least expensive way to transmit single copies of a paper document.

Word processor to word processor is an effective intracompany method for reports or long documents that already exist on word processor disks. It is faster than facsimile once the connection between stations is established.

Computer terminal to computer terminal is an effective method for material that is created on a terminal. It does not make sense for a document that exists in paper form and must be keyed through the terminal.

Each form of electronic mail works best for a specific type of document. In each section above, we provided typical costs. Using these costs and the amount of electronic mail you expect to send or receive, you can determine the practicality of each for your situation. Many organizations use more than one method. If the traffic warrants it, all four methods can be employed.

Telecommunications

The networking ability of digital telephone systems may offer an effective way to tie together dissimilar computers, word processors, and PC's. Owning a programmable switchboard that is located in your own building and under your own control will save a lot of money as you change telephone features or telephone numbers. But changeover of the telephone network from a Centrex or other analog system is a very expensive undertaking.

Owning a digital system may pay off in two to five years. It depends on the number of telephones, number of features, and frequency of moving office locations. This is a very complex issue to resolve. We advise the reader to bring in an outside telecommunications consultant for advice. Do not rely solely on telephone company analysts; you will not get an unbiased review.

Digital systems are the way of the future. They are less expensive to operate, are more versatile, and are able to integrate data and voice transmission. Most digital systems today are made for the large user. Before long, they will become available for small companies.

Deciding between the many competing local area networks is also a highly complex issue. There is no simple formula to apply. On this subject, your company's data processing specialist should be consulted.

Voice Mail

A marriage of computers and telecommunications brings us the concept of voice mail. This is a messaging system designed to avoid the game of telephone tag.

In a voice mail system, the person wishing to leave a message for someone telephones that person's "voice box." This is like a mailbox, but accessible only by telephone. Each recipient has an individual voice box number that is password-protected; only by dialing a password number can the message be heard. The caller speaks the message and hangs up. The voice box is a computer that digitizes the voice message and stores the digital code in a portion of memory accessible only by the recipient's password. When the latter wishes to pick up messages, he or she dials in and hears the message in the sender's own voice.

This concept differs from the telephone answering machine in two important ways. First, you dial the voice box number, not the desk telephone. Thus you know you will not be talking to the person but will be leaving a message. You are mentally prepared to speak the message rather than to hold a conversation. It is like sending a written memo in place of walking into someone's office to make a statement. Second, the recipient hears your voice in high fidelity, feeling your "presence" in a personal way.

Voice mail is available now. It is expensive because it takes a lot of computer memory to store digital voice signals. Like many other new technologies, this one will come down in price with time. Someday it will be competitive with a conventional message service such as we described in Chapter 5.

Teleconferencing

This subject is applicable to large organizations that must coordinate a lot of work among people who are located in different communities.

There are several forms of teleconferencing. Audio conferencing has been available for a long time. This is the familiar conference call in which several people at different locations can each talk to the others at the same time.

Video teleconferencing, a new form, is just starting to be used and comes in several types. The most expensive is full motion video, which is like live television. A camera at each location takes a picture of the person speaking (or of the drawing or diagram the person is discussing) and transmits it to the other locations. If the viewing screen is life-size, it gives the feeling of a real meeting. One- or two-way transmission is possible. An individual can direct the camera and determine what picture is transmitted, or sophisticated electronics can do this.

Freeze frame video takes and transmits one picture every few minutes rather than "live" pictures. The equipment and transmission costs are less, but there is less feeling of participation as well. You don't see facial reactions to a remark, or the other nonverbal clues that let you know when a point has been understood and accepted.

There is also the "electronic blackboard." Participants write on a board, and their markings are duplicated on a screen at the receiving end. You don't see the participants; only the writing on the board is transmitted.

When is video teleconferencing a substitute for travel? It is better than an audio hookup for lectures. The visual image holds the audience's attention and enlivens the talk. Thus the audience is more likely to remember what is said. It is good for meetings that are really lectures to impart information. Questions are asked and answered, but no discussion takes place. It is good for discussion and agreement on changes to a schedule, to blueprints or specifications, or to a plan of action. It allows several people at different locations to look at a chart or drawing together, interpret what they see, and agree on some course of action.

Teleconferencing, however, is not a substitute for professional meetings or seminars. The face-to-face contact established at these meetings is often as important as the content of the formal discussions. It cannot provide this personal rapport. It is not appropriate for brainstorming sessions or for meetings where a truly open exchange of ideas is wanted.

What percent of your travel budget is allocated to meetings for which teleconferencing can be a substitute? It is probably less than half, more likely about 25%. Full motion color video will cost $50,000 to $150,000 per location for the equipment and for setting up a dedicated room. Transmission costs via satellite are about $600 to $800 per hour, which covers transmission in both directions. Freeze frame systems range from $15,000 to $50,000 per station, depending on screen size, camera, and the controls desired. They transmit via modem and telephone lines so transmission costs are the normal long distance rates. Freeze frame does not need a special room. "Electronic blackboards" cost about $15,000 and also use telephone lines for transmission.

Teleconferencing costs will come down, and travel costs will continue to rise. At some point, video teleconferencing will cost less than travel for the midsize company. Which form to use depends on your need. See a demonstration of each; the better systems are quite impressive.

Reprographics

More and more useful features are appearing on conventional central copiers—at a price. While they may be helpful to you, they do not constitute automation. The automation innovations that will have a significant impact on productivity are in the areas of laser printers and the use of word processors as a direct input to the printer, bypassing paper copies.

The advantages of laser printers are book print quality, versatility in layout and type styles, and copy speed. You can also program the type styles, spacing, and formats at the printer, and can change them instantly if you don't like the layout of the first copy you run. Laser printers accept word processing disks as text input.

Because full-feature laser printers now cost over $50,000, they are practical today only for companies with very high printing volumes. Keep an eye on the cost of this equipment. As prices fall, laser printers will be suitable for companies whose printing volume is as low as 100,000 pages per month. When the cost approaches the five cents or so per page that you are paying for in-house conventional copying (including operator salaries and fringe benefits), or approaches your costs for having printing done outside, switch to a laser printer.

Phototypesetting using word processor input is a less expensive alternative. It can be done now using a service operation in your city that has phototypesetting equipment. Costs depend on whether your word processing operators place typesetting codes in the manuscript, or the printer does this step. Codes are needed to designate format changes, type styles, and so on. There are not many codes to learn, but the word processing operator cannot print the document locally to know that all the codes were input correctly. One error can cause some strange-looking type!

Costs of phototypesetting a document from word processing input are not excessive for large documents and long print runs. A 200-page single-spaced typed document (which will condense to 100 typeset pages because of type compression, discussed in Chapter 5) at 500 copies will cost about $3,000 if your operators input the typesetting codes, and $5,000 if the printer does it. Making photocopies at five cents a page would also cost $5,000, and they would not look so professional or be so easy to read as these copies. The cost per page of phototypesetting is lower with higher volumes because most of the printer's cost lies in copy preparation and making plates. You should determine the volume at which use of a local phototypesetting shop is less expensive than internal copying. Be sure that the typesetter can work from the disks of your particular model of word processor.

Computer Graphics

This area is becoming increasingly sophisticated. On many PC's and some word processors you can now draw and print bar charts, line charts, and pie charts.

The vendors call this business graphics. Using a copier, you can make acceptable overhead transparencies from these computer-generated originals. On some equipment the charts can be drawn in color. If you have a plotter with replaceable pens, you can usually print in color as well.

For about $5,000 you can obtain a system that lets you draw any type of chart, graph, diagram, or picture on the screen and print it in black and white. It can place text at any location on the drawing. It can selectively move, enlarge, or reduce portions of the drawings or text. The computer also allows you to make changes in the layout until you like what you see. For about $60,000 you can get a more sophisticated system that also prints in color. Computer attachments allow you to make slides or overhead transparencies of these drawings.

The output speed with such a system is several times that of a graphics artist using pen and a lettering machine. If your organization has a graphics unit that prepares drawings for reports or presentations, computer graphics is an area to watch. Equipment costs will come down. They do not have to fall much further before one graphic artist at a keyboard can substitute for three of four people making drawings manually. When you can obtain equipment that fits your requirements at a cost equal to the annual salary paid a graphics expert, it is time to consider changing to computer graphics.

Records Management

Equipment exists today to read directly from computer memory to microfilm or microfiche without going through a paper copy stage. This is computer output microfilm (COM). Equipment also exists to do the reverse, read from microfilm back into computer memory. This is computer input microfilm (CIM). The combination is very powerful for records storage and retrieval. A COM system costs about $100,000 to $150,000 and CIM from $150,000 to $200,000. COM is available through service companies in some cities, but there are not many CIM systems available.

With greater demand and improved technology, the costs of COM and CIM will come down. When the cost to you of transferring a page of text from computer memory to film reaches about five cents a page, and the cost of going from film to memory reaches about $1.00 a page (you do this much less frequently), it will be time to consider these systems.

Further in the future is video disk storage. It will have the advantage of being an integral part of the computer memory, thus avoiding the transfer steps of memory to film and film to memory. The cost of input and storage of a page on video disk should be close to that of input and storage on film before you consider a change. The latter cost is currently about five cents a page.

Larger computer memories may also significantly change the way in which documents are indexed. The most effective form of document retrieval is key word searching. At present, the key words for a document must be determined by the author, or, preferably, by someone trained in library searching techniques. A computer program can use logic to list all nouns, modifying adjectives, verbs, and adverbs in a document. The key words will be among these. Larger computer memories will permit the storage of this long list so that indexing will be automatic. Searching will be a matter of carefully identifying the word combinations that separate the document you want from all the rest.

Desk Management

This term includes all the features that aid the professional's work habits. Applications include:

1. Maintaining an appointment calendar.
2. Maintaining a tickler file of unfinished business and due dates.
3. Seeing the agenda for forthcoming meetings.
4. Having a scratch pad to write reminder notes to yourself.
5. Being able to call up a telephone or address directory.
6. Being able to call up organization charts.

These features are available today on some equipment. Other features will undoubtedly be added in the future.

Some people will use a terminal for these activities. Others will always prefer to keep little slips of paper on the desk where they can be seen. The matter of personal work habits will make automated desk management very important to one executive and of no interest to another. Calendar programs are useless if the user forgets to call up the program.

To be effective, a desk management program should imitate the role of the secretary. It should be able to bring to a window on the screen a message stating that a meeting will start in five minutes. This is the key to a useful desk management program. Until the programs can do what a good secretary does, it is a moot question to ask how significant a contribution these programs will make in improving personal productivity.

THE AUTOMATION STUDY

We have provided a shopping list of functions that should be considered for automation. We have listed some criteria to help you decide when to consider each one. How do you get agreement on what to automate and on how to do it? How do you sell your conclusions to management? We address the first question now. Selling management is the subject of a later chapter.

A study of automation is different from a study of improving one function as described in Chapter 3. Automation covers the entire organization from top to bottom and from end to end. It covers all procedures in all departments. It affects the working lives of most company employees. Therefore, it must be approached carefully and thoroughly.

The Task Force

To do the study a task force should be formed. This task force must have the full backing of top management, or it will not succeed in reaching useful conclusions, nor will its conclusions be implemented. Some people will not want to cooperate. The continuing support of higher management is necessary to get the information you need.

The study team should constist of the following people:

- Administrative support services manager
- Data processing manager
- Word processing manager
- A consultant
- A financial analyst
- A systems analyst (if available)

The first named should be the chairperson because he or she has the broadest view of needs.

A consultant in office automation is a useful addition to the team to help guide the deliberations and to review tentative conclusions. A good consultant will save enough time to pay for the consulting fee. A consultant, however, should not be asked to perform such a study or make a recommendation alone. The consultant walks away; the organization must implement and live with the results.

Objectives

The task force members have three objectives:

1. To learn what office automation means and what specific system capabilities exist.
2. To learn the specific needs of the company's staff.
3. To match capabilities to needs, and establish a plan for implementing automation.

The first objective involves:

1. Reading and learning.
2. Visiting other organizations that have automated some of their functions.
3. Attending seminars and conferences.

A reading list is provided at the end of this chapter. The consultant can guide you in what to read and which companies to visit. The best of the conferences is the Office Automation Conference held each February and sponsored by the American Federation of Information Processing Societies.[2]

The second objective involves interviewing a selected sample of managers, professionals, and support staff to learn their needs and desires. It is difficult to separate real needs from a wish list. There will no lack of ideas about what should be automated. Most members of the staff will have seen or read of some activity elsewhere that seems much simpler because of automation. Your problem is to sort through the many needs suggested.

You study the paper flow in the organization, though not in as much depth as is done for the productivity improvement studies described in Chapter 3. You select a few areas where automation techniques particularly seem to be needed and examine them more thoroughly. Candidate areas are:

- Filing systems and records management
- Telephone messaging
- Word processing
- Scheduling meetings and conference rooms
- Maintaining lists (telephone, personnel, etc.)
- Computer graphics
- Electronic mail
- Digital telephone systems
- Literature searching
- Local area networks

For its third objective, the task force picks one or two key areas of need. For each, it determines:

1. How strong a need there is.
2. Who is affected.
3. The anticipated improvement in time saved, greater accuracy, etc.
4. Specific equipment to be obtained or system to be used.
5. Appropriate new policies and procedures required.
6. New organizational arrangements, if necessary.
7. Changes required in employee skills.
8. Cost of the automated system.
9. Schedule for implementation.

This information is submitted to management for approval or modification.

There is another part to this third objective of recommending areas to auto-

---

[2] American Federation of Information Processing Societies. P.O. Box 9659, Arlington, VA 22209.

mate. In buying any office equipment, the company should consider the compatibility of such equipment with future automation needs. It is foolish to replace worn-out conventional typewriters with identical models if you can get electronic typewriters at little additional cost. It is foolish to invest in a new conventional high-speed copier if you expect to justify a laser printer in a year or two. The task force should recommend standards for reviewing office equipment purchases.

DECISION TO AUTOMATE

We stated earlier that the initial entry into office automation usually cannot be justified on the basis of cost savings. The savings occur when:

1. There are multiple applications.
2. Most company personnel are on the network.

Management must have faith that productivity improvements will come when these two conditions are satisfied.

However, a cost justification should be made assuming that several applications important to your organization are in place. Identifying these applications is one of the jobs of the automation task force. A financial analyst is made a member of the task force in order to do the cost justification calculations. If automation cannot be cost-justified based on several applications, it is not for your company.

Another necessary condition is a desire on the part of several key managers and professionals to have some aspect of the office automated. Without a dedicated champion, preferably several, automated systems will not happen. There are always problems with an initial installation. There will be ''bugs'' in the system. It will not do all the things that everyone has hoped for. If some of the primary users are not its champions and do not preach patience, the system will be thrown out before it has a chance to prove its worth.

A new system must be implemented in segments. Both those in charge and those using it need to get used to change. They need to learn how to work with the new methods. Problems must be uncovered while the system is still small enough that changes are easy to make. Maybe other features are needed on the equipment; maybe the internal procedures need to be modified; maybe more training is necessary. You will not anticipate all the problems; you learn as you go along. All parties should consider the first installation as an experimental pilot project.

Do not rush into automation. The concepts are promising, but the costs are high, and the problems are many.

SUMMARY

The automation of office functions may not save the company money, certainly not at the start. It does make more information available, saves time, and provides added convenience. These advantages are the real justification for office automation.

The areas that can be automated are discussed individually in this chapter. Wherever you start, the first use will be hard to cost-justify, and faith is required that more applications and more people on the automated networks will justify the system costs. The first application should be considered a pilot process.

Word processing is the usual entry point. A 20% or so improvement in typing efficiency justifies electronic typewriters that are in frequent use. Word processors add about 50% to the efficiency of typing original documents and 300% to typing revisions. Payback of cost is usually under two years.

Personal computers can be justified with as little usage as 15% of a professional's time. More expensive PC's compete with use of the central computer. The choice depends on availability of suitable programs and of time on the mainframe.

Having one's own data processing terminal should not be a status symbol. Data processing terminals are inexpensive, but the cabling to hook up an office may not be. A terminal room close to many users is an alternative.

Electronic mail comes in many forms. Telex usually requires rekeying the message. Facsimile works from paper copies. Most word processors can communicate to like models but not to different models. This restricts their use for electronic mail. Translation equipment to allow unlike equipment to communicate often works on keyboard characters but not on format codes. PC's have the same limitations. Data processing terminals communicate through the mainframe and so avoid this problem.

Telecommunications is a complex subject. Digital systems are the way of the future. Their operating costs are less than current systems; conversion costs, however, are large. Voice mail provides an individual "voice box" in computer memory. Messages left there are retrieved in the sender's own voice.

Video teleconferencing is useful for lectures and some forms of discussion but will not substitute for all travel.

Reprographics is moving toward laser printers which provide book quality and great speed and convenience. Phototypesetting is a less expensive substitute for companies that have a large printing volume.

Computer graphics does an excellent job on business charts. Speed is several times faster than with manual graphics.

Automated records management allows computers to print directly on microfilm (COM) and allows microfilm to be read back into computer memory (CIM).

The combination is very powerful for records storage and retrieval. Larger and less expensive computer memories will allow key-word searching on all words in a document. This will change the manner of indexing documents.

Desk management programs will appeal to some managers and professionals and not to others. Appointment calendars, tickler files, and so on, will be useful only when the program imitates the role of the secretary and reminds the professional of an event just before it is due to happen.

The need for automation should be studied by a task force. Task force members learn what office automation capabilities exist and what the company needs are, determine which areas should be automated, and establish an implementation plan. They should also assure that new office equipment purchases are compatible with future automation plans.

FOR FURTHER INFORMATION

Automation Techniques

Barcomb, David. *Office Automation: A Survey of Tools and Technology.* Bedford, MA: Digital Press, 1981.

Birchall, D. W., and Hammond, V. J. *Tomorrow's Office Today: Managing Technological Change.* New York: Halsted Press, John Wiley & Sons, 1981.

Katzan Jr., Harry. *Office Automation: A Manager's Guide.* New York: AMACOM, 1982.

Ruprecht, Mary M., and Wagoner, Kathleen P. *Managing Office Automation.* New York: John Wiley & Sons, 1984.

Stallard, John J., Smith, E. Ray, and Reese, Donald. *The Electronic Office: A Guide for Managers.* Homewood, IL: Dow Jones-Irwin, 1983.

Electronic Mail

Panko, Raymond R. Options in Electronic Mail, *Office Administration and Automation,* November 1983.

8
Improving the Use of Office Elements

This chapter is written primarily for the professional who is not a manager or supervisor. Here, we back away from the more exotic automation concepts and look at the more conventional office elements. How do you improve your own productivity and effectiveness using the tools that most offices provide today?

HOW TO WORK WITH A SECRETARY

Generally, the first introduction a professional has to office systems is through a secretary. You are introduced: "This is Joan, our group secretary. She[1] will handle your needs." But does she?

Does she realize that you know very little about the office procedures? Is she aware that part of her job is to guide new staff members through the office systems? Only a good experienced secretary will show you how to work with her effectively and introduce you to the office policies and procedures.

Procedures Expert

The secretary is, or should be, an expert on how to get things done. Almost all the paperwork flows through her. Most situations that will occur have happened before. She has the ability to handle these situations as well as the unique cases that come up now and then. The secretary knows the functions of the administrative support groups and the key people in them. She knows the secretaries to these people and can often get things expedited through these contacts.

The good secretary has the experience to handle paperwork better than most professionals and most managers, and she can be the key to easing your administrative work load. When you don't know a procedure, ask the secretary. When you don't understand how to fill out a form, ask the secretary. When you don't know who to see about a particular problem, ask the secretary.

---

[1] Statistics from the Bureau of the Census 1982 Current Population Survey show that 99.2% of the national secretarial work force is female (3,816,000 out of 3,847,000 in this profession). Thus, for easier reading, we refer to the secretary as "she" or "her"—no discrimination is intended.

However, the secretary should be more than an information center. Whatever your need is—following up a purchase request, repairing your calculator, expediting a job through word processing—ask the secretary to handle it. If she does a good job, ask her to handle a more difficult problem such as tracking down the reason for an unexpected entry on the last monthly cost report. Treat the secretary as a paraprofessional—your working life will be made a lot simpler, and your personal productivity will increase.

If the secretary's work load doesn't give her the time to do these things, suggest to your manager that your efficiency and that of the other staff members will increase if some of the secretary's time could be freed for administrative support. Much of the secretary's typing can be done by a word processing center or by a word processing operator assigned to support your department. Her time taking telephone messages can be reduced by using one of the messaging techniques noted in earlier chapters.

If the secretary does not have the interest or ability to do what we suggest here, consider her to be less than a true secretary. The proper role of a secretary is that of a paraprofessional—an administrative assistant. She should be the liaison between the professional and the support groups. Unfortunately, the secretary has been stereotyped as anyone who can take dictation or type. This degrades the real meaning of the job.

Support

There are many ways in which the secretary can help you—and we are not considering personal chores that are unrelated to the office job. Here are some examples of constructive help.

Documents.   When you write a letter or a report, give the secretary the freedom to correct your grammar and spelling. As part of her training, she should be more familiar than most professionals with the rules of grammar. You can also go beyond this. Ask the secretary to critique what you have written:

1. Is it understandable?
2. Do you make your points clearly?
3. Is the sequence of ideas logical?

Few secretaries are editors. But in many instances, if the document is not clear, she can help you.

We cover dictation techniques later in this chapter. The person who transcribes your dictation is the best person to help you improve your dictation habits. Ask the secretary:

1. Are you talking too fast or too slow?
2. Is your enunciation clear?
3. Does your voice fade because you move the mike away from your mouth?
4. Do you dictate all punctuation?
5. Do you spell the unfamiliar words?

Ask for help in becoming a better dictator.

Ask your secretary to proofread what you write. Even if you spell well, it is hard for a writer to catch typographical errors. You tend to read what you know should be on the page rather than what is.

Ask her to assume responsibility for the material sent to word processing, the central copy room, or any other function outside your department. This responsibility will include:

1. Giving clear instructions to the other function.
2. Setting a schedule for return of the material.
3. Follow-up.
4. Checking the returned material both for accuracy and to be sure that the instructions were carried out.

Desk Management.   Make the secretary aware of your appointment calendar and give her the authority to commit you to a meeting time that is not otherwise booked. You'll be surprised how much of your time is saved if you are not involved in scheduling and rescheduling every meeting you must attend. With this goes an obligation on your part to keep the secretary fully informed of appointments you make and their expected duration. You must also indicate those times you want to hold open for uninterrupted work.

Have the secretary provide a listing of the day's events each morning. If there are meetings scheduled, have her obtain the agendas for you to study in advance. Keep the secretary well-enough informed that she can retrieve the pertinent documents you'll need for a meeting without your having to remember all of them.

The secretary should keep a tickler file—a list of dates and times when reports or briefings are due—and remind you far enough ahead of each event that the preparation for it does not become a crisis.

Last, and by no means least, keep the secretary informed. The more information she has, the better the support you'll receive. You should cover:

1. Where you'll be when you leave your office, and when you expect to return.
2. Times and expected duration of all appointments you make.
3. All deadlines that you have.

Table 8-1. Functions That May Be Assigned to a Secretary.

1. Know the company policies and procedures, especially where to locate each subject in the procedure manuals.
2. Know all the department's policies and procedures.
3. Know the purpose and content of all forms used by the department and where to get them.
4. Know who the key workers are in each of the administrative functions.
5. Maintain a file of names, titles, telephone numbers, and functions of important people who may call the professional staff.
6. Expedite requests, orders, deliveries to other functions.
7. Obtain information or explanations from other functions.
8. Critique written documents and help clarify them.
9. Critique dictation and help train dictators.
10. Proofread documents.
11. Provide instructions, follow-up, and review of work going through other departments.
12. Maintain appointment calendar.
13. Commit professionals to a meeting time and place.
14. Take minutes of meetings.
15. Follow up on assignments.
16. Maintain tickler file of due dates of department work.
17. Know the scope and status of projects within the department.
18. Know who in the department is working on what.
19. Read the incoming and outgoing mail and know what is expected when.
20. Maintain confidential files, including personnel files on department staff.
21. Train new staff members in departmental procedures, forms, and other pertinent information.
22. Maintain a list of "how-to's" that can be followed in her absence.

4. Names, titles, and telephone numbers of important people who may call you.
5. The nature of the projects you are working on.

Ask the secretary to read your incoming mail as well as what you send out. This is the easiest way for her to know what instructions, deadlines, plans, questions, and so on, you have been given. Decide together what is confidential and should be opened only by you.

The support roles we have listed define the job of the paraprofessional.

HOW TO DICTATE

We suggested in an earlier chapter that use of dictation can increase your efficiency in writing documents by a factor of eight (see Table 4-1). Despite this, few professionals dictate. Are you part of the silent majority? Why is this? There are two reasons:

1. No one has shown you how to dictate.
2. You are afraid of sounding foolish.

The two reasons are related. When you know how, you won't sound foolish.

Not all documents can be dictated, as we point out later in this section. But more can be dictated than you may think. I worked for several years for a vice-president who was a theoretical chemist. When he wrote for technical journals, few of the pages contained less than three complex equations. These papers were dictated. Anyone can do this the way he did. All you need is to know a few key concepts.

Operating the Equipment

You should be familiar with the dictation equipment. All types have either buttons or slide switches for the following:

1. On–off
2. Listen
3. Record
4. Stop
5. Pause
6. Rewind
7. Fast forward

There may be other controls for special features, but those listed are the key ones.

If you use a cassette desk set or a portable recorder, all controls except the on–off switch are located at the hand-held microphone. You can operate them with the hand that holds the mike. If your system uses the telephone as the dictation instrument, the push buttons or rotary dial numbers perform these functions.

The "pause" control is a very useful feature that not all equipment has. "Pause" stops the cassette tape while you think about your next words. It is usually a spring-loaded button you hold down with one finger. When you release your finger, you are immediately back in the "record" mode. It avoids your having to "stop" and then reactivate "record."

The "rewind" control can be used to retrace a few words or sentences so you can listen to what you just said. If you want to change the last few words you dictated, you use "rewind" to back over the segment and then rerecord over it.

Become familiar with the controls. Be able to find at least the "pause" and "rewind" controls with your fingers without having to think about where they are. Practice talking, listening, backing up, and rerecording over what you said until these steps become second nature. If the equipment is a desk unit or a portable unit, take it home and practice in privacy.

Before Starting to Dictate

Before you start to talk, some preparation is necessary. Just as you would for a handwritten document, write an outline of what you will cover. It can be a list of section headings or a list of the topics for each paragraph. If you are about to dictate a letter, have the name and address of the recipient in front of you. If you plan to reference a document, have that document or the reference handy.

Be fully prepared so that when you start, you can keeping going with as few pauses as possible. This is particularly important if you are on a centralized dictation system. A long pause will disconnect you from the central network. When you reconnect, you will be on another cassette or on a different part of the tape loop. You cannot back up to find out what you said last.

Dictating

Instructions.   The first thing to dictate is your instructions to the transcriber. Identify yourself and give all pertinent instructions for the format of the document. Specifically:

1. State your name.
2. State your telephone extension so you can be called if there is a question.
3. State your department and mail station if the transcribed document is to be sent back to you through the company mail.
4. State your account number if you are charged for transcription.
5. Indicate the type of document to be dictated, e.g., letter, memo, report, etc.
6. Indicate whether the document is a draft or final copy.
7. Indicate single or double spacing and any special format instructions.
8. Indicate the date to be used on correspondence unless you want to use the date on which it is transcibed.

You are now ready to dictate the document.

Techniques.   Talk distinctly at a slow conversational speed. The ideal speed is the speed at which the transcriber types. This is about 60 to 75 words per minute.

The line length in this book averages 15 words. Take any four lines and speak them out loud at a speed that takes you one minute. This is the speed at which you should dictate. Practice until it becomes a normal dictation rate. It will seem slow at first. If the transcriber tells you that she can accept a faster rate, then talk faster. But 60 words per minute is a good rate at which to start. See Tables 8-2 and 8-3 for tips on pronunciation.

Table 8-2. Pronunciation Guide for Numbers.

0:	OH, with a long O.
1:	WUN, with a strong W and N.
2:	TOO, with a strong T and long OO.
3.	TH-REE, with a distinct R and strong EE.
4.	FO-ER, with a strong O and strong R.
5.	FI-VE, with a long I changing to a short and strong V.
6:	SIKS, with a strong S and KS
7:	SEV-EN, with a strong S and V and a well-sounded EN.
8.	ATE, with a strong A and a strong T.
9:	NI-EN, with a strong first N, a long I, and a mild emphasis on EN.
10:	TEN, with a strong T and N.

Here are some other suggestions to make you an excellent dictator:

1. Always spell proper names, company names, street names, and city names if they are not well known.
2. Pronounce numbers very clearly; see Table 8-2 for a pronunciation guide.
3. Spell out sound-alike words, such as "their," "they're," or "there" to assure that the correct word is used; see Table 8-3 for a list of the more common of these words.
4. Spell a word or use a phonetic alphabet, e.g., "Able," "Baker," "Char-

Table 8-3. Common Sound-alike Words.[a]

accede, exceed	accept, except
access, excess	addition, edition
affect, effect	allusion, illusion
assistance, assistants	cease, seize
coarse, course	cite, sight, site
complement, compliment	correspondence, correspondents
council, counsel, consul	decent, descent, dissent
deference, difference	disapprove, disprove
eligible, illegible	era, error
especial, special	finally, finely
formally, formerly	forth, fourth
incidence, incidents	its, it's
legislator, legislature	loose, lose
miner, minor	ordinance, ordnance
passed, past	personal, personnel
practical, practicable	precedence, precedents, presidents
principal, principle	residence, residents
respectfully, respectively	rite, right, write
stationary, stationery	their, there, they're
whose, who's	

[a]Courtesy Association of Information Systems Professionals,

lie,'' if there is doubt that the transcriber will know the word, or if your voice is heavily accented.

5. Spell technical terms.
6. When dictating money values, indicate that you want the dollar sign followed by the numbers (say ''dollar sign, one, three, seven, decimal point, two, five'' for $137.25).
7. Dictate *all* punctuation including commas, periods, quotation marks (say ''open quote'' and ''close quote''), exclamation points, etc.
8. Specify paragraph breaks (say ''end of paragraph'' or ''new paragraph'').
9. Indicate indents, section numbers, and all format changes.
10. Specify capitalized words, and spell abbreviations that the transcriber may not know.

When you change you mind and want to rephrase some of the text, there are two ways to do this. The preferred way is to back up the tape and dictate over the old material. The transcriber will not know that a change was made and will continue to type at full speed. With a lot of practice you can slip in longer or shorter segments than those you erase. If this talk-over is not practical, say on the tape: ''This is insert number one and fits earlier in this document. Type it as a separate section, and I will indicate where it fits in the margin of the transcribed copy.'' At the close of the insert, be sure to state that you have completed ''insert one.'' You will fit in properly when you mark up the draft copy.

In dictating a letter, state how you want the signature block to read. State your job title, if it is to be used; the transcriber may not know you. Dictate the titles of enclosures, and the names of those getting copies.

When you are finished, say: ''This is the end of this dictation. Thank you.''

Special techniques are needed for special types of dictation. When dictating the variable data for a preprinted form such as a purchase requisition, a sales order, and so forth, dictate each open space, even if it is to remain blank. For example, say: ''Space 1: insert Smith Company; space 2, leave blank; space 3, insert $254.76.'' A well-designed form has small numbers at each open space. These numbers should be used to avoid any possibility of error.

Statistical tables with more than two columns or more than three rows should not be dictated. They can be very confusing to the transcriber. Write out the table longhand, give it an insert number, and say on the tape: ''Place the table, insert number x, here.'' Equations and other complex matter are handled in the same way.

What to Dictate

Almost anything can be dictated with practice. For complex material, the straight text is dictated. Handwritten inserts are used for tabular or other complex portions. However, certain types of dictation are not suited to central dictation systems.

Creative dictation requires use of either a desktop or a portable recorder. By creative dictation we mean reports or long letters and memos in which you stop and think for a while as you create the document. Such dictation contrasts to a short letter or memo where you know exactly what you will say before you start and rattle off the words with hardly a pause. It contrasts, also, to dictating the open spaces on a form.

In creative dictation, you may pause for a half minute, or for many minutes while you work out the next section in your head. In a central system you will be disconnected. With a desk set or a portable unit, the cassette stays inside your unit and waits for your next input. It may be the next day—that does not matter. The dictation will be unbroken. Also the tape is always available to rewind and review.

Creative dictation is the hardest to learn. You do not have longhand copy to check to see what you wrote four pages back. You may duplicate a thought you forgot you had covered earlier. You may omit an idea you thought you had stated at the start. Plan on the first transcription's being a rough draft and expect to mark it up drastically.

Until you feel comfortable with the simpler forms of dictation, use longhand for complex documents. But try dictation when the mechanics come easily and you find that you are organizing your thoughts well.

HOW TO USE WORD PROCESSING

Word processing can be an enormous help to the professional. It can also be quite frustrating. The responsibility for making it useful rests with the professional as well as with the word processing supervisor. The concept of word processing was covered in Chapter 4. Here we advise you, the professional, on how to use the function in a way that optimizes use of your time and gets work back to you as quickly and as accurately as possible.

It is important to know what your company's equipment can and cannot do. In Chapter 4, we gave a partial list of functions, Your equipment may be able to do more, or may do less. The word processing group may have a booklet or manual that describes the features. If not, a visit with the word processing supervisor will be worth your time. If you have not worked with word processing equipment before, ask for a demonstration of the capabilities that are of particular importance to your work.

Work Order Forms

Most word processing centers, and many distributed stations, use work order forms to assure that the instructions for each job are complete and are known to the operator who will do the work.

An example of a good work order form is shown in Figure 8-1. The professional fills out everything down to the third black bar. The remainder of the form allows the word processing group to compile their productivity statistics. The form requests your name, department, account number, telephone extension, the document title, and its file number. "Submitted by" permits the secretary to show her name if she is responsible for the document, as advocated earlier in this chapter.

You identify the document as a new document, a revision, or a correction. Corrections take priority over both revisions and new work. In most operations, revisions take priority over new work. You indicate the type of paper required, whether the document is a draft or is final copy, whether it should be single- or double-spaced, who assumes responsibility for proofing, and whether you want the full document or only the changed pages printed. The "date of retention" and the turnaround time are discussed below. When the form is completely filled out, there is no possibility that your needs will be misunderstood by an operator.

Turnaround Standards

A good word processing operation establishes standards for work turnaround time. In companies where most of the work is of one type and length, one standard may be set. Four-hour turnaround is usual for operations that do mainly short correspondence, memos, or filling in the open spaces on forms. Companies that have many types of documents often have multiple turnaround standards. For example, one company has these standards:

- Simple revisions: four hours
- Documents one to two pages long: one day
- Documents three to ten pages long: two days
- Documents over ten pages long: negotiated
- Heavy tabular work: negotiated

The word processing supervisor should define what is meant by a "simple" revision. This usually means changes that do not exceed a half dozen words or lines on each page. The addition of a long paragraph or a change to almost every line does not qualify as a simple revision. These changes will take almost as long as the original input. Revisions that are not "simple" are usually treated under the same standards as new work.

Work turnaround standards are a compromise between the instant turnaround time an author would like and the economics of having the operators kept busy during the ebb and flow of work loads. You should submit work sufficiently far ahead of deadlines to allow for the standard processing times. Standards such as those listed above are reasonable. If the standards are much longer than the

WHITE — WORD PROCESSING
CANARY — WORD PROC-ORIGINATOR
PINK — ORIGINATING DEPT.

CITY OF PHOENIX
CITY CLERK DEPARTMENT
WORD PROCESSING DIVISION
DOCUMENT REQUEST

LOG NUMBER	DOC. SRC.	DOC. TYPE

MUST BE COMPLETED PROPERLY

TODAY'S DATE _____ DATE/TIME DUE _____   ☐ AM ☐ PM

☐ Rush   ☐ Confidential

NOTE: 10 or more pages submitted to Center must have due date scheduled with Supervisor.

AUTHOR'S LAST NAME	FIRST NAME	DEPARTMENT	WORK ORDER NO	EXTENSION

PROJECT TITLE	SUBMITTED BY	DOCUMENT/GLOSSARY NO.

REASON FOR REQUEST	PAPER	PROCESSING	SPACING	DATE OF RETENTION
☐ NEW JOB	☐ LETTER HEAD	☐ ROUGH DRAFT	SINGLE ☐	☐ 10 Days
☐ REVISION	☐ MEMO	☐ FINAL	DOUBLE ☐	☐ 1 Month
☐ REVISION & WP ERROR	☐ 8½ x 11	☐ AUTHOR PROOF	OTHER ☐	☐ 3 Months
☐ WP ERROR	☐ 8½ x 14	☐ WPC PROOF	**PRINTOUT**	☐ Permanent
☐ SPECIAL APPLICATION	☐ OTHER		☐ COMPLETE DOCUMENT	
	☐ PLEADING		☐ CHANGED PAGES ONLY	
	☐ LABEL		☐ NO PRINTOUT REQUIRED	
	☐ ENVELOPE			

SPECIAL INSTRUCTIONS

TIME IN

TIME OUT

CENTER USE ONLY

DOCUMENT NUMBER	TIME STARTED	TIME ENDED	DOCUMENT PAGES	INPUT TIME		PROOFING TIME		PRINTING TIME		S/A		WP ERROR	
				Hrs.	Min.	Hrs.	Min.	Hrs.	Min.	Hrs.	Min.	Hrs.	Min.

P/R _____ Completed by _____

PLEASE TEAR AND RETURN

USER FEEDBACK

Department _____

Comments: _____

IMPORTANT: If this job is in any way unsatisfactory, please notify the Center Supervisor

20-60D REV 5/83

Figure 8-1. Word processing work order form. Reprinted courtesy the City of Phoenix, City Clerk Department.

figures we have quoted, changes need to be made to the word processing operation.

Designating Priority Work

Some documents are assigned special priority irrespective of standards. Examples include: short deadlines for proposal documents, a letter from the president's office, a report required by a contract, a legal filing to meet a court deadline. The system must accommodate them.

One way is to require the signature of a member of management on the input form. This can be awkward if your manager is unavailable for even a few hours when a crisis looms. If the word processing operation charges its costs to the users, a better way is available: a charge rate is set for priority documents that is double the normal rate. Anyone can invoke the priority designation, but your manager will review the charges at month's end and rebuke those people who abuse the privilege. A less formal way is to require that anyone needing priority treatment must first talk to the word processing supervisor, who can accept or deny the priority designation. The decision will be based on other work in progress and the strength of your argument.

None of these methods is ideal. The best advice is to try to avoid priority situations as much as possible but to be reasonable when they do arise.

Filing Codes

Word processing operations file their disks in many different ways. The most common method is by department or by author name. Sequential numbers or dates are used to distinguish the different documents originated by a department or author. Some operations use numeric codes that identify department and date, or alphanumeric systems that use author initials and date. There are probably almost as many filing systems as there are word processing operations.

Whatever system your company uses, you should know what it is. No deadline will be met if the word processing group cannot identify a document you send in for revision and cannot locate the disk that contains the original copy.

On the draft of a document, the file code may be shown at one corner of each page. Some companies place these codes on final copy as well. If the document itself does not carry the code, the returned copy of your input instruction form will show it. Do not lose this identifier! When the marked-up copy goes back for revision, there must be some way for the operator to find the right disk.

Retention Schedules

Disks are reusable. To save money and file space they are erased and used over and over again. Most word processing operations have a policy on disk retention. If you need a document kept on disk for longer than the standard time, you must notify the word processing supervisor. The input form shown in Figure 8-1 has a section titled "date of retention" for this purpose.

Many operations have three levels of retention:

1. Temporary
2. Extended
3. Permanent

Temporary retention usually lasts 10 to 15 days. It is often handled by designating certain disks as "temporaries." The operator uses each disk in the set until she is back to the first disk. She then erases that disk and reuses it. Temporary retention is for transitory documents such as correspondence, memos, or filled-in forms where revisions are infrequent and those that are necessary will occur within ten days.

Extended retention is for documents that will be revised over a longer time but, once completed, need not be further retained. Examples are: long narrative reports, legal briefs, annual plans, annual budgets, the text of this book. Revisions may continue over a period of a week, a month, or longer. The person responsible for the document must indicate how extended a retention is anticipated. Note that once the text is final and has been distributed, there is no longer a need for it in disk form. You have the paper copy. Unless you need to revise it again at some future time, there is no reason to continue to retain it on disk.

Permanent storage is for documents with an infinite life, or whose basic structure continues while parts are periodically revised. Examples are: forms, cumulative accounting reports, policy statements, procedures, telephone lists, and personnel rosters. On these, changes are made from time to time, but on each revision much of the material stays intact. Many companies require approval from a member of management if permanent retention is requested.

HOW TO REVISE A DOCUMENT

Marking up a draft for revision needs to be done as systematically as preparation of the original. You cannot expect to get a correct copy back if you have written all over the paper, tried to insert a whole paragraph in between two lines, written so small that one cannot read what is written, left unclear where some new wording goes, or crossed out a section without clearly showing where to start and end the deletion.

Proofreading

Here are some good habits for correcting drafts:

1. Use standard proofreader marks. (A list of common marks is shown in Table 8-4.)

Table 8-4. Standard Proofreader's Marks.ᵃ

PROOFREADER'S MARKS

∧	insert copy shown	*Cap or* ≡	capital letter
#	insert space	*lc or* /	lowercase letter
ℓ	delete or omit copy shown	(sp)	spell out
◠	close up space	⊙	insert period
∽	transpose, turn around	?/	insert question mark
=/	insert hyphen	!/	insert exclamation point
¶	new paragraph	∧	insert comma
SS	single-space	∧	insert semicolon
DS	double-space	∧	insert colon
TS	triple-space	∨	insert apostrophe or single quotation mark
↻	move copy as indicated	∨ ∨	insert quotation marks
||	align copy	--/	insert dash
stet or...	leave copy as is, restore to original copy	(/)	insert parentheses
⊐⊔⊏⊐	move copy in the direction of the bracket	_or ital	underline or italics
were *was*	change copy as indicated	(?)	query to author

ᵃFrom *Programmed Proofreading* by T. J. Deward and H. F. Daniel, published by South-Western Publishing Co. Used by permission of the publisher.

2. On a single-spaced document, write only in the margins.
3. On a double-spaced document, or space-and-a-half, write only one line of changes between the typed lines.
4. Write long inserts on separate sheets, and show with a letter or number code where they go.
5. If the sequence of the text is to be changed and the document is on a word processing disk, do *not* cut and paste; number the sections and note the location of each numbered section.

HOW TO RUN A MEETING

Meetings represent 40% to 50% of the professional's time. This was one of the findings of the Booz·Allen and Hamilton study cited in Chapter 2. Besides formal meetings and conferences, the percentages include telephone conversations and informal dialogue between individuals. The formal meeting portion of this time is less than half of the total for most professionals, but this is still a significant portion of the work week. In this section we address the issue of making formal meetings more productive and less time-consuming.

Is the Meeting Necessary?

Some managers are meeting-happy. They call a meeting:

1. To avoid sole responsibility for making a decision.
2. Because their superiors hold lots of meetings, and thus they think this is the best way to do business.
3. Because giving a speech to their subordinates provides them with a feeling of power.

Weekly staff meetings, in particular, become a tradition. Nobody questions their value.

Meetings are expensive in both time and money. A two-hour meeting of ten professionals whose average annual salary is $30,000 costs $288. Costs can add up fast, even for meetings involving people at lower salary levels. (See Table 8-5.)

When are formal meetings useful? There are several valid reasons to hold them. A meeting is the most efficient way to:

1. Impart information that everyone in the group needs to know.
2. Review a plan of action when each person needs to know the role of each other person and much of their understanding will result from questions. A question from one person triggers a related question from another.
3. Explore and resolve a problem when the combined experience of the group is necessary to define the issue and brainstorm solutions.
4. Conduct training.
5. Keep a job moving on schedule.

Meetings to impart information should be held only when there is something important to cover. Unless a topic is of overriding importance, it is efficient to

Table 8-5. Cost of a Meeting.

| | COST, DOLLARS PER HOUR | | | |
| | NUMBER OF PARTICIPANTS | | | |
AVERAGE SALARY OF PARTICIPANTS	20	10	7	4
$40,000	385	192	135	77
$30,000	288	144	101	57
$25,000	240	120	84	48
$20,000	192	96	67	38
$15,000	144	72	50	29

save it until a certain time each week, and then cover all such topics at once. This is one rationale for the staff meeting. When there is nothing to impart, the meeting should not be held. An alternative to holding an information meeting is to distribute a memorandum on the subject.

In meetings held to review a course of action, questions and comments must be encouraged. These meetings should not be lectures. Understanding is wanted. Without questions and comments the leader will never know if understanding was achieved.

Meetings that explore and resolve problems are the most open of all meetings. The meeting leader becomes a coordinator—a traffic manager for the verbal interchange. A leader who wants the ideas of the group must not impose his or her own thoughts first. This form of meeting can drag on past the point of useful input. It is both the hardest and the most important to control.

Training meetings are lectures and demonstrations with questions permitted. There are two forms of training meeting. In one, there are specific instructions to impart. Every member of the group is expected to understand and use the information provided. In this type, questions are necessary. There must also be some way to tell if each member of the group understands and can follow the instructions. If at all possible, this type of training should be done on an individual basis rather than as a group meeting.

In the other form of training meeting, the lecturer is imparting general knowledge and does not expect everyone present to remember all the points being covered. Talks at professional meetings come under this heading. Questions are accepted if there is time at the close of the lecture, but they are usually not encouraged. Questions are often asked to show off the questioner's knowledge rather than to acquire understanding.

Meetings to keep a job moving on schedule are partly problem-solving meetings. They also have another purpose. They put pressure on the attendees to meet their respective parts of the schedule.

If a meeting does not fall under one of these headings, question its necessity.

Who Should Attend

The attendees depend on the type of meeting. Group meetings to impart information should include all members of the group. Don't forget the paraprofessionals. Many subjects are also of interest to the clerical and support staff. Review meetings should include only those individuals who have some responsibility for the subject under discussion. The same is true of schedule-status meetings. Problem-solving meetings should involve anyone who can contribute to the subject. This may include people in other departments. Training meetings are for the people who must acquire the knowledge being presented.

A person should not be invited to a meeting just because of his or her title.

Nor should someone be invited simply because he or she asked to come, if that person cannot, in your judgment, contribute to the subject at hand. Nor is attendance at a previous meeting valid, if the phase to which the person contributed is finished. You should expect a specific contribution from each person who is invited.

Agenda

All meetings should have an agenda. When active participation is expected from the group, as in problem-solving and schedule-status meetings, the agenda should be sent to all participants at least a day ahead. This lets each person think about the subjects and come prepared. For information and training meetings, the leader should have an agenda for his or her own use. This assures that all the topics are covered.

If a specific document is to be discussed, it should be referenced in the agenda. This allows the attendee's secretary to locate the document and bring it to his or her attention.

If an agenda has many topics, the expected starting time for each topic may be shown on the agenda. This serves three purposes:

1. It shows the relative emphasis being given each topic.
2. It tells a participant when to arrive or plan to leave if the person need be present for only one topic.
3. It permits the leader to cut off undesired conversation by pleading lack of time.

Meeting Duration

The length of a meeting should be as short as the subject matter allows. All meetings, other than problem-solving and training meetings, should be held to an hour if possible. This is about as long as you can hold the full attention of a group. After this length of time, one's thoughts start to wander. The condition of the room also makes a difference.

Some planning or problem-solving meetings, however, may take days. These meetings must be broken into smaller bites. After an hour and a half, a coffee break is advisable. After two one-and-a-half-hour sessions, a major break is needed. Six hours is the maximum for a day.

Meeting Control

The leader must control the meeting. To do so, you start well before the meeting takes place.

Before the Meeting.   You have drawn up the agenda and made a list of persons you want to attend. The first step is to find a time when all are available and a place where you can meet. Unless you are president of the company, you will have to start working on this many days in advance. Your secretary will help to find the time and place, and will distribute your agenda at least 24 hours in advance.

The meeting room should be cool, pleasant, and quiet. If you will use slides or overhead view graphs, you must be able to dim the lights. Simply turning the lights off is not satisfactory. Some participants will want to take notes, and you cannot do this in an unlit room. A light dimmer control is essential. It should be located near the position where the leader will be standing.

The meeting should start on time. Waiting for a meeting to start is a nonproductive activity. If you habitually start a meeting late because you wait for people, they will come to expect it and so will always come late. The starting time gets later and later, and soon the situation is out of control. If you get the reputation of starting a meeting precisely at the time it is called, people will arrive on time.

Someone should be assigned to take notes. Some leaders do this themselves. However, until you are experienced at running meetings, it is difficult both to control the meeting and to take notes. The notes concentrate on:

1. Decisions made
2. Work assignments made
3. Key arguments presented

During the Meeting.   Open the meeting by stating the first subject for discussion. This may be in writing on the agenda, but state it anyway. The participants arrive with many things on their minds. They are thinking about other subjects while they wait for the meeting to begin. Stating the meeting's first subject focuses each person's attention on the agenda topic.

In a problem-solving meeting, state what the meeting is to accomplish. At its end, do you want a plan of action, a work assignment, a schedule, or what? All the participants now know what they have to do.

Here are some dos and don'ts relating to control of a problem-solving meeting. This is the most difficult meeting to handle because you seek group participation and yet don't want the discussion to get out of hand.

• Do:

1. Invite discussion.
2. Assure that everyone is heard from.
3. Listen more than you talk; be sure you understand each person's viewpoint.
4. Ask for differing opinions.

5. Use visual aids to show complex procedures.
6. Summarize each point of view and conclusion.
7. Keep the discussion on the subject at hand.
8. Break up heated controversy; move to another point or take a short break.
9. Keep the time in mind; don't let one point eat up all the time.
10. Make work assignments at the end of the session.

- Don't:

1. State your opinion before the group is heard from; you may never hear contrary opinions.
2. Come to a meeting ill-prepared, with unread notes prepared by someone else.
3. Let the meeting run itself.
4. Resent challenges to your opinions.
5. Cut off serious discussion with a joke or a derogatory remark.
6. Publicly ridicule or harass a group member.
7. Allow telephone or message interruptions.
8. Allow digressions to continue.

Assignments

After a problem-solving meeting, a summary and assignment memorandum should be prepared by the person who took notes, and it should be approved by the leader. This is not a set of minutes and should not be labeled as such. It is a list of all conclusions reached and of work assignments made to individuals. These are the important results of the meeting. The due dates for each assignment should be shown. If an assignment is made to someone who was not present, the person responsible for notifying the assignee should be indicated.

Visual Aids

First-class meetings are spoiled much too often by the use of visual aids that the participants cannot read. There is no excuse for this. Speakers try to cram too much onto one slide and get nothing as a result. They copy from a book or magazine whose print is too small to be visible when projected. Or they use typewriter copy on which the letters are not sufficiently dark and are too small as well. A few rules will assure first-class readable slides or overhead viewgraphs.

Sheets of paper and the apertures of slide and viewgraph frames are rectangular. Most screens, however, are square. If you fill a slide or viewgraph frame to the edge of the long side, the words may flow off the edge of the screen. Use a seven-inch-square boundary when laying out word slides on a piece of paper.

If you use the seven-inch-square format for a slide or viewgraph, the letters should be 3/16-inch in height with 1/8-inch spacing between the lines. This provides about 20 lines of 35 characters each (including spaces) on a slide. Lettering smaller than this may be hard to read from the back of a room, especially if the projection equipment does not focus precisely, or if the viewer needs new eyeglasses.

If you do not have a lettering machine with 3/16-inch (18-point) letters, use the largest type font you can get for your typewriter or word processor. The orator font is available on a typing ball. Double-strike the letters to get a heavy black image. Examine the final copy for broken letters. If you have equipment to enlarge the image photographically, use narrower margins for typing, and enlarge the image to 3/16-inch letters.

An overhead viewgraph made photographically will show a darker image than one made on most copy machines. If you must use a copy machine, use a central copier rather than a convenience copier because it will provide better quality.

Many people make their slides and viewgraphs using all upper case letters. Upper case letters are larger than lower case by about 25%. This is probably why this habit started. But normal lower case words are easier and faster to read because we are more used to them. The normal upper–lower style is preferred if your lettering is 3/16-inch. If you use orator or pica size typewriter letters, stick to all upper case, or else enlarge the image.

TRAINING

All the techniques discussed in this chapter require training in their use. So does use of any office system that is unfamiliar to you. The training can be self-training—trial and error—which is not very efficient. Or you can ask for and receive help.

Your company may have training programs. If so, embrace them. They are not beneath your dignity as a professional. Community college and university continuing education programs have classes in many of the areas we have described.

If such formal training is not available, your secretary can help with the subjects covered in this chapter, except for running a meeting. Set time aside and ask for her assistance.

Such help and practice are essential. You can read the principles in this book and think you understand them. But until you practice a subject and have someone help you discover where you go wrong, you will not master it. This is no different from mastering the techniques of your profession.

SUMMARY

A good secretary is an expert on company and department forms, procedures, and policies. She should be used to expedite, follow up, track down information, get answers to your questions, and handle the other functions listed in

Table 8-1. She can also help you through a critique of your writing and dictating. She should be fully informed of your activities. The good secretary is a paraprofessional.

Suggestions for improving dictation habits have been provided in this chapter. Desk cassette recorders, or portable recorders, work better than central systems for dictating long reports and memos. Central dictation systems may cut you off.

A word processing operation needs a work order form to assure that the writer's instructions are complete and are known to the word processing operator. The professional must know the standard work turnaround times and how to designate work as priority when it is needed sooner than the standard time.

The document author also needs to recognize the word processing filing codes. If the code is not printed on the document, the form that shows it must be returned to the word processing group so that the operator can locate the disk containing your document. You should also know about disk retention times. Knowing how to show revisions on a document assures their accurate correction.

Meetings can waste a lot of time and are expensive. Valid meetings are those that impart information, review a plan of action, explore and solve problems, do training, or keep a job moving on schedule. All meetings need an agenda. A meeting should be as short as the subject allows.

The meeting leader controls the meeting. The meeting should start on time. Someone should take notes, concentrating on the decisions, work assignments, and key arguments presented. A summary of decisions and work assignments is issued after the meeting.

A list of dos and don'ts has been presented in this chapter for the leader of a problem-solving meeting. Visual aids—slides and overhead viewgraphs—should be designed using seven-inch-square paper. Word slides should use 3/16-inch letters to assure readability.

Professionals need training in these techniques as much as in new developments in their professional fields. Company training programs are often available, as are courses at local community colleges and universities.

FOR FURTHER INFORMATION

How to Work with a Secretary

Horovitz, Bruce. Does Your Secretary Think like an Executive? *Industry Week,* Sept. 7, 1981.
Rosen, Arnold, Tunison, Eileen Feretic, and Bahniuk, Margaret Hilton. *Administrative Procedures for the Electronic Office* (Chapter 1, The Role of the Secretary). New York: John Wiley & Sons, 1982.

How to Dictate

Schrag, Adele F. *How to Dictate.* New York: McGraw-Hill, 1981.

How to Use Word Processing

Foster, Timothy R. V., and Glossbrenner, Alfred. *Word Processing for Professionals and Executives*. New York: Van Nostrand Reinhold, 1983.

Kelley, Susan, and Segal, Robert. *The ABZ's of Word Processing: A Primer for Executives, Professionals and Other Principals Who Submit Work to Word Processing*. New York: Stravon Educ. Press, 1982.

How to Run a Meeting

Kirkpatrick, Donald L. *How to Plan and Conduct Productive Business Meetings*. Chicago: Dartnell, 1976.

Newman, Pamela J., and Lynch, Alfred F. *Behind Closed Doors: A Guide to Successful Meetings*. Englewood Cliffs, NJ: Prentice-Hall, 1983.

9
Budgets and Cost Control*

"It's budget time again!" is a cry that strikes terror into the hearts of otherwise brave managers and professionals. Some professionals are not involved with budgets. But anyone who is a manager, supervisor, or project leader has to go through the budget exercise at least once a year. This chapter is for those people.

There is no mystery to preparing a budget. The forms may look formidable. The written instructions are often much too long and are hideously written. But it is really quite easy to prepare a budget and justify its contents. Follow us as we lead you through the maze.

CALCULATING THE BUDGET

Your company has its own budget forms, which, of course, you will use. Typically there will be a summary sheet and work sheets for each budget element. There will be one or more pages for a narrative justification. We present typical examples of these forms and use them to calculate an annual budget.

Accountants call the year for which you prepare the budget the "budget year." Each budgeted area of cost is a "line item." We use these terms throughout this chapter. The line items we describe are these:

1. Salaries
2. Fringe benefits and payroll taxes
3. Materials and supplies
4. Purchased services
5. Leases and rent
6. Travel
7. Education and training
8. Recruiting expenses

---

*This approach to budgeting is adapted from Davis, Reba, and Balderston, Jack, *Word Processing Supervision,* Indianapolis: Bobbs-Merrill Publishing, 1984, chapter 6.

9. Occupancy costs
10. Other expenses

Work Sheet Summary

The summary page lists each line item that you must estimate. It will resemble the example in Table 9-1. In your company, some of the line items may be combined. Others may be split into two or more entries. But the items listed above cover the main areas of cost, and they suffice to explain how to calculate a budget.

The summary page you get with the budget package should show actual costs for each line item for last year and the estimated costs for the current year. The current year will not be over when you make the budget so these costs must be estimates. If the estimate of current year costs is different from the approved budget, it is better to use the realistic estimate. The three columns on this form are used to compare costs for last year, this year, and next year. If the costs in the "Estimated This Year" column are not realistic, the comparison will be misleading.

The figures in the "Actual Last Year" and "Estimated This Year" columns are placed on the form by the finance department. If it doesn't provide these numbers, ask for them. You will need them to check against your calculations for the budget year.

Table 9-1. Budget Work Sheet Summary.[a]

BUDGET WORK SHEET: SUMMARY
(thousand $)

Department/Project _____   Date Prepared _____
                                                Prepared By _____

COST ELEMENT	ACTUAL LAST YEAR	ESTIMATED THIS YEAR	BUDGET NEXT YEAR
Salaries & Wages	125	159	
Fringe Benefits	38	51	
Materials & Supplies	24	26	
Purchased Services	10	13	
Leases & Rent	5	8	
Travel	5	8	
Education & Training	4	5	
Recruiting	3	3	
Other	2	4	
Occupancy Costs	—	—	
TOTAL	216	277	
No. People, Year End	6	7	

[a] This form is adapted from a work sheet used by the Occidental Research Corporation.

Salaries

Salaries are usually the single largest cost in a department or project budget; thus it is important to estimate this cost very carefully and very exactly. You may be given a work sheet such as we show in Table 9-2. If not, make such a form for yourself. It is the easiest way to perform a salary calculation.

If you are a manager or supervisor, you know the salaries being paid to each member of your staff and to yourself. You also know the salary increases planned for the rest of the current year. Combine these figures to get the annual salaries as of the year's end. This is the calculation performed in the top section of Table 9-2. If you are a project manager, you probably do not have the salary figures for each person assigned to your project. Ask the respective depart-

Table 9-2. Estimating Salaries.

BUDGET WORK SHEET: SALARIES

Department/Project _____   Date Prepared _____
                                       Prepared By _____

Existing Staff

	PRESENT MONTHLY SALARIES	PLANNED INCREASES REST OF THIS YEAR	YEAR END SALARY	ANNUAL SALARY
Alan	2100	200	2300	
Betty	2600	—	2600	
Charles	1700	—	1700	
Doug	2250	—	2250	
Emily	2000	150	2150	
Fred	3000	—	3000	
Ginny (sec.)	1400	—	1400	
TOTAL, EXISTING STAFF			15400 × 12	$184,800

Additional Staff

	ARRIVAL MONTH	ESTIMATED SALARY	ANNUAL TOTAL	
	Mar	1800	18000	
	Aug	2000	10000	
TOTAL, ADDITIONAL STAFF..				$ 28,000
				$212,800

Salary Increases Next Year

Allocation, per guidelines:	7%			
Half of Allocation	3.5%			
TOTAL SALARY INCREASES	3.5% × $212,800			$ 7,448
SUBTOTAL				$220,248

Utilization Factor

Use 89%: (89% of $220,248 is $196,021)

BUDGET YEAR SALARIES $196,000

ments, or the financial or employee relations departments, for the total salary amount for the named individuals at year end.

If you plan to increase staff next year, estimate a monthly salary for the persons you will hire or transfer in. Estimate the month in which each person will arrive. For each person, multiply the estimated salary by the number of months remaining in the year. Total these. This is the second section of Table 9-2. If you know that someone will leave, subtract the appropriate portion of his or her salary from the total.

The size of salary increases planned for the budget year is set by management. The number to use is included in the budget preparation instructions. This number is usually expressed as a percentage of year-end salaries. Use this percentage; do not deviate from it without approval from the budget department. If you and others deviate, the organization's total salary budget will be overstated. If you know that you will give salary increases that exceed the guidelines, request approval to deviate. If you don't get it, note in the narrative section that salaries are understated because the guidelines are too low for your situation.

In most companies, salary increases are given throughout the year. Some people get theirs early in the year, others toward the end. Therefore the average employee has the benefit of the increase above his or her January 1 salary level for only half the year. Thus, if 7% is the quota for increases next year, the salary of the average person is increased by this amount for only half the budget year. Therefore, to calculate the effect of salary increases, the guideline quota should be divided by two. This is shown in the third section of Table 9-2.

The salary utilization factor is a difficult concept. Its application depends on the accounting structure of your organization. In some organizations, especially universities, a person's full salary is charged to the salary account regardless of whether the person is working, on vacation, enjoying a national holiday, absent, or sick. In this case the utilization factor is unity. Most organizations, however, have separate accounts for vacations, holidays, sick time, and so on. These costs are charged to overhead, specifically to the fringe benefit accounts. Therefore an amount less than the full salary of each person is charged to the department or project. The utilization factor represents the portion of gross salary that is charged to the department or project budget.

Typically, the following percentages of gross salary flow to the fringe benefit accounts:

Vacation	4% (2 weeks)
Paid holidays	4% (10 days)
Absence	1% (20 hours)
Sick time	2% (5 days)
Total	11%

The utilization factor is one minus the percentage charged to fringe benefits. In the above example it is 100% less 11%, or 89%. If your company has more paid holidays, or if your sick and absence times are higher than shown above, the total percent of gross salary that flows to fringe benefits will be higher. The utilization factor that applies to you will be lower. Use of the utilization factor is shown in the fourth section of Table 9-2.

In summary, take the existing salaries as they will be at year end, add or subtract salaries for staff increases or decreases, increase total salaries by half the amount of planned salary raises next year, and apply the utilization factor. This gives total salaries, as shown at the bottom of Table 9-2. This total is also entered on the ''salaries'' row of the budget work sheet summary, Table 9-1.

Either on the summary or on the salaries work sheet, you will be asked to show the number of people planned at the start and end of the budget year. This shows management the planned rate of growth or of decrease. If you are called on to justify your salary budget, a planned increase in staff will be the first item for discussion.

Fringe Benefits

These costs are not under your control. They are fixed by law or by company policy. They are directly related to the number of people you have and to their salaries. Companies consider fringe benefits and payroll taxes as part of the cost of labor.

The more common elements included in fringe benefits and payroll taxes are:

1. F.I.C.A., commonly called social security taxes; the company contributes an amount equal in size to the amount deducted from your paycheck.
2. Unemployment insurance taxes.
3. Paid holidays.
4. Paid vacation time.
5. Paid sick time.
6. Medical insurance plan premiums.
7. Pension plan contributions.
8. Profit-sharing plan contributions.
9. Matching funds in employee savings plans.

Three of these—holidays, vacation and sick time—are the amounts subtracted from salaries by the utilization factor.

These fringe benefit costs typically add 30% to 40% to total salaries. The percentage to use for the budget year is estimated by the financial department and given to you in the instruction package. Your only role is to apply the given

Table 9-3. Calculating Fringe Benefits.

BUDGET WORK SHEET: FRINGE BENEFITS

Department/Project _____   Date Prepared _____
Prepared By _____
Fringe Benefit % from guidelines 35%
Total Salaries $196,000
TOTAL FRINGE BENEFITS (35% × $196,000) . . . . $ <u>68,600</u>

percentage to your estimate for salaries and enter this on the work sheet. The calculation is shown in Table 9-3.

Materials and Supplies

This line item is easy to underestimate. You are probably unaware of many of the supply items charged to you and their costs. Look at the summary sheet which shows actual last year and estimated this year. If this line item is relatively small, say, 10% or less of the total cost, project next year's total by extrapolating from prior- and present-year costs. This is as accurate a way to estimate a small total as trying to list all the material items and price each one. If the line item is large, determine the major items that are part of it and estimate your need for each of them. Extrapolate from past history for the balance.

To extrapolate, first decide what it is that the quantity of material and supplies primarily depends on. Is it the number of people on your staff? Or is it the population of the whole company, the amount of space occupied, or something else? Divide the material and supply costs for last year and this year by the respective sizes of this independent variable. This gives you the history ($ per person or $ per square foot) for the past and present years.

If this ratio is consistent for the two years, and you see no reason for it to change other than cost inflation, use it as the basis for the budget year line item. For example, if the independent variable is your head count and you plan to increase your staff by 30% next year, increase materials and supplies by the same factor.

In the past year or two, the cost of supplies has not risen as dramatically as it did in the early 1980s. If cost inflation is only 5% per year or so, it can be ignored. If it is higher, ask your purchasing department for an estimate of price inflation. Add this factor to your estimated total. A calculation done in this manner is shown in Table 9-4.

Purchased Services

Many things are included under this heading. The more common are equipment maintenance agreements, consultant contracts, temporary-help-agency person-

Table 9-4. Estimating Materials and Supplies.

BUDGET WORK SHEET: MATERIALS & SUPPLIES

Department/Project _____ Date Prepared _____

Prepared By _____

Dependent Ratio

Last Year: M&S $24,000; Head Count 6 = $4,000 per person

This Year: M&S $26,000; Head Count 7 = $3,700 per person

Budget Year, use . . . . $3,800 per person

Budget Year M&S: $3,800 × 8.2 (Avg. Headc't) = $31,160

Price Inflation

Inflation factor: 10%

Budget Year M&S: Inflation 1.10 × $31,160   = $34,276

---

nel costs, and charges from contractors who work on a time and materials basis.

For this line item, you must determine what has been charged to it in the past. If you do not know, talk to your accounting analysts. Take each major element and project it individually. Add a factor for miscellaneous requirements.

You cannot reduce this line item to a ratio as we did for material and supplies. Purchased services are not similar to materials. They are not repetitive items that are repurchased as they are used up. Many of the services are one-time expenses that will not be repeated. For example, last year a consultant was hired at a cost of $6,000 to help with a study of office automation; that study is now done, and the consulting services will not be needed next year. A subcontract was let to engineer a complex part; this expense will not recur. One type of item that is predictable is maintenance agreements. If you purchased your computers, copy machines, word processors, typewriters, and other equipment, you probably have a purchased service agreement to maintain them in working order.

We present no table for purchased services. If you are given one as part of the budget work sheet package, it will be a series of blank lines on which to list individual jobs or contracts and to note the anticipated amounts for each. You will probably be asked for a brief narrative to justify each one.

Leases and Rents

The cost of anything that is leased or rented rather than bought shows in this line item. If you are in a rented building, a part of the rent may be allocated to you based on the number of square feet you occupy. Alternately, this cost may be shown as an occupancy expense, which is discussed later. Lease costs on equipment such as computers, copy machines, and word processors are part of this line item. If you are involved in maintenance or construction, you lease specialized equipment that you use for only a few weeks or months during the year.

Ask your accounting analysts for the company's policy on leasing. If during the budget year you plan to acquire an item that may be leased, explore the probable cost treatment with them. Sales tax is applied to leases in many states. Installation costs may be added to the basic lease cost. Leases may or may not include service and support from the vendor or lessor. Be sure your estimate includes all the costs charged to this line item.

If you are projecting the continuation of an existing lease into the budget year, know the terms of this lease. Does it contain a cost escalation clause? When does the lease expire? If you plan to add additional items to an equipment lease, call the lessor for an estimate of what the additional items will cost.

The work sheet for leases and rents will be a list of all the items showing their anticipated annual cost.

Travel

This is not usually a major cost, at least not of the same size as salaries or materials. It is sometimes budgeted as a separate line item to make it easier to control. Travel can become a sizable item if all employees are allowed to go wherever they wish.

Travel includes trips out of town and also trips in town for which mileage is reimbursed. Some of the reasons for travel are:

1. Seeing customers
2. Talking to suppliers
3. Visiting other company locations
4. Attending technical meetings
5. Attending educational seminars
6. Picking up supplies locally

Out-of-town travel costs include:

1. Airfare
2. Lodging
3. Meals
4. Taxis and airport buses
5. Car rentals
6. Mileage to and from the airport and parking fees

It is useful to determine an average cost for out-of-town trips and use this number for the budget estimate. Divide out-of-town travel into two parts:

1. Part 1 is the fixed cost—getting to and from your destination.
   (a) Pick a city to which your group travels frequently or whose distance from your city is an average of all trips taken.
   (b) Look up the round-trip airfare and add the cost of getting to and from each airport.
2. Part 2 is the per diem cost.
   (a) Figure the average daily cost of lodging, meals, car rentals, and taxis.

Estimate the average duration of your trips. Multiply the duration by the per diem cost and add the fixed cost. This is the average cost per trip.

Add an allowance for local mileage reimbursement to the out-of-town travel. The accounting analysts can tell you how much your group spends on mileage.

The budget work sheet may ask for the number of trips planned as well as for a dollar amount. If you use the approach suggested above, you have full justification for your budget numbers.

Education and Training

This line item covers the registration costs for training seminars, workshops, and meetings for you and your staff. If a meeting is purely for education or training, such as an American Management Association workshop, travel costs may be charged to the education and training line item. If the workshop is held as part of a professional meeting, travel costs may be charged to the travel line item. Check with your accounting analyst for the policy your organization uses.

Registration costs are always shown in the brochures that describe seminars and workshops. Multiply the registration cost for each meeting by the number of people you plan to send to the meeting, and total these costs for the budget year. Add lodging, meals, and travel if these costs, when resulting from workshops, are charged to the education account. Add these costs to the travel line if that is where they are charged.

Training done by your company training group may be charged to you, as might reimbursement of fees for courses taken at college and universities. Check with the accounting department analyst on these points also.

Recruiting

This item may be shown separately or be part of the "other" category. If you do a lot of recruiting through professional recruiting firms and if you are expanding, this can be a major cost. In that case, recruiting may be requested as a separate line item. If you hire mainly through advertising and word of mouth and your employment level is steady, this is probably not a separate item.

The cost of hiring a professional employee includes:

1. Fees to recruiters
2. Advertising costs
3. Travel costs for interview trips
4. Relocation costs for the new employee

The employee relations department maintains cost figures for each of these factors.

The number of people you plan to hire is not just the number of additional staff positions. Some people will leave and must be replaced. You must allow for this contingency as well. Data on turnover rates for the professional staff are also kept by the employee relations department.

Determine an average cost to recruit one professional. Multiply this by the number of professionals to be hired.

Other

This is the line item for all expenses that are not called out separately. Find out what charges usually appear in this miscellaneous category. Dues to professional societies may be here. Reimbursed business meals may be also. Find out what items are in last year's "other" costs as shown on the budget work sheet summary. Project similar costs into next year.

Always put at least a small amount in this "other" category. You do not know what unexpected costs may arise during the budget year.

Occupancy Costs

This is a form of rent for the floor space you occupy. Not all organizations charge a department or project with occupancy costs. If you do not find this on your budget form, that is why.

Occupancy costs typically include the costs of power, heat, telephone, building maintenance, janitorial, and other expenses related to the building. Building rent or depreciation and purchased equipment depreciation may also be included. The total cost of all these items is usually charged to departments on the basis of the number of square feet each occupies.

You have no direct control over these costs. You can reduce the amount charged to you by giving up space. You will increase the charge if you expand into more space. These actions, of course, do not change the company's total cost; they merely change the way it is allocated. Any change of the total requires a joint effort by the entire staff to reduce power consumption, telephone calls, and so on.

An occupancy cost rate for the budget year is determined by the financial analysts and given to you in the budget work sheet instructions. You may be given a single dollar figure based on the space you now occupy, or you may be given a dollars-per-square-foot number. If it is the latter, you will also be given the footage you now occupy and be asked if you plan to increase or decrease this amount of space. If you plan no change, you merely multiply the two figures provided and place the product on the summary work sheet. If you plan to increase or decrease space, you use the new footage figure to determine the product.

Completed Work Sheet Summary

You have completed calculating each line item for the budget year. The resulting numbers are placed on the summary work sheet (see Table 9-1). A sample completed work sheet, incorporating the calculations we have described, is shown in Table 9-5.

Before turning in the summary, look at the budget year figures in comparison to the current year and last year. Are the changes reasonable? Can you explain each of them? If a number looks odd, go back and check it.

CONTINGENCY PLANNING

There is a very serious game played at budget time between the person who prepares a budget and the managers and accountants who review and approve it. Some call it contingency planning; others call it padding the budget.

You, the preparer, are legitimately concerned that you will be charged for

Table 9-5. Completed Budget Work Sheet Summary.

BUDGET WORK SHEET: SUMMARY
(thousand $)

Department/Project_____ABC_____   Date Prepared___9/12/8–

                                       Prepared By_____JLB_____

COST ELEMENT	ACTUAL LAST YEAR	ESTIMATED THIS YEAR	BUDGET NEXT YEAR
Salaries & Wages	125	159	196
Fringe Benefits	38	51	69
Materials & Supplies	24	26	34
Purchased Services	10	13	11
Leases & Rent	5	8	8
Travel	5	8	10
Education & Training	4	5	5
Recruiting	3	3	5
Other	2	4	5
Occupancy Costs	—	—	—
TOTAL	216	277	343
No. People, Year End	6	7	9

items that you cannot anticipate. You may have forgotten to include something or may have neglected a lot of small costs that add up to a significant sum. You want a small contingency amount in the budget to cover the items you miss. Those who review and approve budgets must assure that the grand total for the whole organization is acceptable to management. Since the total of what all preparers submit is always higher than what management will accept, a process of budget cutting starts.

Budget cutting is rarely a logical process. It is too often an approach that says "cut everybody by 5%." Even when one function is cut more and another less, the amounts that are cut are usually arbitrary. The experienced budget preparer anticipates this process and builds in enough contingency dollars to survive after the cuts take place.

Contingencies are most easily provided for in the supplies, travel, education, and miscellaneous line items. Since these items are hard to estimate with precision, you merely estimate on the high side. If asked to justify increases from the present year, you quote inflation in supply costs, the importance of going to a certain meeting or of coordinating with a company group located across the country, the need for advanced training, and whatever else occurs to you. You may never do any of these things, but this puts money in the budget.

It is harder to add a contingency amount to salaries, despite the size of this line item. The arithmetic is too straightforward once the size of the staff is set. If you are hiring, you can budget for an opening a few months earlier than you really expect to hire a person. That is about all you can do.

The budget reviewers, of course, know all the hiding places for contingencies. They will come to you or your manager and suggest reducing supply and travel costs to the present-year levels, and so on. Your ability to be persuasive, and your manager's ability to play the contingency game, determine the outcome.

A contingency amount of about 2% of the total budget is reasonable, particularly for the professional new to budget preparation. You will need it and use it. There are always unexpected costs. As you gain experience in forecasting and controlling costs, there will be fewer unanticipated events in the budget year. You can work the contingency amount down to 1% or so.

NARRATIVE JUSTIFICATION

The budget instructions usually require a narrative justification for changes in the level of staff and for other major changes and unusual situations. The budget work sheet for this, if there is one, will be a series of blank lines for you to write on.

Justifying Additional Staff

The only reason for additional staff is an addition to the work load. Work may increase because there is more to be done or because you take on additional responsibilities.

You are estimating and justifying your staff needs for the 12 months of next year. The end of that year is a long way off. Yet the budget forms ask you for the anticipated staff level at the end of the budget year. The level you show is the number the budget reviewers will concentrate on. It is an important number to forecast and defend because you may be stuck with it for a whole year. If the budgeting and cost control process is rigorous, you will not be allowed to hire a person unless that addition to the staff is part of the approved budget.

How do you determine the size your work load will be a year from now? There are guidelines that cover the work level for the company as a whole. They are usually called the annual plan. You must determine what this plan means to your department or project.

Project or Primary Department.   Are you a department head or project leader working under a contract or a plan of action? If so, the approved plan will contain a chart showing staffing levels. If your group is one of its line items, a reference to these levels is your narrative justification. If your group is part of a larger entity whose staff level is the line item, you and the others in that entity must agree on the staff distribution.

What if the staffing levels are unrealistic in light of recent events? That is a bigger problem than preparing next year's budget. It must be resolved at the appropriate levels of management and a revised plan agreed to. Only then can new approved staffing levels be forecast. What if there is not enough time to have this issue resolved before the budget's due date? Some companies will tell you to use the present plan and revise your budget after the issue is resolved. Others willl ask you to use your best judgment. The former approach reduces gamesmanship, whereas the latter gives more realistic totals—if everyone is honest.

Support Department.   Is yours a support group? If so, determine:

1. The proposed staffing levels of the departments you support.
2. Whether a greater or lesser fraction of their work will flow to your operation, and why.

Talk to the head of each department you support. Document what you are told. These statements form the basis for your narrative justification.

This two-part approach to determining the work load from each department gives you more accurate data than asking the simpler question: How much work will you be sending me next year? The latter question gives only the subjective opinion of the department head. If that person is concerned about his or her budget, you may be shortchanged. It is quite common for project managers to underestimate how much of a project budget goes to supporting groups. Sometimes this is done deliberately to hang on to a larger fraction of the available money, to build up or retain the project group's own staff.

The first of the two determinations tells you whether each department you support will grow or decline. The work that you get should follow the same trends unless reasons can be given to the contrary. The second determination addresses whether such reasons exist.

Additional Responsibilities.   If the responsibility you will assume already exists in the company and you are taking it over, information on past and present staff levels exists. Estimate this new responsibility separately. Add it and the existing operation together in submitting the budget, but in the narrative justification show how the staffing level for each of the two parts relates to each of the prior levels.

If the responsibility has not existed before, an implementation plan should exist. It should contain a proposed staffing table, and reference to this is the justification. If no such plan exists, you should reach an agreement with the appropriate level of management for the staffing and dollar levels. This agreement becomes the justification.

Justifying Materials, Purchased Services, and Minor Line Items

The narrative statement should justify any significant change in one of these line items from the levels of the present year and the prior year. If the change is in the same ratio as the change to your staffing level, a statement to this effect is sufficient. If not, state the reason for the dollar figure you placed in the budget work sheet. In the discussion on calculating budget amounts, we suggested some reasons for higher or lower levels.

THE CAPITAL BUDGET

Usually you prepare a second budget, the capital budget. Capital assets are purchases that have a long useful life, usually defined as two years or more, and that cost more than a certain amount. The threshold amount varies from company to company, but the range is between $200 and $1,000. The principal difference between capital assets and materials is that the latter are consumed as the operation progresses, whereas capital assets remain to do the job again and again. Office equipment—furniture, typewriters, personal computers, word processors, copiers—is capital equipment.

The capital budget applies to you only if you are buying the equipment.

Leasing the equipment is generally part of the operations budget already described. If the budget preparation instructions do not make clear whether an item you plan to buy should be in the capital or the materials budget, ask the accounting analysts.

The capital budget is a separate financial plan. The two plans—the two budgets—are not interchangeable. If you are running out of funds in one category, you cannot transfer funds from the other. Capital funds are recovered through equipment depreciation, which continues over several years. Capital dollars are thus more precious dollars than operations dollars.

If the amounts you enter on the capital budget are significant, you will be asked to itemize them and to justify each item.

The most persuasive justifications for a capital asset are these:

1. Its use saves the company money.
2. It is essential to perform a function.

The cost-saving argument should use one of the cost-justification methods described in Chapter 3. A payout period of two years or less is good justification.

APPROVAL CYCLE

When you have completed the budget forms and the narrative justification, your manager will review them. You must convince your superior that your assumptions are valid, the numbers are realistic, and the justification is supportable. Your manager, in turn, will have to support this budget to his or her superiors, and so on up the line.

Expect probing questions. Why do you need two more people next year? Can you justify the work-load estimate? Did you use the work-load levels shown in the approved plan of action? Do all the departments you support agree to the increased work load? These questions are not criticism. Your manager needs the answers in order to support the budget submittal at the next higher level of review. If you cannot justify your numbers, expect to be told to cut back.

Your manager may also want to make changes based on the judgment that an increase in some item will not be accepted by higher management at this time. Making these judgments is part of your manager's job. If you cannot convince your manager to support your position, you will have to back down.

After the budget has been submitted to the finance group, you will hear nothing for many weeks. The financial department is consolidating all the budget work sheets and presenting the totals to top management for their review and decision. Finally, at a time close to the start of the budget year, the approved figures will be distributed. They may or may not be the same as those you submitted.

If you are cut back, this is not a reflection on your judgment. Generally it means that the overall budget submittal was too high to let the organization make its desired profit. All or most functions were cut back. Accept this gracefully; you are a member of the management team. Figure out what the reduction means in terms of people, supplies, travel, training, and so on. Can you live with it? Unless it is completely impossible, you have to try. That is part of your job. Tell your manager what the approved budget does to your operation and what problems you foresee. But adjust your plans to fit the approved numbers.

MONTHLY SPREAD OF THE BUDGET

After the approved budget is released, you may be asked to spread by month the annual total for each line item. The monthly figures will be entered in a computer program that calculates monthly variances of costs from budget. You will be given a work sheet for this.

If you believe that costs for a line item will be spread fairly evenly throughout the year, divide the total budget by 12 and enter that number for each month. If costs can be shown only to the nearest thousand dollars, juggle numbers just above and below the average to reach the correct total. The problem of where to place zeros and ones on the smaller totals is ever present. Space them so that the monthly totals remain about steady. Table 9-6 shows such a work sheet balanced to the budget totals of Table 9-5.

The salaries line requires special attention. Spread the budget on a slowly rising basis to reflect the salary increases coming throughout the year. If you are hiring, show an increase in the planned month of hire that reflects the new

Table 9-6. Monthly Spread of the Budget.

BUDGET WORK SHEET: MONTHLY SPREAD
(thousand $)

Department/Project ABC   Date Prepared 12/18/8–

Prepared By JLB

LINE ITEM	J	F	M	A	M	J	J	A	S	O	N	D	T
Salaries	14	13	14	16	15	16	16	18	18	18	19	19	196
Fringe Benefits	5	4	5	5	6	6	6	6	7	6	7	6	69
Materials	2	3	3	3	3	2	3	3	3	3	3	3	34
Purch. Services	—	—	—	1	1	3	3	1	1	—	—	1	11
Leases & Rent	1	1	—	1	1	—	1	1	—	1	1	—	8
Travel	—	—	1	3	—	—	—	3	1	—	2	—	10
Educ. & Training	1	—	—	—	2	—	1	—	—	1	—	—	5
Recruiting	—	—	—	2	—	—	1	—	2	—	—	—	5
Other	—	1	1	—	—	1	—	—	—	1	—	1	5
Occupancy Costs	—	—	—	—	—	—	—	—	—	—	—	—	—
TOTAL	23	22	24	31	28	28	31	32	32	30	32	30	343

person's salary. You may adjust for the varying lengths of each month, but most organizations do not request this degree of sophistication.

If you know when a training seminar, a trip to attend a professional meeting, or some other specific event will occur, budget its cost in the month after the event. Costs show on the cost reports at the time they are posted to the accounts or are paid. This is usually a month after you turn in your expense report or after an invoice is submitted.

CONTROL OF COSTS

After you get into the budget year, you receive a monthly report on costs. If you have a good cost control system, you will get a summary report that shows actual costs on each of the line items you budgeted. You will also get a detailed report showing all charges against each account for which you are responsible.

Cost Summary Report

Figure 9-1 is an example of a good monthly summary report. The top part is a cumulative graph. It shows two lines. One is the cumulative budget through the latest month; in this example it is the dashed line. It is plotted from the "total" row of the monthly spread sheet. The solid line is cumulative costs.

The graph serves two purposes. It shows at a glance whether any differences between cost and budget are diverging or converging. It also shows whether the cost line is concave, straight, or convex. This is helpful when you are extrapolating costs to year end.

The three-line middle section shows the year to date in tabular form. The three rows show the cumulative costs, cumulative budget, and cumulative variance between them. These are the same data as plotted on the graph. If the two lines on the graph virtually coincide—which is the ideal situation—the table shows which is higher. On this chart, the dollars are rounded to the nearest thousand, which is sufficiently accurate for purposes of cost control.

The cumulative variance line is the most important line on the form. If it is at or near zero, you probably have no worries. If it is negative—an overrun— you may have to take action. If it is both negative and diverging, you have a large problem.

The table at the bottom third of the page shows monthly costs on each of the line items budgeted. To the right of this table, there are two columns showing actual costs to date and the amount over or under—(O)/U—the budget to date for each line item. The (O)/U numbers are calculated from the monthly spread of the budget described earlier and shown in Table 9-6. If you have a problem, the (O)/U column is the place to start your analysis. It shows which line items are causing the problem.

As well as the summary report, you get a detailed listing of costs charged

Department Spending Summary

Month ending _____   Department_____

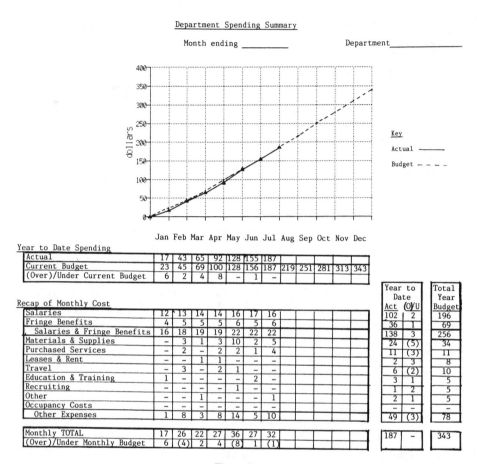

Year to Date Spending

	Jan	Feb	Mar	Apr	May	Jun	Jul	Aug	Sep	Oct	Nov	Dec
Actual	17	43	65	92	128	155	187					
Current Budget	23	45	69	100	128	156	187	219	251	281	313	343
(Over)/Under Current Budget	6	2	4	8	–	1	–					

Recap of Monthly Cost

	Jan	Feb	Mar	Apr	May	Jun	Jul	Aug	Sep	Oct	Nov	Dec	Year to Date Act	(O)/U	Total Year Budget
Salaries	12	13	14	14	16	17	16						102	2	196
Fringe Benefits	4	5	5	5	6	5	6						36	1	69
Salaries & Fringe Benefits	16	18	19	19	22	22	22						138	3	256
Materials & Supplies	–	3	1	3	10	2	5						24	(5)	34
Purchased Services	–	2	–	2	2	1	4						11	(3)	11
Leases & Rent	–	–	1	1	–	–	–						2	3	8
Travel	–	3	–	2	1	–	–						6	(2)	10
Education & Training	1	–	–	–	–	2	–						3	1	5
Recruiting	–	–	–	–	1	–	–						1	2	5
Other	–	–	1	–	–	–	1						2	1	5
Occupancy Costs	–	–	–	–	–	–	–						–	–	–
Other Expenses	1	8	3	8	14	5	10						49	(3)	78
Monthly TOTAL	17	26	22	27	36	27	32						187	–	343
(Over)/Under Monthly Budget	6	(4)	2	4	(8)	1	(1)								

Key
Actual ———
Budget — — —

Figure 9-1.

that month to each account that is a part of the project or department total. This is usually a computer-generated report. Its purpose is to show the detail behind each of the summary totals. You should be able to go from the summary report to the appropriate section of the detailed report and see what payments represent that month's total. It should show you what department and what person charged time to your project, what purchase orders were paid, what expense reports were included, and so forth.

Analyzing Costs

Again referring to Figure 9-1, in this example you are seven months into the year that you budgeted. The budget figures used are taken from Table 9-6. The cost figures shown are exaggerated to point out some of the techniques used to analyze costs.

The key question you must answer is this: Do you have a problem in meeting the year-end budget? The year to date total is right on target! You budgeted $187,000 through July, and that is exactly what you have spent. So you have no problem, right? Not necessarily. Let us look at the situation, line item by line item.

Salaries and fringe benefits are slightly under budget. If you compare costs to the monthly budget spread shown in Table 9-6, you find that the April increase of $2,000 you had budgeted was not spent. The arrival of a new staff member, forecast for April, did not occur until May. This resulted in an April underrun of $2,000. This is the amount by which salaries are still under budget. Therefore all the other elements in the salary total, such as the amounts and timing of salary increases, are on target.

Looking at the balance of the year, however, there will be a problem. The company management has just announced a cost of living increase in all salaries of 5%, effective September 1. This will add $4,000 to the salary total and about $1,000 to the fringe benefit total. Thus the present underrun in salaries will become zero.

Materials and supplies is $5,000 over budget. You were under budget until May when a huge payment occurred. This was payment of a major supply order that will last you until late fall. Will you still meet the $34,000 budget? Forecast your remaining needs. If it looks as if you'll run over, by how much will you do so? Let us assume you'll be over by $6,000.

Puchased services is definitely in trouble. You had an unanticipated charge in February for a consultant who is due to return in August. By year end, you'll have overrun this line item by the $2,000 charged in February and probably by an additional $3,000 for charges in August.

Travel is the other line item in difficulty. In January there was an unanticipated meeting in your Dallas office. Two members of your group spent a week there. The costs appear in February. If you stick to your travel plans for the rest of the year, you'll be over by $3,000

What about the items that are running under budget? Leases are under budget. You think you'll end the year at $5,000 rather than the budgeted $8,000. Education costs are being paid later than forecast. Seminars forecast to be paid in May were charged to you in June. The $1,000 forecast for July has been spent; the cost will probably show in August. Therefore the apparent underrun for the education line is not real. The cost of recruiting the person who arrived in May was less than anticipated; this explains the current underrun in recruiting. But the August arrival involves an expensive relocation cost, and there was also an interview trip in late May that has not been recorded on the books yet. You may save $1,000 on recruiting costs, but not more. The "other" costs are running a little under budget and look as if they will end the year $1,000 under.

Let us recap this. Your estimate for year end, in relation to the budgeted amounts, looks like this (all $ numbers in thousands):

Salaries	(2)	over
Fringe benefits	—	even
Materials	(6)	over
Purchased services	(5)	over
Leases	3	under
Travel	(3)	over
Education	—	even
Recruiting	1	under
Other	1	under

The total is a potential $10,000 overrun!

You reached this conclusion by looking at the costs line item by line item. You recalled what you budgeted for the last five months of the year, and estimated whether the anticipated events would still occur. The zero variance on the total cost is misleading. There is a problem. What can you do?

Cost Control

Having analyzed the situation, you must now exercise control. What alternatives do you have?

One alternative is to announce the cost overrun and request an increase in your budget to cover it. In most companies, a budget increase will only be granted after you convince your superiors that you have tried all reasonable avenues to reduce costs. So the first step is to look at each element and see what can be done to reduce its costs. Do not look only at the line items that will overrun—look at all of them. It does not matter which items you extract funds from, if you can thereby balance the budget.

Start with salaries. If you are not already committed to a starting date for the staff member you are about to hire, and if your work load permits, can you delay his or her arrival for a month or so? Each month's delay saves $2,000 in salary and $700 in fringe benefits. If one of your staff is leaving, can you delay replacing that person? Can you persuade some of the staff who were planning to take their winter vacations after next January 1 to take them in December instead? Their salary is not charged to your salary budget during vacation time but becomes part of the fringe benefits account. Each week of vacation taken this year subtracts about $500 from the salary total.

On materials and supplies costs, can some orders be canceled? Can delivery of some supplies be delayed until next January? Doing this moves their cost into next year. If you were underrunning your total budget near year end, you could use this same technique to accelerate material deliveries and move costs from the next year into the current year.

On all the other items, question what you can postpone. Can you put off the planned educational and training seminars until next year? Can you postpone a consultant or a lease or a trip? Review all these options and see if you can avoid the potential $10,000 overrun by taking action now. Review the situation with your manager and point out the options and their consequences. If the actions needed to come in on target are too harmful, your manager may opt to request a budget increase.

Sometimes an amount will appear on the summary and detail reports that makes no sense to you. You have no idea what it represents and why it is charged to you. Mistakes happen. Someone may have put your account number in error on a purchase request or charged time to your account by mistake. If a questionable charge appears, investigate it. Ask the financial analysts to check it out. If it is wrong, ask that it be corrected. Such vigilance may save you from overrun problems.

SUMMARY

Each company has a set of work sheets with which to calculate annual budget submittals, including a summary section, detail pages for the major line items, and a narrative section. The line items most frequently budgeted are salaries, fringe benefits, materials and supplies, purchased services, leases and rent, travel, education and training, recruiting, other expenses, and, in some companies, an occupancy expense.

On the summary page, actual costs for last year and projected costs for the current year should be shown for each line item. As each requested amount is calculated for the budget year, it is entered in the budget-year column of the summary.

Methods for calculating each of the budget line items have been presented in this chapter.

Contingency planning is the process of adding 1 or 2% to cover unforeseen costs. It also cushions against cutbacks that accompany the process of budget review and approval.

The narrative justification covers all line items where the amounts being requested are significantly different from the present- and prior-year costs. Changes in staff level always require justification.

The capital budget is a separate budget. It covers purchased items having a useful life of several years and a value higher than some threshold dollar figure. The capital and operations budgets are not interchangeable.

The budget approval cycle starts with your manager asking probing questions to assure that your budget numbers are realistic and supportable. Your manager in turn supports the proposed budget at the next higher level. If, when the approved budget levels are distributed, your portion is less than you submitted, determine what effect the cutback has on your plans, and review this with your manager.

After budget approval, a monthly spread of budget line items is often requested.

A cost summary report has been described in this chapter. The cost variances from budget are the most important set of numbers on the report. They show overall status and also which line items are above or below budget. In analyzing costs, you examine each line item and project its costs to year end.

Cost control means adjusting your plans to assure that you meet the budget total. Suggestions have been made regarding actions you can take to affect future costs. You analyze the effects of all possible actions and review them with your manager. Mistakes may appear on the cost reports. If a number appears that makes no sense to you, it should be investigated. If it is an error, it should be corrected. This precaution may avoid overruns.

FOR FURTHER INFORMATION

Davis, Reba, and Balderston, Jack. Chapter 6, Preparing a Budget and Controlling Costs in *Word Processing Supervision,* Indianapolis, IN: Bobbs-Merrill Publ. Co., 1984.

Montgomery, A. Thompson. *Managerial Accounting Information.* Reading, MA: Addison-Wesley, 1979.

Sweeney, Allan, and Wisner, John N. *Budgeting Fundamentals for Non-Financial Executives.* New York: American Management Assoc., 1976.

10
Leadership

You have just been made supervisor, group leader, or project manager. Your boss has shaken your hand, congratulated you for a fine performance over the years, and expressed confidence in your ability to take on this increased responsibility. If you were lucky, you got a raise, or at least a free lunch. You also got a new office with more buttons on the telephone and a secretary outside the door. Friends have dropped by to tell you how much you deserved this promotion.

Now that they have all left, reality has begun to set in. Help! What do you do now?

This chapter is for the newly appointed group, project, or department head and for anyone else responsible for completing a task with the help of other people. In it, we discuss leadership styles and the different roles that a manager must play. We start with a subject that underlies all forms of leadership: motivation.

MOTIVATION

In this book, we rarely describe theories of management. Our approach is pragmatic. There are two useful concepts, however, that can guide you as a leader to get enthusiastic compliance and complete cooperation from your staff. They suggest which buttons to push to motivate each person. The theories are the hierarchy of needs concept originated by Abraham Maslow and the motivation–hygiene concept developed by Fredrick Herzberg.

Hierarchy of Needs

Maslow[1] suggests a five-layer pyramid of personal needs that each of us strives to satisfy. The pyramid is shown in Figure 10-1. Needs are met in sequence from the lower levels to the upper ones. At any given time, a person's needs lie primarily at one of these levels, and the person is motivated to satisfy the

[1] Maslow, Abraham H. *Motivation and Personality,* 2nd ed. New York: Harper & Row, 1970, pp. 35–38.

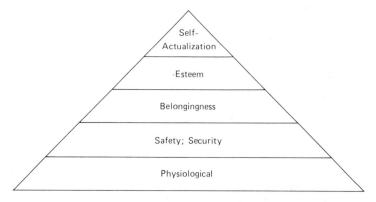

Figure 10-1. Maslow's hierarchy of needs.

needs at this level. The needs at lower levels are already sufficiently satisfied and are no longer motivators. Needs at the higher levels are not yet in focus. They, too, are not motivators at this time. The strongest motivators are those that apply to the level at which a person currently stands.

Reading from the bottom of the pyramid upward, this is what each level represents:

1. The lowest level, the *physiological,* is the need for food and shelter. If one is starving, the need for food dominates all other needs until it is satisfied.
2. The second level, *safety and security,* includes the need for job security and reasonable and safe working conditions. In times of high unemployment, and when your fellow workers are being laid off around you, this need dominates your thinking. Anything that assures that you are not part of the next layoff is a very strong motivator.
3. The third level, *belongingness,* includes the need to be part of a working group or team. The social interaction at work addresses this need. On a less positive note, so does the clique or in-group.
4. The fourth level, *esteem,* includes the need for recognition from your manager, your peers, and your friends. It also includes your need for a job title that fits your level of responsibility and the satisfaction of being consulted on subjects you know well.
5. The top level, *self-actualization,* is the need to feel fulfillment for a difficult job well done, and a difficult challenge overcome. It is the wish to live up to your full potential. It includes the desire to advance to a more important position with more responsibility.

Using the Hierarchy of Needs.   What does this mean in practical terms? Each person is primarily at one level of needs. Find out where each person stands in this hierarchy and tailor your motivation actions accordingly. For example:

- A secretary who has a family and whose spouse is out of work is at the physiological and safety levels of need. A steady job and steady pay are most important to this person. Appeals involving recognition or greater achievement have little meaning at the moment. Appeals suggesting job security and higher pay are the ones that will motivate this person.
- The paraprofessional who has a working spouse and a full bank account may be at the belonginess level. If this person sees herself or himself as the second income in the family, it is the fun and togetherness of the group that holds this employee. If this social satisfaction is lost, the person may leave. None of the safety or physiological factors, including salary, will motivate this person if belongingness is reduced. It is at this social level that motivation will be most effective.
- The professional, unless concerned with job security, is more likely to be motivated by appeals to the top two levels of the Maslow pyramid than to those at the bottom. Recognition by superiors and peers is a reward at the esteem level. The opportunity to write an article for a professional publication or to give a talk at a professional society meeting is important to this person. A mention in the company paper for an important achievement, or a "salesman of the month" award are strong motivators at the esteem level.

The leader should recognize each individual's level and address the person accordingly.

Motivation–Hygiene Theory

This concept from Fredrick Herzberg[2] lists specific elements in the working environment that create or block job satisfaction. Herzberg suggests that a higher level of satisfaction on the job brings better performance, and a lesser level of satisfaction brings lower performance. You can get better performance from your staff, therefore, by increasing the factors that satisfy and by decreasing those that dissatisfy. In this sense, you increase the staff's motivation. This concept applies primarily to the motivation of subordinates. However, knowing what factors bring satisfaction and what factors block satisfaction can also be used to motivate ("sell" an idea to) peers and superiors.

Herzberg lists two sets of factors. The set that increases personal satisfaction he calls the *motivators*. The set that blocks satisfaction he calls the *hygiene* fac-

---

[2] Herzberg, Fredrick. One More Time, How Do You Motivate Employees? *Harvard Business Review*, 46,1 (Jan.–Feb. 1968): 53–62.

Table 10-1. Herzberg's Motivation–Hygiene Theory.

MOTIVATION FACTORS	HYGIENE FACTORS
Achievement	Company policy and administration
Recognition	Supervision
Work itself	Relationship with superior
Responsibility	Work conditions
Advancement	Salary
Growth	Relationship with peers
	Personal life
	Relationship with subordinates
	Status

tors. The list of principal motivation and hygiene factors is shown in Table 10-1.

Note that salary is listed as a hygiene factor, not a motivator. Not being paid a salary that you think is fair leaves you dissatisfied. Raising it to a fair level removes the dissatisfaction. Raising it further to a level that you know is unusually high may motivate you to greater efforts for a short period, but the motivation is temporary. Salary alone will not keep the juices flowing and a person working at full pitch.

Using the Motivation–Hygiene Theory.   What does Herzberg's concept mean in practical terms?

- You do not motivate an unhappy employee with a raise, unless the dissatisfaction is related solely to money.
- You should eliminate or reduce the hygiene factors. Listen to complaints and gripes; determine which are significant; change the conditions if you can; work on higher management to change conditions where they can.
- Motivation factors are open-ended. There is no upper limit. You can continually reinforce the level of satisfaction and add to it. Look for opportunities and grab them.

How can you use the five motivation factors listed in Table 10-1? Try the following:

1. Achievement
   (a) Provide a challenging task.
   (b) Delegate more responsibility.
   (c) Allow the employee to work on a task from start to finish.
2. Recognition
   (a) Give the person a pat on the back.
   (b) Pass along a compliment from a customer or the user of a completed job.

(c) Encourage the publication of an article or the making of a presentation at a professional meeting.

(d) Encourage accepting a leadership role in a professional society.

(e) Mention the person's name in the company paper.

(f) Give an award, which need not be monetary.

3. Challenging work

(a) Spread the interesting and important work among all staff members able to handle it.

(b) Be sure that the significance of each task is explained.

(c) Enhance the content of each job as much as possible.

4. Greater responsibility

(a) Delegate the full task to one person rather than divide it among several people.

(b) Encourage individuals to become expert in a task or function.

(c) Reduce controls placed on the way a job is performed while retaining employee accountability for results.

(d) Allow employees to answer questions and describe procedures in their areas of expertise.

(e) Invite comment, ideas, and even criticism on your orders and ideas.

5. Advancement

(a) Assure that a career path is available to each person.

(b) Provide and encourage participation in training and education courses that can lead to more responsible positions.

(c) Be realistic about growth opportunities and the evaluation of employee potential.

Survey after survey confirms these concepts. What the professional who is at Maslow's esteem or self-actualization level wants most is not a higher salary; it is challenging work, recognition, and more responsibility.

LEADERSHIP

Supervision has been described as getting work done through people. Leadership is the process of getting people to do the necessary work. The supervisor, the manager, and the project manager are leaders. Their positions carry titles that show authority over people. But leadership, as we use the word here, can also exist without that formal authority. We define a leader as a person who is responsible for accomplishing a task, or portion of a task, and who has a group of people working on that task. The professional who has no formal title may be the leader on a segment of a task because of his or her expertise on the subject. In the work environment, almost everyone is a leader in some area.

Leaders lead in many ways. They can give a direct command: "Do this!" or "Do the job this way." This is authoritarian leadership. They can also say: "Let's work out together the week's schedule of activities," or, "Have you tried this method?'' This is participative or democratic leadership. The way in which the leader gives direction is the style of leadership. Leadership style is very important. It makes the difference between a good leader whose orders and advice are followed enthusiastically and a poor leader whose orders are followed resentfully. It makes the difference between high morale and a well-knit team where each member helps the other, and poor morale with an uncooperative staff who obey the letter of a command but do no more.

There are many concepts of leadership. The most important thing to know is that no one style applies to all situations. One cannot say that democratic leadership is good and autocratic leadership is bad. One cannot say that a leader should always be people-oriented or should always be work-oriented. Flexibility is the hallmark of a good leader. The form of leadership that should be employed depends on the situation.

One useful way to look at leadership was first suggested by Robert Tannenbaum and Warren Schmidt,[3] who describe leadership as a sharing of influence over a decision by the manager (in our terms the leader) and the nonmanagers (the task group). This is shown in diagram form in Figure 10-2. The leader can assume almost 100% authority over a decision, in which situation he or she is completely autocratic. The leader can also delegate almost all the authority to the staff, which makes the leader highly democratic. There is a continuum of leadership styles in between these extremes.

Democratic or participative leadership must be distinguished from the absence of leadership. In the latter situation, the designated manager or leader simply does not make a decision. The subordinates or team members are left on their own to determine what to do. This is not a style of leadership; it is the abdication of leadership. In participative leadership, the group makes a decision within a defined set of rules and circumstances; the group members know when they can and cannot act. When there is abdication of leadership, the group is left to drift on its own. Unfortunately, some supervisors and managers sometimes abdicate their responsibilities. Faced with two choices, or with a divided opinion within the group, they continue to postpone making a decision.

Leadership Styles

Figure 10-2 shows the two extremes of leadership style and five positions on the continuum between. For ease of discussion, we have numbered them from left to right. The good leader employs different leadership styles along this continuum, depending on the circumstances. Let us look at the seven styles.

At the very left side of the diagram, the leader makes the decision with no participation by others. This is the traditional army-style command: ''Forward,

---

[3] Tannenbaum, Robert, and Schmidt, Warren. How to Choose a Leadership Pattern. *Harvard Business Review*, 36,2 (May–June 1973): 162.

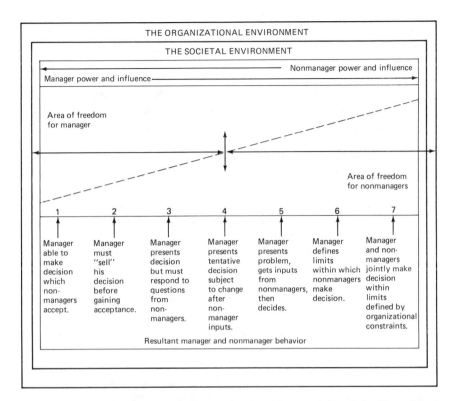

THE ORGANIZATIONAL ENVIRONMENT

THE SOCIETAL ENVIRONMENT

Nonmanager power and influence

Manager power and influence

Area of freedom for manager

Area of freedom for nonmanagers

1	2	3	4	5	6	7
Manager able to make decision which non-managers accept.	Manager must "sell" his decision before gaining acceptance.	Manager presents decision but must respond to questions from non-managers.	Manager presents tentative decision subject to change after non-manager inputs.	Manager presents problem, gets inputs from nonmanagers, then decides.	Manager defines limits within which nonmanagers make decision.	Manager and non-managers jointly make decision within limits defined by organizational constraints.

Resultant manager and nonmanager behavior

Figure 10-2. Continuum of leadership styles. Reprinted by permission of the *Harvard Business Review*. An exhibit from "How to Choose a Leadership Pattern" by Robert Tannenbaum and Warren Schmidt (May/June 1973). Copyright (c) 1973 by the President and Fellows of Harvard College; all rights reserved.

march." "Do this job next." "Here is the new procedure I have written. Follow it." This is the pure authoritarian style.

In the second style from the left in Figure 10-2, the leader "sells" a decision. There are two types of "selling." In one, the leader makes an authoritarian decision, as in style number one, but decides that some persuasion or motivation is necessary to obtain the group's compliance. The leader may point out how the decision benefits group members. "If we get the report on project X to management by Monday morning, there is a much better chance of it becoming one of the major programs next year. Therefore, we are going to work this weekend . . ."; or: "Here is the new schedule you will follow. If you meet all the deadlines, you won't have to work over Thanksgiving weekend." This is a positive form of motivation.

In the other form of "selling," the leader may say: "Here is what I think. Don't you agree?" Some managers consider this democratic because they have not given a direct order. They have given the group a voice in the decision. Subordinates and group members recognize this type of statement as a disguised order. Whether anyone will disagree depends on the leader's tone of voice and his or her previous reaction when someone did disagree. Only the brave will speak up, and then only if the decision is clearly wrong. The group members have been given a very small degree of freedom in the decision process.

In the third leadership style, the leader gives his or her opinion first and then asks for comments: "Here is what I think. Do you have any questions?" The questions the leader wants are questions aimed at clarifying the decision, not questioning it. This style, while still autocratic, is less threatening to the team. It is easier to express disagreement through a question than to be forced to say outright, "I disagree with you." There may be aspects of the decision that have been ignored; questions can bring them out. The decision can be modified without anyone's ego being bruised.

The fourth and middle style is the first that really allows an open discussion. It is the first that is not authoritarian. The leader still states a position, but clearly indicates that it is tentative. The leader shows that he or she wants input from the group members: "I'm inclined to favor the following approach, but I want your opinions before I decide for sure." This invites discussion, but limits it initially to the leader's suggested approach. Focusing the discussion in this way keeps it brief and to the point. However, in this fourth style, better alternatives may not be raised.

The fifth style differs from the fourth by inviting a completely open discussion: "Project Zebra seems to be stuck. Who has ideas about how to get it going again?" This is the first of the participative or democratic leadership styles. All participants are placed on the same footing. Ideas are solicited from everyone. The leader makes it clear that he or she will make the decision. The leader also makes it clear that he or she wants the group's help. The leader wants to hear all ideas and points of view. In this leadership style, the group members feel that they are full-fledged participants. Their abilities and knowledge have been recognized by the leader. Besides getting a lot of information from which to make a better decision, the leader motivates those group members who are at Maslow's "esteem" level using Herzberg's "recognition" and "greater responsibility."

In the sixth style, the leader defines a problem, sets limits within which the group can operate, and then lets the group make the decision. "The company's new flex-time policy allows each of us to start work at any time between 6 A.M. and 9 A.M. and work our full eight hours. However, because so much of our work is joint team effort, we need everyone here together for seven out of the eight daily hours. This means limiting the variation in your starting time to one hour. You decide together what the starting limits will be, and let me know." The limits on the decision on starting times are that they vary only by one hour and that the variation must occur between 6 A.M. and 9 A.M. This is the ultimate phase of participative leadership.

At the extreme right side of the chart, in the seventh style, the leader acts as if he or she were simply another team member, and the team as a whole makes a decision. Tannenbaum and Schmidt cite a research group as one of the few examples where this happens. The group as a whole defines the research problem, develops procedures for solving it, and picks a solution from the alternatives available. The leader acts as a leader only in assuring that action takes place and that the problem selected lies within the group's charter and, perhaps, in communicating the status of the project to higher management. In doing its work, the group as a whole makes the decisions.

When to Use Each Style

It should be apparent by now that there is no one style of leadership appropriate to all situations. No one style is best. When should you use each style? There is no simple answer. It depends on three things:

1. The leader's personality
2. The style of the organization
3. The circumstances

Leader's Personality. If your nature is autocratic, you will find it difficult and unconvincing to be democratic. It's hard to imagine General George S. Patton at the right-hand side of the leadership chart. You must be yourself and act in the way you feel comfortable. Your staff will generally adapt to you if you are consistent and fair. The worst style of all is inconsistency.

Organization's Style. Every organization has a dominant style, usually set at the top and filtering down through the ranks. Some companies are autocratic. Traditionally, all decisions are made by management, none by the informal leaders. Decisions are made further up the management chain than is the case in less autocratic companies. The president becomes involved in many decisions that elsewhere would be delegated well down in the management ranks. In these organizations it is hard to use a participative leadership style.

Other organizations believe in delegating a decision to as low a level in the organization as possible. People are encouraged to assume responsibility. The atmosphere is less formal. Participative decision making is encouraged. In these companies, it is normal for leaders to use a style at the right side of the chart.

Circumstances. Although your personality and the organization's style set a pattern, the circumstances surrounding a decision are the most important consideration in choosing the proper leadership style.

Autocratic. Sometimes an instant decision is needed. Should one job be pushed ahead of another? Should all members of the group be pulled from their current assignments to work on a sudden crisis? This is no time for a debate or even to ask for opinions. You need a decision now. When time is critical, the autocratic leadership style (number one) is appropriate and essential.

The other circumstance that leads toward an autocratic decision is its importance. If it involves who is to be hired, or how to cut costs to meet budget, the manager makes the decision. The manager may ask one or two specialists on the staff for advice or comment on an aspect of the situation, but the decision will be the manager's alone.

Whether style two rather than style one is used is a matter of tactics. If the leader feels that motivation is necessary and can spare the few minutes required to phrase motivational remarks, this style is more effective than style one. However, when a leader who is normally democratic uses an autocratic style, the nature of the crisis is often so obvious that no explanations are needed.

Interpretative questions should always be encouraged. The group may not understand the leader's order, or someone may not understand his or her role. The situation must be clarified if the order is to be carried out promptly and correctly. For style three, however, what Tannenbaum and Schmidt mean by "questions" is a give-and-take session in which the implications of an order are discussed, and the manager's reasoning is presented. If time is so pressing that an autocratic order is needed, explanations should be given later, not before the order is carried out. Even in the most democratic of organization climates, employees recognize the necessity for immediate decisions on some matters and accept the manager's role in making them.

Participative.   The fourth style is the one in which participative decisions start to be made. If time and importance permit, all decisions should involve at least this degree of participation. This fourth style is for situations where the leader is not sure what to do, and time is short. By presenting a target decision, the discussion is focused and brief.

The fifth style takes time, often a lot of time. In this leadership style, staff meetings are often used to present and discuss a problem. The leader stays neutral and listens. After all points of view have been presented and the discussion seems to be repeating itself, the leader reaches a decision, stating it and the reasons for it. This style produces the most ideas. It maximizes participation and motivation. It appeals to the higher levels of the Maslow pyramid, and uses Herzberg's motivation factors. This is the style that should be used whenever possible.

The sixth style is for decisions that the leader is willing to have the group themselves make. Generally, these will be problems of lesser importance, although some important task forces will result from use of this style. Group decision making is a good leadership training ground for the participants. A wise manager finds a few issues where this style can be used so that everyone in the group has a chance to participate in a decision-making role.

As noted earlier, the seventh style is used only in unique circumstances where the leader virtually abandons the role of leadership and joins the group in a joint decision effort. There will be few such cases outside of research.

Within the limits discussed, the closer your leadership is to the fifth style on the leadership chart, the more you motivate, and the better decisions you are likely to reach. Morale will be higher. The staff will be more willing to help you work out problems or to work extra late or extra hard in times of crisis. They will identify problems you were not aware of. They will provide ideas you had not thought of. The productivity and accomplishments of the group will be higher, and the leader will be seen as a better leader.

RESPONSIBILITIES OF MANAGERS

All professionals must motivate other people. All will find themselves in a leadership role many times in their career. The professional who holds the position of supervisor or manager has additional responsibilities. A few words are appropriate to list what else, besides motivation and leadership, the manager and supervisor must do. The extent of a manager's or supervisor's functions often is not appreciated by the staff who aspire to these lofty positions.

Management comprises the following elements:

1. Planning: what needs to be done, and how it will be done.
2. Organizing: who does what.
3. Controlling: assuring that plans and promises are met.
4. Staffing: hiring and training.
5. Directing: motivating, leading, communicating, appraising, rewarding, resolving conflicts, and handling organizational power and politics.

Figure 10-3 shows these functions. M. K. Badawy, author of the book from which this figure is taken, includes staffing as a part of organizing. We have chosen to list it separately because the functions of hiring and training people are continuous, whereas other aspects of organizing may be temporarily static.

All managers perform these five functions, regardless of what area they manage. We discussed motivation and leadership earlier in this chapter. Here is a summary of the other functions.

Planning

We discussed planning for change in Chapter 3. The manager has the responsibility to plan change in his or her department, but has a much broader responsibility as well. All planning starts with one key question. It is:

• What does top management want from the operation the manager heads?

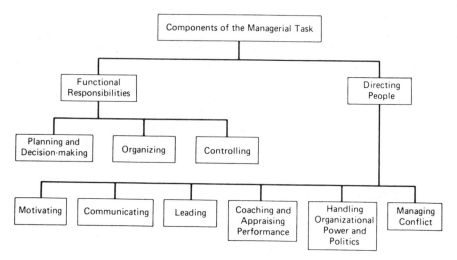

Figure 10-3. The functions of managers. From *Developing Managerial Skills in Engineers and Scientists,* by **M. K. Badawy. Copyright (c) 1982 by Van Nostrand Reinhold Company, Inc. Reprinted by permission of the publishers.**

Until you know this, you cannot plan. It is impossible to give a universal answer to this question. The answer depends, of course, on the particular department being managed. Our point is this: Whatever the department, the manager should not assume a priori that he or she knows management's goals for that department. There are usually several possible goals. Find out which of them is important to your management.

Here are some examples. For the purchasing department, is the goal to achieve the lowest possible cost consistent with adequate quality and reasonable delivery times? Or is the emphasis on meeting delivery time at a reasonable cost and with adequate quality? Or is the emphasis on quality, with cost and delivery secondary? Which of these three variables is the most important? In most consumer goods companies, minimizing cost usually dominates. In the space program, quality and dependability were paramount. Which of the three variables is most important to your business? The answer makes a difference to department policies and procedures.

For manufacturing operations, does management place the emphasis on unit cost, the quantity to be produced, or the quality produced? Advertisements from the major automobile companies suggest a change in their manufacturing emphasis in recent years. In engineering, is the product designed to last one year, five years, or fifty? What reliability factor is desired? What are the production cost targets? For each department in a company one can draw up a comparable set of questions.

Once you know management's goals for your operation, you can plan at the department level.

Planning involves:

1. Establishing department objectives and policies
2. Establishing operating procedures
3. Forecasting needs
4. Allocating available resources

Department *objectives* and *policies* are derived from management's goals for the department. These objectives define what needs to be done. The manager keeps an ear tuned for changes in corporate goals and reviews the department policies when change occurs. Do not assume that someone will hand you a neat package that says, "Effective next Monday the corporate goal will be. . . ." That doesn't happen. Goals usually change by evolution, not revolution. Corporate planners rarely know what the impact of a change will be at all department levels. The good manager senses these changes, asks questions of middle and higher management, and acts accordingly.

Procedures, which follow from policies, show how jobs get done. We covered the preparation and writing of procedures in Chapter 3. Standards are required. There should be standards for quality and for productivity. Both procedures and standards should be reviewed at least annually to see if underlying conditions have changed.

Forecasting of needs includes the following:

1. Funding
2. Staffing
3. Equipment
4. Materials
5. Space

The forecasting of needs starts with forecasting the department work load. Each of the five elements listed flows from the work load. In some organizations, management's assumption may be stated in an annual plan. More often, the annual plan covers only the major elements of sales, production, and inventory. Supporting departments must determine their work from these data. Also, as corporate sales, production, inventory, and so on, change during the year, the good manager senses the effect of these changes on his or her department.

Funding needs are expressed through the operating and capital budgets. We described how to prepare budgets in Chapter 9. Staffing needs are work load translated to number of people required. The elements of equipment, materials, and space likewise are derived from the forecast work load.

The *resources* available to the manager comprise the size of staff, funds, equipment, materials, and space. Because the needs that were forecast are often not granted in full, the manager must achieve the department's objectives with whatever is made available. Allocating insufficient or partly obsolete equipment among members of the staff, conserving materials, and crowding people into inadequate space are among the planning problems the manager faces constantly.

Organizing

Organizing consists of the following activities:

1. Dividing the department's goals into tasks.
2. Assigning to individuals the responsibility for each task or element of a job.
3. Delegating suitable authority to each person to handle his or her segment of a job.
4. Establishing work relationships and necessary coordination among the staff.

• Department *tasks* or projects are described in writing if there are many and if the department is large. These written plans of action show:

1. The objective.
2. The work description.
3. The schedule.
4. The budget.
5. The name of the person responsible.
6. The names of those assigned to the task.

In smaller departments, or ones that do only a few tasks repeatedly, the precise definition of each task and of the method to perform it resides in the manager's head. As a task is assigned to a new employee, the manager—or someone to whom this responsibility is delegated—shows the employee the purpose and procedure involved.

• *Responsibilities* are usually defined in writing in the form of job descriptions. These show:

1. The job title.
2. The reporting relationship.
3. The overall function of the job.
4. In specific detail, each duty and responsibility the person has, or each task the person performs.

• Lines of *authority* are specified by organization charts. In a large department with more than one level of management (i.e., a manager and several supervisors), the chart specifies who has authority over each segment of the department. In a small department, a chart will not be needed if it has a single point of authority (the manager) and only a few informal task leaders. It does not take long to learn who these task leaders are and the scope of their authority. The key issue is delegation:

1. How much authority does the manager delegate to each supervisor or task leader?
2. Is this amount sufficient to get the job done expeditiously, or does the task leader have to check with the manager whenever an unusual circumstance occurs?

The supervisor or task leader should be given as much authority as his or her knowledge and judgment permit.

• Establishing *work relationships* and coordination is perhaps the hardest part of organizing. For coordination with other departments, questions that must be considered are:

1. What tasks require coordination with other departments?
2. At what stage of the work is this coordination needed?
3. Who is the coordinator for our department, and who for theirs?
4. Who acts if a coordinator is unavailable?

For coordination within the department:

1. What are the working relationships among the staff?
2. How is work transferred from one individual to another?
3. What are the precise functions that each person performs?

Organizing is not done once and then neglected. Responsibilities and work relationships must be reviewed as:

1. The nature of the tasks changes.
2. The quantity of work changes.
3. The staff members change.

They are also reviewed when:

4. The present operation is not working well.

Controlling

Control follows directly from planning. In planning, the manager establishes standards for performance. Control is the process of:

1. Measuring actual performance.
2. Comparing actual performance to the standards.
3. Correcting deviations where found.

A budget is a plan and a standard for performance. In this case, the performance measurement is usually done by the accounting department, which may also prepare the report that shows the variance of actual costs from budget. Accounting has done the first of the above steps, and part of the second. The budget status reports show gross comparisons, but the manager must usually dig deeper to find out what item caused a deviation. Determining how to correct or compensate for a deviation is one of the manager's most important functions.

A schedule is also a plan and a standard for performance. In controlling schedule performance, the manager usually performs all three steps, determining where a job stands on the schedule, whether it is ahead or behind, and planning how to work around slippages and to catch up on the schedule.

There are standards for quality and quantity, and there are other standards or goals for the department. Everything promised in the planning stage is a candidate for control.

Staffing

Hiring is more than adding people during department growth. There is continuous attrition of personnel through promotion, transfer, and termination. These people must be replaced. Each staff member has a unique set of knowledge and talent that the manager, we hope, has used to the fullest. When that person leaves, the replacement will not have the identical abilities. The job content and assigned responsibilities should be reviewed each time there is a staff change.

The process of hiring involves:

1. Determining the attributes of the position to be filled.
2. Determining the degree of knowledge, skill, experience, and personality attributes required for the position.
3. Locating sources of job candidates.
4. Screening applications.
5. Interviewing applicants.
6. Selecting the best candidate.

We discuss techniques for interviewing and selecting staff in Chapter 11.

Training and education are a continuing part of staffing. Employees will ask approval to attend training classes, education courses, professional seminars, and workshops. The manager, however, should do more than just react to such requests. The department's needs in terms of knowledge and skills are always in a state of change. The manager should predict needs six months or a year ahead and persuade the appropriate members of the staff to prepare themselves for the opportunities that will arise.

Directing

Directing represents the bulk of the manager's time. It is a day-by-day, hour-by-hour job. Its elements are:

1. Motivating
2. Leading
3. Communicating
4. Coaching and appraising
5. Rewarding
6. Resolving conflicts
7. Handling organizational power and politics

These elements were shown in Figure 10-3.

We discussed motivation and leadership earlier in this chapter. We reserve verbal communications for Chapter 11. It is a vital and lengthy subject that is as important to all professionals (and paraprofessionals and nonprofessionals) as it is to managers. This leaves items four through seven on the above list to discuss here.

Coaching and Appraising. Coaching is the informal process of helping someone handle a new job or prepare for the next job or set of responsibilities. It is less structured than a training program which follows a set outline. It responds directly to the needs and questions of the individual. All employees who are given a new responsibility need coaching. If the manager is sufficiently familiar with the new job, he or she should be the coach.

Newly appointed managers also need coaching. There are many responsibilities—we have listed several of them—for which the new manager can get no formal education or training. The best coach is the new manager's own superior, provided the superior is a good manager and knows how to show by example. Next best is a specialist from the employee relations department or an outside management consultant.

Appraising the performance of employees is another important facet of the management job, and one that many managers dislike. They may feel they are playing God with someone's destiny. True, they are affecting a person's career and livelihood, but this is part of what managers are paid to do.

There are five reasons for performance appraisal:

1. To establish the basis for salaries and salary increases.
2. To inform the employee whether the manager's expectations are being met.
3. To learn how the employee views the work and his or her future.
4. To establish work and career objectives for the next six months or one year.
5. To document the employee's progress and problems throughout his or her company career.

Methods for handling performance appraisals are covered in Chapter 11.

Rewarding.   Establishing salary levels and the size of salary increases is one part of rewarding. Nonmonetary rewards are just as important. Several of these were mentioned in the section on motivation.

Ideally, the ranking of the staff in terms of salary earned should be the same as a ranking in terms of value to the organization. Value is a function of:

1. The importance of the job
2. The person's performance within that job

In most company salary plans, each job lies within a family of salary grades. Each step on the ladder of grades represents jobs of different value to the company. Thus a grade 14 job is seen as intrinsically more valuable than a grade 13 job, which, in turn, is more valuable than a grade 12 job, and so on. Each salary grade has a maximum and minimum salary level. Each person doing that job is worth a salary somewhere between these values, depending on the person's relative performance as measured by the performance appraisal. This is the theory behind most salary plans.

In practice, the theory is tempered by practical considerations:

1. You normally don't reduce a person's salary.
2. Passing over a person for a raise is often viewed as a hint to look for another job.
3. A very small raise (e.g., 2%) is definitely viewed as such a hint.
4. Some skills are so rare that you must pay more to retain that person than salary theory suggests.
5. An employee with important talents may have had little opportunity in which to use them. Greater use of these talents is expected, and the salary should reflect that.

6. Performance varies with time. A high performer one year may be low the next and high the year after. Some averaging is necessary.
7. Not all raters rate the same. Manager A's high performer may be manager B's low performer.
8. Some older professionals have an intangible worth in company experience (knowing other old-timers, company evolution, results of numerous decisions, etc.) that has real value but is hard to measure.

With all these modifiers, practice usually differs from theory.

Managing Conflict.   Conflict is the normal situation within a company and even within a department. There are fewer supervisory jobs than people who wish to become supervisors. There are fewer exciting tasks than routine ones. No matter who is promoted or who is assigned an exciting task, several others will be certain that they were better qualified. Staff egos and personalities will conflict. Someone will be sure the manager is playing favorites. There are endless causes of real or imagined hurts and conflicts.

The manager has the unenviable job of resolving these tensions in a way that retains a maximum of motivation for all parties. The manager becomes as much a psychologist as a technical expert.

Organizational Power and Politics.   The conflicts bring power politics to the organization. Cliques are formed. One group will not talk to or help another even in a common cause. Rivalries abound. If you're not for Mr. A, then you're against him. If rivalries are very strong, you can rarely be neutral or apolitical; you are placed in one camp or the other. If your man moves up the ladder, you are more likely to be promoted. If he doesn't, you may not either.

Knowing when to ally with one faction or another and when to avoid entanglement is an important skill. So is judging who will succeed as well as who is right. Some people are born knowing how to handle power and work within a power structure. They have a strong advantage.

Politics is the art of compromise. This is as true of corporate politics as of national politics. Politics is adjusting between what is technically best or right, and what is acceptable to higher management, to your own staff, and, sometimes, to your users or customers. Successful national politicians are good role models. Study them, or consult one of the references cited at the end of this chapter.

SUMMARY

Two concepts of motivation have been described, Maslow's hierarchy of needs and Herzberg's motivation–hygiene theory. Maslow suggests there are five levels of personal needs, and each person's needs are primarily at one of these levels at a given time. Motivation should address the level where each person currently is. Herzberg lists elements that create or block job satisfaction. Motivation is achieved by reducing or eliminating problems within the hygiene factors and enhancing the motivator factors.

There is a continuum of leadership styles between the pure authoritarian or autocratic and the pure participative or democratic. Seven styles have been described, in which the leader grants increasing amounts of influence over decisions to subordinates. The good leader uses all leadership styles, the choice depending on the circumstances. Autocratic leadership is necessary for immediate action and when a decision is of vital importance. Democratic leadership is used for matters where the time and subject are of less importance. An intermediate style, wherein the views of the subordinates are obtained and weighed, is best for most situations.

Managers have the responsibility to plan, organize, control, staff, and direct. Planning must start by knowing what top management wants from the manager's department. That goal is translated into department work objectives, policies, procedures, and needs. Organizing divides department goals into tasks, assigns responsibility, delegates suitable authority, and establishes the work relationships and necessary coordination between people and departments. Control measures actual performance, compares performance to the planned standards, and corrects deviations that are found. Everything promised in a plan is a candidate for control.

Staffing is hiring and training. Hiring involves determining the attributes of the position and the person who should fill it, locating sources of candidates, screening applications, interviewing applicants, and selecting the best candidate. Directing takes most of the manager's time. Besides motivating and leading, it includes communicating, coaching and appraising, rewarding, resolving conflicts, and handling organizational politics.

FOR FURTHER INFORMATION

Motivation

Herzberg, Fredrick. One More Time, How Do You Motivate Employees? *Harvard Business Review,* 46,1 (Jan.–Feb. 1968): 53–62.
Maslow, Abraham H. *Motivation and Personality,* 2nd ed. New York: Harper & Row, 1970.

Leadership

Argyris, Chris. *Increasing Leadership Effectiveness.* New York: Wiley, 1976.
Blake, Robert R., and Mouton, Jane S. *The New Managerial Grid,* Houston: Gulf Publ., 1978.
Tannenbaum, Robert, and Schmidt, Warren. How to Choose a Leadership Pattern. *Harvard Business Review,* 36,2 (May–June 1973): 162.

Responsibilities of Management

Drucker, Peter F. *Management: Tasks, Responsibilities, Practices.* New York: Harper & Row, 1974.

Maccoby, Michael. *The Gamesman.* New York: Simon and Schuster, 1976.

Melcher, R. D. Roles and Relationships, Clarifying the Manager's Job. *Personnel* 44,3 (May–June, 1967): 33–41.

Pascale, Richard Tanner, and Athos, Anthony G. *The Art of Japanese Management.* New York: Simon and Schuster, 1981.

Peters, Thomas J., and Waterman, Robert H., Jr. *In Search of Excellence: Lessons from America's Best-Run Companies.* New York: Harper & Row, 1982.

11
Person-to-Person Communication

Have you ever played the parlor game where people stand in a circle and one person whispers a phrase to his or her neighbor, who whispers it to the next person, and so on around the circle? By the time it gets back to the originator, the phrase is unrecognizable! To a large degree, we hear what we want to hear. We block out disquieting information. Our brains tune in and out of a conversation. We interpolate what we think was said in between the parts we really heard. Usually we interpret correctly. Sometimes we don't.

Oral communication is the subject of this chapter. It is the lifeline of any organization. Without it, nothing happens. With good oral communication, what happens is what is wanted. With poor communication, what happens is anybody's guess. Improved communication will enhance the professional's own productivity and that of all the functions with which he or she interacts.

Oral communication is a two-way street. There is a speaker and there is a listener. The speaker gives an order or makes a statement. The listener hears the order or the statement. What the listener hears may or may not be what the speaker intended. The problem may be that the speaker was not clear. It also may be that the listener tuned in to a different message.

We need good oral communication. In a person-to-person situation this should always be possible. In this chapter we look at it from the points of view of both the speaker and the listener. We look at communication with your superior, with fellow workers, and with your supporting staff. We look at the special situation of communicating with a job applicant you may want to hire. But before we do this, we must discuss a subject that underlies all forms of communication—understanding.

UNDERSTANDING

Understanding means that what is said is what is heard, and, further, that the meaning of the message is clear. There are three parts to understanding:

1. A clear message is spoken.
2. The identical message is heard.
3. The message heard is interpreted correctly.

Problems can occur along any one of these three paths.

The Speaker

It is particularly important that the speaker be clear. If a listener fails to understand, only that one person will not get the message. But if the speaker fails to communicate, there is very little chance of the message's getting through to anyone.

The speaker knows what he or she wants to say. Most of us are pretty good about choosing the right words, keeping our grammar simple and correct, and following a logical pattern as we present our case, explain a situation, or give an order. Most people talk more clearly than they write. But there are danger signals, things that some speakers do that make understanding difficult if not impossible. The four most common faults of speakers are:

1. Using key words that the listener doesn't know, that have more than one meaning, or that are incorrect.
2. Using a sentence structure that is awkward and hard to follow.
3. Not using a logical progression of thought in moving from a problem statement to a conclusion.
4. Talking in a dull and monotonous way.

Words that are used infrequently will not be understood by many listeners (e.g., "procrastination" for delay, "reprehensible" for bad, "ambivalent" for uncertain). Words that are special jargon in one field will not be understood by those who are not professionals in that particular field. To people who were not in the army, the word "echelon" may mean nothing. If the speaker is describing an organization structure, the word "level" is more likely to be understood. Engineers use the phrase "critical mass" to suggest a minimum size that makes something work. Many people do not understand what "critical mass" means. Computer experts are particularly guilty of carrying jargon over to everyday conversation.

The use of substitute words and the use of abbreviations and initials also cause misunderstanding. The first time I heard the word "waste" substituted for "kill," I did not know what was meant. A "ginny mae" has meaning to investors in government securities, but probably to few others. Use of "AOP" or "P&L" is second nature to an accountant. Does everyone know that these initials stand for Annual Operating Plan and Profit and Loss?

Poor sentence structure can leave the listener trying to work through the grammar to find the subject, verb, and object of a statement. While pondering one sentence, the listener will not hear the next several sentences. People whose native language is not English often have this syntax problem. Leaving verbs to the end of a long sentence is particularly hard on Americans.

Words made negative by use of the prefix "in-" or "un-" should be avoided. The listener may not hear the "in" in "inappropriate" or "insincere," and may get the opposite impression. The use of "not" is better. "Blue jeans or shorts in the office are inappropriate attire" is more likely to be understood if phrased "Do not wear blue jeans or shorts to the office."

A speaker whose logic moves from *A* to *C* to *B* to *E* to *D* to *F*, and so on, leaves everyone behind. Example: "We have a problem with excessive employee tardiness. I can dock the pay of everyone who is late. This lost time is costing us money. Whatever I do it will come out of my pocket. The other idea is a free lunch for the person with the best attendance each month. We're going to try the lunch idea." Rather confusing—especially when the actual telling takes ten minutes. Rearrange these short sentences (which are written in *A, C, B, E, D, F* sequence) to a logical *A, B, C, D, E, F* sequence and see if the concept is more understandable.

As noted below, listeners tune out a good fraction of what is said. This fraction increases if the speaker is dull and monotonous.

The speaker can increase the proportion that is heard by:

1. Being more personal.
2. Putting life into his or her voice.
3. Using visual aids.
4. Changing the pace of the meeting.
5. Emphasizing and reemphasizing the key concepts.
6. Having the room cool and reasonably comfortable so that extraneous matters such as physical comfort don't distract the listener.

The Listener

The listener must hear the message that is spoken. This is not always easy, even when the speaker is absolutely clear. The main problems the listener has are:

1. Hearing the pleasant information and blocking out the part that is disquieting.
2. Interpolating between the segments that are not heard.

It takes considerable concentration to listen to all that is said.

If a speaker says something nice, our ears perk up. We hear that. If someone mentions our name, we hear that. If a speaker goes on for five minutes about the food he or she just ate, we quickly tune out. What does this mean? We listen to what we think is important, and we rest our brains—or think about something more important—while trivia is being discussed. Only 20% or so of what is said is heard and retained.

What can the listener do to hear more of what is said? In Table 11-1 we

Table 11-1. Listening Problems and Suggested Actions.[a]

HABIT	CAUSES	SUGGESTED ACTIONS
In-out	Most people think four times as fast as the average person speaks.	Write down whatever you were thinking that caused you to stop listening. This will enable you to recall what you were thinking at that time. Then get right back to listening.
Red flag	Some words, when we hear them, upset us and we stop thinking: for example, "layoffs," "behind schedule," "strike," etc.	Write the word down. Listen. Is the speaker using this word correctly or adding a new meaning?
Closed mind	We often think there is no reason to listen because we will hear nothing new.	Set an objective to listen to see if in fact the speaker is saying anything new. This will force you to listen.
Day dreaming	Frequently, we hear a word or idea that causes us to think of something else.	If you sense, before the meeting, that you have too many other ideas on your mind, don't go to the meeting. If you find your mind wandering during the meeting, note the thought and then concentrate on listening.
Too technical or complex	You may attend a meeting thinking the topic is too complex or technical for you to understand.	At the meeting, follow the discussion. Prepare before the meeting. Read articles or skim a book on the topic.
Mind guarding	You may not want your pet idea, prejudice, or point of view challenged. You stop listening, become defensive, and even plan a counterattack.	Listen! Find out what the speaker has to say. Get the other side of the question. This leads to better understanding and enables you to reply in a calm and reasonable manner.
Court reporter	You try to record everything said. However, the speaker speaks faster than you can write.	Jot down the key words. Later put them in an outline format.
Hubbub listening	Distractions are always present in a meeting.	Practice tuning out these distractions and concentrate on what the speaker is saying.

[a]From Newman, Pamela J., and Lynch, Alfred F., *Behind Closed Doors: A Guide to Successful Meetings*, Englewood Cliffs: Prentice-Hall, 1983, pp. 94–96.

present a checklist of common listening problems, their causes, and suggested corrective measures. In summary:

1. If the meeting is a lecture, take notes. Pretend that you have to write the minutes of the meeting and all the issues and points of view must be represented. This forces concentration.
2. If a word or a thought disturbs you or starts you thinking about something else, jot it down for later consideration. Go back to listening.
3. If the meeting is a discussion, become involved even if you are not vitally concerned. Pick out one or two active participants and decide that you will support or disagree with what they say. To do so, you will have to hear and understand them.

There will always be times when your attention wanders and you will have to guess at what was said in between the parts you heard. I remember vividly someone I once worked for who spoke at a very slow speed. I would hear the start of a thought, decide I knew where that idea was headed, tune out for a full minute while I worried about a problem I was working on, tune back in to hear where the message stood, and so on. There were a few times when the message was not what I thought it would be. These times were very embarrassing. This practice is not recommended. Try the note-taking trick or any other ideas that work for you.

The Interpreter

The listener must do more than hear the message; the listener must interpret it in the same way that the speaker meant it. Our interpretation of words depends on our individual backgrounds. In different cultures, the same words will have a different meaning. "Please drop by the next time you're in town" is not an invitation in some circles. In fact, the speaker would be quite upset if you did drop by. In other circles it is a sincere invitation. "Come to dinner at seven" will be interpreted as 7:00, 7:15, 7:30, 8:00, or even 8:30, depending on the culture you are in.

In a business situation, the command "Start this job now" will be interpreted by one person as: "Drop everything you are doing and start the new job this second." Another person will interpret it as: "At a sensible break point you reach in the next five minutes or so, put the present job aside and start the new job." The interpretation depends on the listener's conditioning from both parents and superiors. If the speaker means "drop everything" and the listener continues doing the old job for several minutes, the speaker may get quite angry. If the speaker means "within five minutes" but the listener stops immediately and therefore must start the present job all over again later, the speaker may also be unhappy. In each case, the listener hears exactly what the speaker says. The interpretations are different.

Involvement

If good communication is to happen, the listener must be motivated to understand; the listener must become involved in the subject being discussed. We discussed motivation at length in Chapter 10. The principles described there, particularly Maslow's concept of a hierarchy of needs, apply also to communication.

You must have a reason to listen. If you know that an order is about to be given that affects you, you listen for it. You know you'll be in trouble if you don't hear it. You become involved. If the speaker is explaining something you want to understand, you listen. You will learn something you are interested in. You are involved. A good speaker suggests motivations to the listener before launching into a presentation. The listener picks up the motivating words and tunes in.

There are not many motivators for listening. Nearly all are some variation on these three themes:

1. A command is to be given.
2. Information is to be presented on a subject you are interested in.
3. Rewards or compliments are being handed out.

COMMUNICATING WITH SUPERIORS

Communication with your manager is probably the most important of all your communication links. If it fails, you are in trouble. You are responsible to your manager for your performance on your job. There must be good communication on:

1. What your manager expects from you.
2. What you have actually done.

Expectations

It seems trite to write that you should know what your manager expects from you. You think you know. But do you really? Many people form an opinion about what their boss expects only to find out the hard way that they have misjudged the expectation.

Check expectations in the following areas by asking your manager these questions or by stating your understanding and asking for confirmation:

1. Output (if there is some measure of output to your job—number of drawings, number of analyses, number of orders written)
   (a) What measure does your manager consider as acceptable performance?
   (b) What measure does your manager consider as outstanding performance?
2. Quality
   (a) What degree of accuracy is desired?
   (b) How many errors are acceptable? ("None" is not an acceptable response; everyone makes some mistakes.)
   (c) How much slippage is acceptable, if any, in following procedures, follow-up, documenting your work, etc.?
3. Plans and objectives
   (a) What innovations are expected this year?
   (b) What objectives have you mutually set?
   (c) What schedule is agreed to for meeting each objective?
4. Responsibilities
   (a) Do you know your job description?
   (b) Is it current? Does your manager agree with it?
   (c) Where does your authority start and stop?
5. Reporting
   (a) What written reports does your manager want from you?
   (b) What format and level of detail are desired for each?
   (c) On what matters does your manager want oral reports?
   (d) On what subjects do you interrupt your manager, what subjects wait for the manager's convenience, and what subjects accumulate for a weekly or monthly meeting?

The issue of where your authority starts and stops is always tricky. What issues can you decide, and what issues does your manager want to handle? This is impossible to define in writing and difficult even to talk through. There are too many "it depends" situations. With time, you develop a feel for your authority limits. You make a decision and your manager steps in; you have found out that this issue lies on the manager's side of the boundary. You bring some issue to your manager's attention, and a tone of irritation, or lack of interest, tells you that you should have handled the subject.

Do not expect complete consistency from your manager even if you have a good understanding on all the above issues. Sometimes you will find your manager involved in seemingly trivial situations. Perhaps someone at a higher level of management has shown an interest in the subject and so your manager has decided that he or she should become personally involved. It may also be simple curiosity, the desire to learn firsthand how something is done. If you don't understand why your manager did or did not become involved in a decision, ask.

Accomplishments

Most people are quite good at blowing their own horns and telling their managers when they have done something well. They are usually not so good at speaking up when they have failed. Knowledge of your failures is just as important to the manager as knowledge of your successes. Failure to inform your boss of a problem is the worse sin you can commit.

Check the following:

1. Accomplishments
   (a) Does your manager know your exact progress on the job you are doing?
   (b) How often do you give your manager an update? Is this the frequency you agreed to?
   (c) Are you as honest about failures as about successes?
   (d) Do you both agree on what your significant accomplishments have been over the past year?
2. Schedule
   (a) Do you both agree on which jobs or events were completed on or ahead of schedule, or are progressing on or ahead of schedule?
   (b) Do you both agree on which jobs or events were finished behind schedule or are running behind schedule now?
   (c) Do you review schedule recovery plans with your manager before taking action?
3. Costs
   (a) Do you tell your manager of potential budget overruns as you discover them?
   (b) Do you both agree on the cost projections?
   (c) Do you review cost reduction plans with your manager before implementing them?
4. Performance
   (a) Do you inform your manager of problems in meeting specifications or meeting objectives as soon as they arise?
   (b) Do you review your suggested solutions with your manager before putting them into effect?

If your responses to all the above questions are positive, you have no communication problem with your manager. But in order to be sure, ask your manager if he or she agrees. You may think you are doing everything right, but the person who counts most may not agree. In summary, remember the maxim: *Never let your boss be surprised!*

COMMUNICATING WITH COLLEAGUES

This is the most relaxed of the communications channels. There is no implication of giving or receiving orders. This is equals talking to equals. Work-related, nonsocial interaction with fellow workers nearly always involves giving or receiving information. This is generally the easiest form of communication.

We define colleagues as fellow professionals who are working on the same task and who are in the same profession or a closely allied field. Colleagues are members of a work team getting a project done.

With professional colleagues there is a shared interest, as well as a shared vocabulary and jargon that aid communication and help to knit a group together. Within a colleague group, the involvement that must underlie good communications is strong.

If you are giving information to a colleague (i.e., you are the speaker), you are the expert on the particular point being discussed. You want the other person to understand and agree with you so that you retain and enhance your position as the expert. You are strongly motivated to achieve understanding.

If you need information to continue doing your job (i.e., you are the listener), you are motivated to hear and understand the speaker. Your success depends on it. People in the same professional field have few communications problems with vocabulary or technical concepts. The conditions for communicating effectively are all present.

There is one barrier, however—professional jealousy. We all know people who want to hog the spotlight, or who believe that they can do everything themselves and do not want to share. This is a personality problem. As long as it exists, there will be poor communication, if any at all. The group manager can order an uncooperative professional to impart or accept information, but if done reluctantly, the communication is likely to be poor. The good manager must find a way to motivate the uncooperative person to change his or her attitude. Motivational techniques were discussed in Chapter 10.

COMMUNICATING WITH THE ADMINISTRATIVE STAFF

There is another category of professionals with whom you communicate. They staff the support groups in the administrative functions. If you are a professional in one of the primary departments, you spend several hours a week with administrative specialists. If you are one of the administrative staff yourself, you use specialists in the other administrative groups for support; this section still applies to you.

You and the administrative professional are not colleagues as defined in the previous section. You are in different professions. You don't share the involvement of working together on a task, the involvement that makes colleague-to-colleague communication simpler. Communication with the administrative functions involves one person who needs something, the requester, and another person who must provide it, the performer. This is different from giving and receiving an order and different from giving and receiving information.

The need must be communicated by the requester and understood by the performer. There are three aspects to the need:

1. What is needed.
2. When is it needed.
3. How much it can cost.

Much of this information should be shown on forms. For simple requests, the form alone communicates these three elements. Nothing more is needed. But there are complex requests where an oral explanation is helpful. There are also times when a requester is unsure of exactly what is required and needs to talk to the administrative professional to help define the need. Unusual or difficult purchase requests, maintenance requests, word processing requests, duplicating requests, and so on, are handled more smoothly if an understanding is reached on "what," "when," and "how much."

Administrative support personnel want to be helpful. That is their professional role. But they also want to optimize their own efficiency. We noted in Chapter 6 that this can lead to suboptimization of the administrative functions. The time and effort of those who perform the support work is optimized rather than the time and effort of the requesters. Good communication helps to eliminate suboptimization. It shows the performers the importance of a request and how the request fits into the requester's job. It makes the performers feel that they are a part of the work team rather than outsiders. It results in faster and better support.

The performer who receives a request form has only the information shown on that form. The performer does not know how the request ties into your work or how you plan to use the result of the request. He or she cannot infer information that is not on the form. Do not assume that information not required on a form is too obvious to be worth adding to it or calling the performer to explain. What is obvious to you may not be obvious to someone who does not know what you are doing. Everyone in engineering may know that there is one critical tolerance in a certain specification. But purchasing or facilities people will not know this unless the requester remembers to tell them.

What Is Needed?

If the requester needs help in defining the need or is not aware of what materials or services are available, he or she should call the appropriate support department and talk to the person who will do the job or to that person's supervisor. If the requester wants to be part of a negotiation because the specification of a part or the definition of a service is critical, this should be told to the person who will negotiate. If the requester wants to review or inspect what is going on at certain times in the process, this needs to be said. If the request form does not show some information the performer should know, a note should be added calling for a meeting with the performer before action is taken.

It is very helpful if the performer understands the use to be made of the material or service requested. Then there are two of you checking to be sure the instructions are complete and correct.

The communication between requester and performer must reach an understanding on:

1. The complete specification of the item required or the service to be performed.
2. The use to which the item will be put.
3. The times or procedure steps at which a review or an inspection will be made by the requester.

When Is It Needed?

There are two parts to scheduling a request. The first involves the processing time within the administrative group. The second is the time given a vendor who supplies a requested material or service. We discuss the internal processing first.

All requesters want their needs handled immediately or as soon as possible. Requesters should know that most administrators put ASAP (as soon as possible) requests at the bottom of the pile. They do this because they see so many ASAP's and because they feel that the request cannot be critical if no specific date and time are stated. ASAP items are handled in normal sequence or, perhaps, last.

There are usually standard processing times for support activities. We discussed turnaround times in the word processing section of Chapter 8. Turnaround times are used by most other administrative functions as well, though they may not always be published. The heads of purchasing, facilities, reproduction, and so on, will usually tell you what their standard processing times are. If you cannot predict your needs far enough ahead to live with these times, you must request priority treatment.

Priority treatment disrupts the support group's normal routine. It is more expensive to process a priority request than a normal request, and so the organization does not want too many priority requests. To get priority status, you may have to convince the supervisor of the administrative group, or perhaps your own manager, or both.

Oral communication is necessary if priority treatment is requested. In this case, an understanding should be reached on:

1. The importance of the request.
2. The reason for the date and time needed.
3. Why the request could not have been initiated earlier.

If the requester communicates this, the full cooperation of the performer will follow.

The time allowed a vendor is a matter of negotiation. The vendor will quote a delivery time and cost based on his current work load. Faster delivery can usually be negotiated but at an increase in price because it disrupts the vendor's schedule or requires overtime. Another vendor may be used who quotes a higher cost but promises faster delivery. Cost and schedule are usually intertwined. A purchasing buyer will normally accept the lowest cost that meets the specification and has a reasonable delivery.

If a certain delivery date is critical, rather than "It would be nice to have it by . . . ," the buyer must be told this. For later audit, the purchasing file must show why a higher bid was accepted. The buyer must understand your need, and you must understand the extra price you are paying. The communication must cover:

1. What the critical date is.
2. Why it is critical.
3. Any change to the required date that occurs as it approaches.
4. The price of meeting this date and, if necessary, approvals to spend the extra money.

How Much Can It Cost?

Not every request has an upper limit on cost. But when one exists, the performer must know what it is. The request form may have a space for "estimated cost." Requesters usually make a guess and enter an approximate number in this space. Only if the real cost will be significantly different does the performer call the requester and ask if he or she wants to go through with the order. If the cost figure entered is a true upper limit rather than an estimate, and the requester will alter the specifications rather than exceed this limit, the performer must be told this.

Communications relative to costs should cover:

1. How much the requester expects to pay.
2. Whether this figure is an estimate or an upper limit.
3. How large a deviation is permitted before the performer must notify the requester.

Feedback

Communication, of course, goes both ways. The performer should:

1. Always notify the requester when the requested job is expected to be completed, unless a published standard turnaround time exists that defines the completion time.

The requester should also be notified if any of the following circumstances exists:

2. Any part of the specified instruction cannot be fulfilled.
3. The delivery time expected is different from that requested or has changed since a prior notification.
4. The cost as quoted or estimated is significantly different from the requester's estimate.
5. There are additional requirements or costs that the requester may not have considered.

If communication takes place on all the subjects noted for each transaction between a professional and the administrative support groups, there will be no surprises. Effective communication will have occurred.

COMMUNICATING WITH SUBORDINATES

This is still another aspect of communication. In this situation you can give orders. By now you realize that this does not necessarily mean that the orders are understood.

Expectations and Accomplishments

All the points made in the earlier discussion of communicating with your manager apply in reverse to communicating with your subordinate. Every question in that section can be rephrased by placing yourself in the position of the manager and seeing if you and your subordinate understand each part of your expectations and the subordinate's accomplishments. We will not repeat the list here. We remind the reader that communication is a two-way street, and both parties are responsible for its success. Hence professional-to-manager communication also means manager-to-professional (or subordinate).

There are two additional forms of communication initiated by the manager, supervisor, or leader.

Discipline

Nobody likes to discipline another person, but there are times when it must be done. Communication in a disciplinary situation is extremely important and also difficult. This is an emotionally charged situation. Discipline done well can be a positive motivator. If done poorly, it leaves a bad taste that will take a long time to eradicate.

When a situation calls for disciplinary action, the worst thing of all is to ignore it. The sooner it is faced, the easier it is to handle. All organizations have rules. Many are for the well-being or safety of the staff. Others assure that company policies and procedures are followed, or that legal requirements are carried out. Rules must be enforced equitably. All personnel must be treated alike. Therefore, if someone breaks a rule, there must be discipline.

Discipline usually starts with a verbal warning, unless the act was so flagrant as to endanger life or property. Being habitually late to work calls for a warning. Ignoring this situation would be unfair to the conscientious people who start work promptly. The initial warning may be a mild hint: "The workday starts at 8 A.M., George." If the hint is not taken, the next step is more formal.

The formal warning is a threat to invoke a penalty if the behavior is repeated: "If you are late one more time this month, George, I will dock you half a day's pay." The employee relations department must be consulted in advance of a formal warning and must agree to the threatened penalty. It is their job to assure that all employees are treated alike throughout the organization. You should not be more lenient or more strict than other managers.

There are three important things to remember about warnings:

1. Never discipline someone in public.
2. If you promise to impose a penalty if the offense is repeated, always follow through.
3. Document all warnings and actions.

If you are going to give a warning, call the person into your office and close the door. Be calm, be direct, and make your point without any preliminary conversation. Don't dilute the point by discussing anything else or allowing George to bring up anything else. Other matters can be discussed at other times. If there is a history of poor behavior, put it all on the table. Be sure your subordinate understands why he or she is being disciplined. Be sure, also, that the action to be taken if the subordinate ignores the warning is specific and clear. A general statement such as, "If you do this again, I'll have to take action," is meaningless. It is also unfair because the person is given no concept of the consequence. Spell out the penalty.

A warning is a promise to take action. Always follow through. If George is late again that week, invoke the penalty you promised unless there is an over-riding excuse: "But, boss, my mother died this morning." OK. If you think George is lying, you can do some discreet follow-up later.

All disciplinary conversations must be documented in writing. This is done with a memo to the individual and a copy to the employee relations department. Notes you write to yourself and place in a private folder are not appropriate. If there is a question later as to whether the warning was given, the note in your drawer is not good evidence. If the employee and the employee relations department both have copies, there is no question that the warning was authentic.

Performance Reviews

Another form of communication unique to the manager and subordinate relationship is the annual or semiannual performance review.

One purpose of these reviews is to help establish the size of the next salary raise. Salary is, or should be, based on performance. Another purpose is to inform the employee how you, the manager, see that person's performance. An annual performance review should not be the only feedback the employee gets on how he or she is doing. Praise and criticism should be almost a daily affair as jobs progress. But it is useful to step back occasionally and take a longer-range look at the person's performance over time.

Appraisal Forms.   Many organizations use forms for performance rating. These measure such attributes as:

- Judgment
- Knowledge
- Creativity (originality)
- Quantity (productivity)
- Communication (expression, quality of presentation)
- Initiative
- Interaction (interpersonal; effectiveness with people, working with others)
- Dependability

One or more attributes concerning leadership are often added to identify those who have managerial potential. The form usually has a line on which to judge overall performance and a section for comments.

On the performance review form the supervisor or manager rates the employee's performance against each attribute. A five-segment scale is typical:

- Superior
- Exceeds expectations
- Meets expectations

- Needs improvement
- Unsatisfactory

The rater should be able to indicate "insufficient opportunity" if the employee has not had a chance to demonstrate a particular attribute, or if the rater does not know the employee's performance in the particular area well enough to give a valid rating.

Use of the appraisal form can enhance communication, but it also can kill it. It depends on how you, the manager, handle the situation. You do not hand the employee the form you have filled out and say, in effect, "This is what I think of you." You use it as a summary of an appraisal interview you hold with the employee. Equally important, you use it to prepare for the interview, to assure that you consider all the attributes of the job and not just recent events. Think of examples that illustrate good or poor performance on each attribute. Make notes of them.

The appraisal form covers past history. You are also interested in the future.

1. What are the person's ambitions?
2. How do the person's ability and potential fit your future staffing needs?
3. Is there a prospective need that the person should start to prepare for now?
4. What task assignments or special training will prepare the person?

List these points so that they will be discussed in the appraisal interview.

Appraisal Interview. The performance appraisal interview is a dialogue between you and the employee. It is as important for you to know how the employee rates his or her strengths and weaknesses as it is for the employee to know your judgment. This interview should cover at least the following points:

1. Areas of strength.
2. Areas of weakness.
3. Plans for training or other actions to overcome the weaknesses.
4. Goals for the next six months or year.
5. Problems.
6. Ambitions.
7. Actions planned to help achieve the ambitions.

Give the employee at least a week's notice before the interview so that he or she can be ready. Show the employee a blank appraisal form, and explain how you fill it out and what happens to it. State that the two of you will talk about the completed form and about performance and goals in general. Say that you want to hear the employee's self-evaluation and opinions.

When it is time for the discussion, treat it like any other interview.

1. Clear your calendar for an hour and do not allow interruptions. If an hour is not enough time, the interview should be done in two parts. This is an emotionally draining time for the employee; one hour at a time is enough.
2. Put the employee at ease. Smile. This interview is a positive action even if some of the discussion will be negative. Together you will decide on steps to enhance use of the employee's best abilities and to improve those that are poor.
3. Start with a compliment on some task well done. Ask what recent tasks the employee is particularly proud of. This leads naturally into a discussion of strengths. Reach agreement on what you both see as strengths.
4. Ask what tasks have been giving difficulty. This leads naturally into a discussion of weaknesses. When discussing weakness, ask what help you can provide: additional training? more experience on certain applications? a course on some subject?
5. Ask about near-term and far-term ambitions. If these ambitions seem realistic, explore how job assignments, formal education, and training can help prepare the employee. Agree to a personal development plan.
6. Mutually set goals for the next period of six months or a year. These should be specific events, not generalities; for example, to complete project X, or to learn a certain skill.

As you go through each of these subjects, get the employee's opinion before you state your own. If you start to discuss each subject with a dogmatic judgment, you will never find out what the employee sees as strengths and weaknesses and what ambitions the person has. Be sure, however, that you do make your judgments clear before the interview is over. Your subordinate deserves to know exactly what you think.

If you find that you and the employee disagree on what is a strength or a weakness, or on what was a good job and what a mediocre one, discuss it until you find the cause of the disagreement. There is probably a misunderstanding about your expectations for the person. Occasionally your evaluation may be wrong. If this happens, admit the error and correct it.

Close the performance interview with a mutual agreement on goals for the next period and training or other actions to correct the weaknesses. No matter what the evaluation, this closes the interview on a positive note.

INTERVIEWING THE JOB APPLICANT

The interview with a job applicant is one of the most important forms of communication that a manager or project leader participates in. The performance of your group depends on how well you pick your staff. Few people come naturally to interviewing. It is a learned ability and requires practice.

Job Attributes

Applicant interviews require considerable preparation. First, what are the attributes of the job you are hiring for? They should be described in terms of:

1. Knowledge (what fields, subjects, specialties)
2. Experience (how many years, at what level, in what type of organization)
3. Skills (specific to equipment or to a craft)
4. Attitude (maturity, team spirit, cooperation)
5. Leadership (planning, organizing)

Be very specific. If you need someone with experience doing a certain type of calculation, list that type. If you have a certain model of computer and need someone with experience using it, name the model. Describe each attribute in such a way that its presence or absence can be measured. For example, "ability to write reports" is not a measurable characteristic. However, "two years experience as editor or lead writer for project reports and publications" is an attribute you can check "yes" or "no." Make a list of the attributes required for the job.

Next rate these attributes for their relative importance. First mark those that are mandatory. If the job applicant lacks one of these, that person is out of the running regardless or how well he or she measures up on the other attributes. There should not be too many mandatory attributes. Next, mark those that are important but are just short of being mandatory. Finally mark those that are desirable, but not essential. Rework your list so that the mandatory attributes are at the top, the important ones next, and the desirable ones last. This listing of job attributes should be done before you start to look for job candidates. It may be used by the employee relations interviewers as a way of screening job application forms. You will also use it later to compare the qualifications of job candidates.

Questions

Next, prepare a series of open-ended questions that give you information about each of the job attributes. An open-ended question is one that cannot be answered "yes" or "no."

Questions about knowledge, experience, and skills are relatively easy to prepare. The question, "What experience and knowledge have prepared you for the position we are offering?" demands specific data from which you can judge the adequacy of these attributes.

Attitudes can be judged by such questions as:

- "Which of your jobs did you like best? Why?"
- "Which of your jobs did you like least? Why?"
- "What are your hobbies?"
- "What are your short-term goals? long-term goals?"

The Interview

When you meet the applicant, put him or her at ease.

1. Introduce yourself.
2. Find some common ground for a minute or two of small talk.
3. Offer a cup of coffee or a soft drink.
4. Take notes, but first ask the applicant if this is all right. The request will help to calm the applicant's nervousness.
5. Start with a couple of general questions that you know will start the applicant talking, such as, "Tell me about your present (last) job."
6. Slowly work in the other questions. It is best if the questions are not asked as abruptly as written above but allowed to flow smoothly into the conversation.
7. Don't make every question a critical one. This is tiring for the applicant and keeps you very busy writing.
8. Listen more than you talk. The listen–talk ratio should be about three or four to one. One way to tell whether you are a good interviewer is to measure how much time you spend talking rather than listening.

Many inexperienced interviewers start an applicant interview by describing the job to be filled and the group and the company. They usually speak with a lot of enthusiasm. This approach is wrong. You should describe the job and your organization only after you have the information you want on the applicant. There are two reasons for this:

1. You may be so enthusiastic and talk so long that there is not enough time left to learn about the applicant.
2. If the applicant is unsuitable, it is a waste of your time and unfair to the applicant to "sell" the applicant on the position.

If you decide that the person across the desk may be a good addition to your staff, however, pull out all the stops in selling the advantages of working in your company and your group.

Selection

After each interview, summarize your judgments using the list of job attributes. Prepare a form with the attributes in the left column and add a series of columns, one for each candidate. For each person, put a ''plus,'' ''zero,'' or ''minus'' oposite your rating of each attribute for that person. A double-plus or double-minus can be used to show outstanding ability or lack of it. When you have completed all the interviews, this form becomes the summary of your evaluations. Eliminate everyone with a minus on any mandatory attribute. Of those left, look for the most plus marks on mandatory and important attributes. That person is your best candidate.

SUMMARY

Oral communication is the lifeline of any organization. It involves a speaker and a listener. Understanding requires that the speaker's message be clear, that the listener hear the message, and that the listener interpret it in the way the speaker meant it. Confusion can occur at any of these three stages.

Common faults of speakers are using words the listener does not know, that have more than one meaning, and that cover up or substitute for the right word. Among other faults are using a sentence structure that is hard to follow, using an illogical progression of thought, and speaking in a dull, monotonous way.

The listener blocks communication by hearing only pleasant information and blocking out the disquieting messages. The listener listens only a fraction of the time and interpolates between the sections that are heard. A few tricks to improve concentration are suggested in this chapter. Besides hearing the message, the listener interprets it. Whether this interpretation is the same as the speaker's meaning may depend on the listener's previous conditioning and the culture in which he or she was raised.

Communication problems with a superior often involve expectations and accomplishments. There can be misunderstanding on what the manager considers acceptable and superior performance, about current plans, about responsibilities and authority, and on the type, content, and frequency of reporting.

Communication with colleagues generally involves giving or receiving information that pertains to your present work. You are aided by a common jargon and a strong motivation to understand. The primary barrier is professional jealousy.

Communication with the administrative staff involves someone requesting a service and someone performing that service. There must be understanding on what is needed, when it is needed, and how much it can cost.

Communicating with subordinates carries the same problems as communicating with superiors, this time as seen from the other side. Two additional forms of communication are unique—disciplinary action and performance reviews. A formal disciplinary warning is a threat to invoke a penalty if an undesired act is repeated. The warning must be documented, and if the act is repeated, the penalty must be carried through. Performance reviews rate job attributes as superior, exceeding expectations, meeting expectations, needing improvement, or unsatisfactory. The manager also wants to know the employee's ambitions and their fit to future work plans. The appraisal interview covers areas of strength, weaknesses, training plans, goals, problems, ambitions, and actions to help achieve the ambitions.

Before interviewing a job applicant, the manager prepares a list of job attributes, rating each as mandatory, important, or desirable. Open-ended questions are prepared and asked that give information on each applicant's ability on each attribute. For each, the applicant is rated as plus, zero, or minus. A minus on a mandatory attribute eliminates an applicant. A comparison of pluses on mandatory and important attributes shows the best candidate.

FOR FURTHER INFORMATION

Understanding

Bonner, William H. *Communicating Clearly: The Effective Message.* Chicago: Science Research Assoc., 1980.

Oral Communication

Linver, Sandy. *Speak and Get Results.* New York: Summit Books, Simon & Schuster, 1983.
Morris, John O. *Make Yourself Clear.* New York: McGraw-Hill, 1982.

Performance Appraisal

Johnson, Robert G. *The Appraisal Interview Guide.* New York: AMACOM, 1979.

Interviewing

Fear, Richard A. *The Evaluation Interview,* 2nd ed. New York: McGraw-Hill, 1978.
Stanton, Erwin S. *Successful Personnel Recruiting and Selection.* New York: AMACOM, 1977.

Written Communication

Easton, Thomas A. *How to Write a Readable Business Report.* Homewood, IL: Dow Jones-Irwin, 1983.
Ewing, David W. *Writing For Results,* 2nd ed. New York: John Wiley & Sons, 1979.
Gallagher, William J. *Writing the Business and Technical Report.* Boston: CBI Publishing Inc., 1981.

12
Selling a Change

"That's a good idea, but management will never buy it." Has your manager ever said this about an idea that you were sure would solve some inefficiency in your organization? It is true that sometimes top management won't buy an idea that will benefit the organization, and a department head won't buy an idea that will benefit a department's operation. Like everyone else, they must be sold on the benefits of a new concept, and on changing their present habits. Is it true that management will "never buy" the new idea? Or do you just need to know the right selling technique?

In the preceding eight chapters we discussed elements that will improve an organization's operation and your own personal productivity. If the changes you want to implement affect the office operations, they must be sold to management. In this chapter we describe how to sell a change.

INFORM AND EDUCATE

The first barrier to overcome is:

- Not knowing there is a problem.

Even when the existence of a problem is known, it may be tolerated because no one knows there is a way to solve it. Thus there is a second, related barrier:

- Not knowing there is a solution.

Overcoming these barriers requires informing and educating the appropriate levels of management.

Presenting the Problem

We described planning for change in Chapter 3. We stated there that you, the reader, will be in one of three situations:

1. You are in charge of a group or function in which you want to make a change.

2. You are a member of a task force or advisory group looking at a function that is a candidate for change.
3. You are an individual with ideas of what needs to be done, but without official sanction to investigate or initiate change.

If a task force or advisory group exists, the existence of a problem has been recognized. If you are in charge of a group or function and are willing to say that you see a problem within your function, that statement alone carries a lot of weight and will overcome the first barrier. Who should know better than the person in charge? Only if you are without official sanction do you need to convince management that a problem exists.

Until you can make the study suggested in Chapter 3, acceptance of your statement that a problem exists must rest to a large extent on your reputation, your expertise, and the record of your previous judgments. If you can gather and present a few supporting facts, this will bolster your case. Try to determine through the literature or through colleagues:

1. That other companies have identified and are working on the same problem.
2. That the performance or the procedures of other organizations are better than yours.
3. That cost standards in general use are lower than yours.

The most convincing argument you can present to management is that other companies have the same problem or that other companies do the function more effectively and at less cost.

Showing That Solutions Exist

If management agrees there is a problem but seems willing to tolerate it, your need is to convince them that the problem can be solved, that there are better ways to do the job.

Once again, the best argument is the experience of other companies, preferably other companies of about the same size and in the same line of business. The experience of a bank will not influence the executive of a consumer products manufacturing company. The experience of a manufacturing plant will not influence the executives of a retail store. But within the same field, examples of what another company has done to solve the problem will influence your management.

Sources for these examples are business periodicals—such as *Fortune, Business Week,* and the *Wall Street Journal*—trade publications, and the daily newspaper. Reports by the National Industrial Conference Board or by industry-wide associations are also excellent. The reports and findings of professional societies will not be accepted quite as readily as these sources, but are

better than no supporting information. When you see an article, clip it, duplicate it, and send a copy to each of the key decision makers.

The author worked for a while for a company whose heads did not believe
in adopting office automation techniques until they were in common use. Manual office systems were tolerated that could be significantly improved by using
some of the techniques described in Chapter 7. My strategy to make management aware of these techniques was to clip everything I read on office automation that involved a company in our particular line of business. I circulated
these clippings to the key decision makers with an ''I think you'll find this interesting'' cover slip. There was no hard sell, for I thought that would defeat
the purpose. The executives had to convince themselves that these office automation techniques were real and were being used by our competition. Slowly,
a ''that's not for us'' attitude changed to a ''let's look into it'' approach, and
after about a year, an office automation task force was established.

The key ingredients of a campaign to inform and educate are:

1. Find written descriptions of successful solutions or current approaches to
   the problem you have identified from companies:
   (a) In your own line of business.
   (b) Of about the same size as your company.
   (c) That are known and respected by your decision makers.
2. Clip the descriptions and send them to the decision makers with a ''for
   your information'' or ''I think you'll find this interesting'' note. No hard
   sell is necessary.
3. Repeat your message at every opportunity.

THE KEY DECISION MAKERS

In Chapter 3 we suggested the following approaches to convince management
that a problem exists or to sell your solution to it:

1. In companies that have tight control, work through line management,
   starting with your own manager.
2. In companies that go ''by the book,'' start with your manager but also
   convince the specialist in the systems and procedures group.
3. In companies open to suggestions, use quality circles and informal discussions as well as working through your manager.
4. In authoritarian companies, find out who makes the decisions and who is
   close to that person. Work through a member of the ''in group.''
5. In companies with a true open door policy, walk through that door.

Who, specifically, are the key decision makers you need to influence? They
are not always the people you would expect from looking at the organization
chart. This chart, however, is the place to start.

Since our subject is office systems, the vice-president of administration, or the person with a title equivalent to that, is the individual in charge of most office operations. The controller, if this is a separate position, will influence those parts of the office function that involve accounting and finance. If data processing reports to the financial function, the controller will be involved in any changes that affect the role of data processing or the use of computers. The president is the final authority on all matters, but it will be unusual for a president to become involved in matters of administrative procedure and policy except in very tightly controlled or very authoritarian organizations.

However, others holding line or staff positions may be the key people. A staff assistant to a vice-president or controller may be the power behind the throne. This is especially likely if the vice-president is involved in many activities and delegates the procedural details to his or her staff. The decisions are made and the directives are issued by the executive, but the executive follows the advice of the staff most of the time. It is the staff assistant you need to reach and convince.

If the organization has a systems and procedures group, the executives may look to its manager for advice and accept this advice on almost all occasions. This manager, and perhaps one or more specialists on the systems and procedures staff, are those you must reach. If the subject involves office systems automation, the data processing manager or a specialist on that staff may be one of the key people. Computers have baffled many executives, and some executives have abdicated their authority in favor of the data processing experts.

Determine:

1. Under whose authority a change will be made.
2. Who influences that individual.

Reach and convince the latter person or persons.

WHAT IS IMPORTANT TO MANAGEMENT

The Decision Criteria

To sell the concept of investigating a problem or to sell a solution to the problem, learn first what is the single most important criterion on which a decision will be based? Find out if it is:

1. Return on investment
2. Reducing overhead costs
3. Reducing administrative personnel
4. Image
5. Speed of operation

6. Accuracy of an operation
7. Flexibility of an operation
8. Something else

Theory suggests that management decisions are based on maximizing an organization's *return on investment* (ROI). Reality says otherwise. ROI is one very important consideration, but other factors include executive job security, short-term profit, aversion to taking risks, and fear of the reaction of stockholders and security analysts. All of these are interrelated and tend to make for short-range and conservative decisions.

Image is important. One executive may like to be a pioneer and to be written up in the business press for such leadership. This person will embrace change if a reasonable argument can be made that it improves effectiveness. Another executive prefers the conservative image. This person watches the successes and failures of the pioneer and enters a market (or adopts a new technique) only when it has been proved practical.

Speed of operation refers both to the speed with which decisions are made and to how fast a response can be provided by the office support operations. Speed is important to those executives who put a high value on time that is lost or ineffectively used while the productive staff wait for support to occur. It is less important to executives who see the extra cost of faster support and do not value the intangible loss of time.

Accuracy is always important, but almost all organizations have reached a state where they are satisfied with the present degree of accuracy (error rate) in handling orders, shipments, invoices, and so on, as well as being satisfied with their accuracy rate in making decisions. Improved accuracy costs money to implement. The savings that will accrue through less follow-up, less rework, and better decisions are guestimates. If an organization is currently considered successful, executives will be reluctant to raise costs in the hope that more accuracy will lead to greater success and profit.

Flexibility refers to having people and equipment that can adjust readily to new situations. Most production lines are inflexible. Their machines are designed for maximum efficiency in performing one process. When that process is no longer required, the machines are useless. Multi-function tooling is starting to appear, in which software programs control the function of the machine. When one production run is completed, a software change makes the equipment usable for the next run. Such equipment costs more initially, but has a much longer useful life. Some executives will opt for the long-range view. Others will look to this year's profit statement.

The *something else* category is added because it is not safe to think you know all possible reasons that may favor or oppose a change. I worked with one executive whose primary interest in office automation was to have a calendar management program on a terminal in his office. Any system that the organization could consider had to do that function. The emotional issue of executive job security—the don't-rock-the-boat syndrome—is also a real consideration one must face. It can be overcome, but a lot of analysis and solid documentation that proves savings are required.

One illogical reason for not making an improvement needs to be stressed. The *appearance* of inefficiency, even when it is false, influences some executives. Increasing the number of paraprofessionals will improve the professional's and manager's productivity. But it will also increase the ratio of support to production personnel, which is a ratio sometimes used to measure administrative efficiency. Some executives will not increase this ratio or allow an overhead rate to rise no matter how much more productive or effective an operation will become. The appearance looks bad to an auditor or analyst not familiar with all the facts. The safe decision is to hold the ratios within accepted limits and to hold or reduce the overhead rates.

Determining Importance

How do you determine which of the criteria are the key issues to the decision makers?

This is one time when asking a direct question is not the right approach. If you do this, you will get the "correct" answer, probably one of the first three on our decision criteria list. This may not be the real answer. In this case, actions speak louder than words. The real answer is determined from the prior actions of the decision makers, not from their speeches or writings.

Employees who have worked for an executive for a year or more can predict that superior's actions with considerable accuracy. They have seen many decisions made and know the circumstances surrounding these decisions. They know how the boss thinks, what influences him or her, and what values are important. The old-timers in the organization can tell which of the eight criteria we listed will dominate an executive's thinking. If you are not among the old-timers, ask some colleagues who are. Ask people who have had direct dealings with the decision makers you want to influence. If you ask several, you may be surprised how close the agreement is among them.

COST BENEFIT ANALYSIS

If your presentation is to initiate a study of change, you should have data that show what benefits can accrue and a rough idea of what the change may cost. These may be actual data from another company, estimates from the business literature, or estimates you make based on your own knowledge and that of the colleagues with whom you have discussed the situation.

If you are selling a specific solution to a problem, you need a more exact cost benefit analysis. We discussed cost justification in Chapter 3. That is the "cost" part of cost benefit. The "benefit" side is a listing of the advantages that accrue to the organization if your solution is adopted.

The easiest benefit to sell is:

1. A cost savings

If your solution results in a cost savings, you are three-quarters of the way around the bases. Frequently, however, the benefit is not a cost savings but is:

2. Faster operation
3. Improved accuracy
4. Improved professional productivity
5. Improved decision making

The last benefit listed is the least tangible and probably the most important.

The second through fifth benefits listed may cost money in terms of additional people or automated equipment. How do you show that the benefits outweigh the costs?

List all the benefits that will result from the proposed change. They will probably fall in more than one of the categories noted above. If there are savings of time, price these savings in terms of the salary and fringe benefit costs saved. Speeding up an operation saves time. An improvement in accuracy saves time by reducing rework and follow-up. An improvement in productivity saves time.

The dollar value of time saved is called *soft dollar* savings. The organization has not reduced its costs. The salaries of the people involved are still being paid. Instead, these people are now doing other work that could not be done before because of lack of time. It is this new work that is the real benefit. Show both the soft dollar savings and the activities that will be done with the time saved.

Soft dollar savings can be translated to *hard dollar* savings by reducing staff through attrition (not replacing those who leave) or by termination. Hard dollars are real cost savings. But staff reduction must occur in units of whole people; you cannot reduce 500 work hours a year. Unless the time savings are close to the 2000 hours that represent a work year (or some multiple of 2000), the benefit of time saved must be in terms of alternate work to be performed in the saved hours. If you cannot suggest important alternate work, there is no benefit.

Another form of benefit is *cost avoidance*. In this case, costs that are now incurred or are budgeted for the future can be avoided because of the suggested improvement. In this category are:

1. Overtime
2. Temporary help
3. Planned staff increases

These are hard dollar benefits.

A cost benefit analysis should be done even when the decision maker's most important criterion is not a reduction of costs or return on investment. Whatever the real basis for a decision, the executive will want a cost benefit analysis to support the decision that is made.

THE PRESENTATION

Most decisions are sold in oral presentations, either in informal conversations or in formal meetings. A written presentation is often required, and is important to document what you say, but the written presentation is rarely the means by which a concept is sold.

Individual Conversations

These are the best means to get your point across. You are face to face with a key decision maker. You can watch his or her expressions and body language for clues to which points are being accepted and which are not, what is understood and what causes puzzlement. You can counter the arguments that the decision maker presents. You can tailor the presentation as you go along. If you have done your homework, you know the decision criteria important to the person you are talking to. Appeal to them. The greatest advantage of a series of face-to-face conversations is that you can make a different appeal to each person.

The following are the key ways to make a persuasive presentation. They fit both individual conversations and formal meetings.

1. Appeal to the decision maker's interests. At the start, bring up the executive's specific concern that your concept will resolve, and say that the concept will solve this concern.
2. State the specific problem and, if necessary, facts to support its importance.
3. Present the conclusion next. Show *what* change you are suggesting, or *how* you propose to resolve the problem.
4. List the benefits to the individual you are addressing and to the organization as a whole.
5. Show the costs and the problems you anticipate.
6. Counter any arguments you expect before they are raised.

7. At the end, summarize the proposed action, and request approval to proceed.

Formal Meetings

A formal meeting held to hear, discuss, and perhaps approve your concept is chaired by the decision maker. You have no control over the agenda or the way the meeting is run, and it may not follow the precepts listed in Chapter 8 for a good meeting. You should follow the advice on the use of visual aids we presented in Chapter 8 if you intend to use them.

Your presentation is not a simple exposition of facts. It is not like a presentation to a professional society or to an in-house seminar on your work. This presentation is to *persuade* certain key people to accept your point of view. Always keep this purpose uppermost in your mind.

The seven points listed above also apply to the formal meeting. In addition:

1. Know the purpose of the meeting. Is it merely to hear your concept, with no action expected? Or is it a decision meeting? If it is informational, are you sure that the chairperson will not make a decision? Tailor your talk accordingly.
2. Interact appropriately with others in the meeting. Are the key decision makers present? If so, address your points to them. Be polite and responsive to other participants, but concentrate on the key people. If no key person is present, treat the meeting as a rehearsal; you'll have to do it again.
3. Don't expect as much reaction or disagreement from participants as you get in face-to-face conversation. Watch the key people. If they nod in agreement, go to the next point. If they seem bored, go to the next point. If they frown, muster your best argument, but don't belabor it.
4. If you know that one of the participants supports your concept, involve that person in any discussion of the merits of your position: "Mr. A, I know you've studied this subject. What do you think?"
5. Hold to the scheduled ending time for the meeting, even if it started late.
6. If a key participant is called away, modify your talk, if possible, to delay key points until that person's return. Summarize what the person has missed, without making it obvious that you are doing so.
7. Offer to meet individually with any participant who would like to discuss the matter in more depth.

Written Report

The written report should always start with a summary section. Many executives may not read beyond it. A suggested outline for the report is as follows:

1. Summary
2. Objective or purpose of the proposal or study
3. Findings or data
4. Evaluation and alternative actions considered
5. Recommendation
6. Cost benefit analysis
7. Proposed implementation schedule
8. Appendixes showing: list of study participants, methodology of the study, important raw data or information.

The summary section should show, in sequence:

1. The problem being addressed
2. The recommendation
3. The benefits and costs
4. The request for approval

Your concept should have merit to be accepted, but merit alone does not sell good ideas. The techniques we have listed will.

SUMMARY

In order to sell management on changing the way a function is handled, they must be convinced that a problem exists and that a solution is possible. Showing that other companies are working on or have solved similar problems bolsters the argument.

The key decision makers must be identified. They may be shown on the organization chart as the executives in charge of the functions where you desire change. They may also be staff specialists or other managers. There are many criteria on which a decision to change may be based. These include: return on investment; reducing overhead or administrative costs; image; speed, accuracy, or flexibility of an operation; executive job security, aversion to risk, fear of stockholders or security analysts, and the appearance of an operation to others. The relative importance of each criterion to the key decision makers is determined from their actions, not their words.

A cost benefit analysis is required. All benefits that will result from the change should be listed, including time saved. Time saved provides a soft dollar benefit. The activities to be performed with that time are identified, or the savings are converted to hard dollars by the attrition or termination of employees.

Decisions are sold in oral presentations, either face-to-face conversations or formal meetings. The presentation should first appeal to the executive's interest, then present the conclusion, list the benefits, show costs and problems, counter all arguments, summarize, and request approval to proceed. In formal meetings, address remarks primarily to the key decision makers. A written report documents your position.

FOR FURTHER INFORMATION

Ewing, David W. *Writing for Results,* 2nd ed. New York: John Wiley & Sons, 1979.
Linver, Sandy. *Speak and Get Results.* New York: Summit Books, Simon & Schuster, 1983.

13
Implementing Change

The best concept in the world is of no value if people will not accept the change. These people may not actually sabotage changes they do not like, but they find the minor flaws that inevitably exist at the start of a new system and blow them up to disastrous proportions. Those who want a system to succeed are patient with such flaws, will help to fix them, and will work with you continually to improve the concept.

We need the staff on our side. Handling resistance to change is a major part of implementing a change. In this chapter, we discuss how to handle resistance. We also discuss the other actions that are part of implementing change.

HANDLING RESISTANCE TO CHANGE

Fear of Change

Any change, even one for the better, evokes anxiety. This anxiety, conscious or unconscious, includes fear of:

1. Losing one's job
2. Losing a familiar and comfortable routine
3. Losing status
4. Change in personal relationships
5. Implication that the job is being done poorly
6. Needing to learn new skills and procedures
7. Failure in the new routine
8. Career paths being changed or eliminated

Here are some of the concerns that accompany each of these fears.

Loss of Job. Whenever someone comes around investigating what you are doing, you will worry that your job may be abolished. A memorandum from management that the operation of a certain department will be improved may bring joy to those who use the services of that department, but it brings fear and concern to those in the department. Even a promise that no one will lose his or her job may not put such fears completely to rest—that depends on management's prior record in keeping such promises. From the time the investigation begins until its results are made known, the rumor mill may suggest that jobs will be abolished, downgraded in salary, or changed in some drastic manner. Everybody has plenty of opportunity to worry.

Loss of Routine. Everyone of us, professional, paraprofessional, or support staff, develops a routine way to handle the functions of the job. We do certain functions first thing in the morning. We follow the same general sequence or pattern in the way we work. We take breaks at certain times. We chat with certain people, often about the same subjects. We establish a familiar routine, and we are comfortable in it.

The team investigating change promises that improved methods will be suggested. What methods? Any change will disrupt our routine. A whole new way of working will be required, not only in the routine of the job but also in social contacts. Until we know what will happen, there is bound to be anxiety.

Loss of Status. We all become expert in our particular segment of the overall job. A professional has been doing a particular set of calculations for years and can do them faster and more accurately than anyone else. A clerk knows the filing system by heart and takes pride in being able to locate a document in seconds. A secretary learns the procedures and staff assignments in her department and can answer almost any question put to her.

Change may affect how the calculations are made, the documents filed, the procedures handled, and the staff assigned. The pride that comes from knowing one is the best, and the status that comes with recognition from one's friends and colleagues, may be shattered. One or more of Herzberg's motivators is eliminated, and the worker may drop a rung or two on the Maslow pyramid.

The problem of status is particularly important in changes that affect the manager–secretary relationship. To many managers, the secretary is a status symbol. To many secretaries, having one boss rather than handling a group is also a mark of status. The desire to hang onto this status by both parties is a real source of resistance to any change that could disrupt the current relationship.

Change in Relationships. The professional works closely with other professionals, paraprofessionals, and certain support staff. The manager has a close working relationship with the secretary. Relationships also are established with people in other departments who assist from time to time and whose judgment one learns to accept. A mutual respect and trust are built that simplify the job and add social pleasure to the work.

Change may break these bonds. The introduction of word processing has broken the boss–secretary relationship in many companies with unforeseen and unfortunate results. When relationships are broken, it takes time and effort to establish new ones. Most people are reluctant to have to do so.

Implication of a Poor Job.   If someone wants to change our job, one natural assumption is that we were not doing something right. Despite statements that it is the job design, not its execution, that is wrong, many individuals will continue to believe that somehow they are at fault. Based on this assumption, they will anticipate that their positions and salary will suffer when the changed system is installed.

Need to Learn New Skills.   The person performing well in his or her present job has mastered the skills and knowledge required. It may have taken months or even years to do this. Long experience in a position also gives insight as to what will be needed, so that the incumbent can often anticipate a request before the manager makes it.

Any change alters the procedures in use. Duties must be reassigned and, probably, new techniques learned. If the change involves automation, it will require use of a terminal. The staff will have to learn a series of codes to input data and instruct the computer to read out whatever information is desired. If a person is afraid of learning, perhaps because of age or poor experiences in school, this need to learn is viewed with varying degrees of concern.

Possibility of Failure.   A series of good or superior performance reviews attests to the ability of most of the staff to do their present jobs well. A series of salary increases has provided the reward. Further salary increases can be expected if performance continues to be adequate or better. Each individual has seniority in the particular position held. No one is likely to come along and oust the person from that spot.

The change, however, starts everybody over again from scratch. The younger whiz kids may have an advantage in an automated system over the old-timers. Much of the latters' value lies in knowing the right people, the procedures, and the history of prior successes and failures. The older person may find it difficult to understand computer-dominated systems. Not only may seniority and expertise be lost, but also the ability to perform in a superior manner.

Career Path Change.   In each department, the line of job advancement is usually clear. In the professional ranks, the need for specialists in your particular field may be increasing, and you can anticipate a promotion as your group grows. The junior secretary sees advancement to department secretary and then to executive secretary. The paraprofessional works toward professional status.

A procedural change will have little effect on this, but a major upheaval, such as that caused by office automation, can severely jumble career paths. There may be fewer executive secretaries and more paraprofessional staff assistants.

Many clerical jobs may disappear and be replaced by jobs requiring computer understanding. The expectations of some individuals will have to change. The after-hours training that some have taken may turn out to be for naught.

With all these factors causing anxiety, is it any wonder that change—any change—causes fear and resistance?

Overcoming Fear of Change

What can be done about this anxiety?

1. Recognize its existence.
2. Involve employees in the evaluation phase.
3. Determine each individual's desires and concerns.
4. Allay the concerns, and sell satisfaction of the desires.
5. Provide adequate training and time.
6. Expect mistakes and lower initial productivity.
7. Implement in stages; show success in one before moving to the next.
8. Have patience.

We discuss each of these practices.

Recognize the Resistance.   The reasons for resistance were listed earlier in this chapter. No more need be said on this point.

Involve Employees.   As many as possible of the staff who will be affected by a change should be involved in the evaluation and design phases. By being involved, they will see the need for change, have their views and their problems considered, and understand what will happen. They are more likely, then, to accept and become committed to the change. The involvement may take several forms; these employees may:

1. Be members of the task force.
2. Participate by submitting data on the present work flow.
3. Participate through a spokesperson appointed to represent a group of employees. The spokesperson participates in task force discussions.
4. Be interviewed and asked for ideas on improving the present system.

All employees must be kept continually informed of what is being done and why. This point is mandatory.

Determine Desires and Concerns.   You, the change agent, may think you know the desires and concerns of those who will be affected by a change. Indeed you may, but your knowing does not have the same impact as allowing the staff to express their views individually or through a spokesperson. Knowing that one's concerns and opinions have been heard and considered, even if they are not adopted, goes a long way toward eventual acceptance. Resentment is strongest when an action is taken that greatly impacts a person's job and livelihood without that individual's being consulted or allowed any voice in the matter.

Allay Concerns and Sell Improvements. Individually, or in a general meeting, talk about the concerns and anxieties you have discovered, and those unspoken ones you suspect exist. Be open and honest. Some concerns are valid, and you'll need a strategy for handling these situations. Some people will need new skills; stress to them that training and time to learn will be provided. Some jobs may be abolished; stress that no one will be laid off. If layoffs are a part of the plan, talk to the people and groups involved as early as possible. If the company will help each person relocate, emphasize this point.

Concurrently, describe how the employees' desire for job enhancement and growth will be satisfied under the changed system. Show how the dull and routine aspects will be replaced with more exciting and important work. Remember the Herzberg motivators? Stress all those that apply to the changed operation. Explain how the whole organization will be better off, costs will be lower, market position enhanced, and so forth, and how this can lead to growth and greater opportunity for everyone.

A good technique is to visit other organizations that have implemented the type of system you are adopting. Take along those people who exhibit the greatest anxiety, and let them see the new system in action and talk to people who are using it.

Provide Adequate Training. Promise that wherever a job is changed, training will be provided and enough time allowed for each employee to become proficient in the new methods. Don't leave training up to each supervisor. Bring in people who know how to train, and set up formal training sessions.

Expect Mistakes and Lower Initial Productivity. Mistakes and reduced productivity will occur as the changeover is made, and will continue for several weeks or months afterward. Each person has a different learning speed, and some changes will take longer to absorb than others. The change from using a typewriter to superior proficiency on a word processor takes from three to six months, depending on the equipment make and model. In the first few weeks, output is lower than before the change. There is a learning curve for all new functions.

Implement in Stages. Some changes, usually the smaller ones, must be done all at once. The old procedure is scrapped and the new one started as of a certain date. But other, more drastic changes, such as introducing word processing or other office automation techniques, should be implemented in stages. The new system should be introduced in one department or function or floor of a building at a time. In this way, the problems and errors can be uncovered and fixed while the operation is still small. Staged implementation permits a demonstration of the new system to those whose concerns and anxieties remain. The initial success causes those who are not yet on the system to want to participate. Concern is replaced by desire.

Have Patience. The change agent needs lots of patience. Not everyone will see the advantages you see. Some will refuse to be convinced, no matter how successful the trial. There will be problems during implementation. People will be upset, and management will be anxious for results. All this goes with the territory. Relax as best you can and continue plugging away. If your concept is good, it will work out properly in the end.

SELLING THE CONCEPT

From the previous discussion it is clear that the new concept must be sold, not only to management but to all users of the system being changed, and to all those who perform the function being changed. Selling management was the subject of Chapter 12. Management's acceptance brought the concept to the point of implementation. Part of implementation is selling it to everyone else.

Those whose jobs are affected by the change are the most likely to resist. Techniques to reduce resistance were discussed above. It is essential that they be used whether the change is big or little.

You may think that those whose work will benefit from the change—the users of the office systems being improved—will be overjoyed and give you no problems. If so, you are wrong. They, too, must be sold on the change.

Users will be skeptical. They have probably been promised utopia before and have yet to get there. Their comfortable routine is also being upset; they will have to learn new ways to get administrative support. They have complained of the present methods, but complaint is a form of therapy, and you are removing its source. You can expect resistance to change from the complaining users too!

How do you handle users? In much the same way as you do those whose jobs are affected by change. Involve them in setting the specifications for the changed system. Point out how the new system handles areas of complaint, and show the improvement in productivity and the decrease in turnaround time anticipated. Be enthusiastic and try to convey this enthusiasm to your listener so that he or she will also enthusiastically anticipate the new system. Do not oversell. Point out that there will be problems initially. Suggest that you'd like the listener's help in finding and overcoming whatever problems occur. Enlist the users on your side. Leave them wanting to see the change and willing to support you in making the new system work.

SELECTING EQUIPMENT

If the change involves automation, a key issue in implementing the chosen concept is selecting the right equipment. The automation study team described in Chapter 7 should have suggested the types of equipment and the features that the equipment must have. It probably did not select specific makes and models. Selection is a lengthy process and requires more detailed knowledge of specific equipment models than a task force needs to have. More important, the individual who will be responsible for operating the equipment and making it work should be the person who makes the equipment decision.

The principles below apply to the selection of personal computers, word processors, data processing equipment, printing or copying equipment, microfilm systems, or any other system whose successful operation depends on using the proper equipment.

The Selection Steps

Capacity.   First determine:

- The work load you expect to process on the equipment.

This determines the capacity of the unit, or the number of units required. PC's are different; by their definition they are one to a customer. Allow a large factor for work expansion, or assure that the equipment selected can be upgraded to handle an expanded work load.

Configuration.   Next determine the system configuration. Will it be:

1. Centralized in a single location to cover the entire organization?
2. A series of mini-centers in different buildings or on different floors of the buildings?
3. A series of localized units placed conveniently in user departments or groups:
4. Some mix of centralized units and localized convenience units?

The decision depends on the cost of the units, the need for operator training, the importance of user access to the equipment operator, and the importance of features that may be available only on larger units. (Again, the PC's are an exception.)

Features.   Third, establish a list of requirements for equipment features and options. A different set may be appropriate for each of the locations in a decentralized operation. The list should identify the available features as:

- Mandatory: you won't accept any unit without this feature.
- Desirable: it is nice to have at little or no extra cost but not essential.
- Unnecessary: you don't need it or want it.

Also check each possible vendor's performance record on:

- Service: time from placing a trouble call until the service representative's arrival.
- Support: training and help when the equipment does not behave as expected.

And check the vendor's:

- Financial condition.
- Commitment to future product improvements.

Site Visits.   Fourth, visit other organizations using equipment models that have the mandatory features you have listed. See if their type of work is the same as yours. If it is, ask the following questions of the person in charge of the equipment:

1. What are its best features?
2. What are its worst features?
3. What aspects have been especially helpful?
4. What aspects have been disappointing?
5. What features are used most frequently?
6. What features are never used?
7. What type of equipment failures have occurred? How frequently?
8. How long does it take an operator to reach full effectiveness?

Also ask about the vendor's service and support.

Vendor Demonstrations.   Fifth, see vendor demonstrations of models still in the running. Be wary. Salespeople will express enthusiasm for the better qualities of their product while not mentioning the shortcomings. The visits to users make you aware of some shortcomings; use vendor salespersons to tell you the rest.

1. Ask whether improvements have been made on the vendor's equipment to handle problems you know about.

2. Ask the vendor how his equipment's features are superior to others' equipment. Mention the good points of a competing model, and ask the salesperson's opinion of it.

The second question provides a list of the shortcomings of other vendors' equipment.

At vendor demonstrations:

1. Bring examples of the type of work you do to see how the equipment works with your samples.
2. Ask if the programs being demonstrated are those released and available now, not prototypes or special demonstration programs.
3. Perform the functions on the equipment yourself, or use one of your better operators; you will not know how easy or hard the equipment is to operate by watching a trained demonstration artist.

Supplies.   Sixth, check on the cost and availability of supplies. On some equipment, supplies are only available from the vendor and may be quite expensive.

The Decision Process

Select the specific equipment model or models by a process of elimination. Eliminate all equipment that:

1. Does not have the mandatory features.
2. Is difficult to use.
3. Needs an excessively long training program.

Also eliminate equipment whose supplier has a:

4. Poor service and support record.
5. Poor financial condition.

From what is left, select on the basis of price and the list of additional desirable features.

UTILITY NEEDS AND PROBLEMS

If you are changing the work layout within a department, or bringing in new equipment, you must lay out the space and know the new utility requirements. You should also know about some of the equipment operating problems that can result from poor utility design. We discussed work layout in Chapter 6. Here are a few additional comments pertinent to bringing in equipment.

Electrical Needs

The standard electrical circuits in office buildings are 115 volts, 20 amps. Some equipment may require a 220-volt outlet or a 115-volt circuit rated at 30 amps. It usually is not a difficult problem to provide these, but special wiring will be required from the nearest circuit box. The building electrical crew should be informed as early as possible so they can determine whether the power capacity is available and anticipate any problems in routing the wiring.

Some types of equipment—including data processing equipment and some word processing equipment models—require dedicated circuits. This means that no other appliances such as lights, clocks, and electric pencil sharpeners can be plugged into these circuits. Such equipment is sensitive to electrical noise which can be caused by fluorescent lights and motors, even as small a motor as that in a clock or pencil sharpener. Electrical noise may cause false readings within the equipment or even shut it down. If the dedicated line has unused outlets, the prohibition against using these outlets for anything other than the specified equipment must be enforced.

Electrical problems are common in the operation of sophisticated automation equipment. Voltage surges or drops can cause loss or alteration of memory in data and word processors and PC's. When blackouts and brownouts occur, you are aware of them and know you have probably lost data and need to recheck all work that was being done at the time. But you are not usually aware of momentary voltage fluctuations that last a fraction of a second. However, this is long enough to affect work being done.

If voltage outages are frequent, you should consider having backup power that cuts in instantly. For voltage fluctuations, consider an isolation transformer. The source of these fluctuations may be inside your building. The start of an air conditioning compressor or of an elevator motor may cause a momentary voltage drop. The source may also be outside the building in the main power lines. If strange things keep happening to the equipment, call in an electrical expert to check the voltage situation.

Proper grounding of electric equipment is also very important. In some cases, the third prong of a three-prong outlet is not sufficient. You may need an additional ground wire and perhaps even an isolated ground to which no other equipment is connected. Static electricity can be a major problem in dry climates. A person walking on carpet can build up a potential of over 10,000 volts. If this person touches an improperly grounded cabinet or another part of some delicate electrical equipment, an unwanted signal may be generated within the equipment. As little as 500 electrostatic volts, an amount you probably would not feel, can cause a false signal. If there is static electricity, replace carpet with tile or with specially treated mats or grounded carpeting.

Heat and Noise

The advent of microchips with the resulting reduction of electrical power needs has also reduced the amount of heat produced by office equipment. Power consumed by the equipment ends up as heat; so the lower the power needs are, the less heat generated. In a normal air-conditioned office, about 4000 watts of equipment power can be handled in a 20 ft. by 20 ft. room without overtaxing the air system. Above this amount, special venting or cooling will be required.

All equipment has temperature limits within which it is guaranteed to operate. These are shown in the equipment specifications. If your building has an energy savings program, the air system may be turned off during evenings and weekends. Do not operate equipment when the temperature is above or below the specified operating limits; it could be damaged. There usually are operating limits for relative humidity as well. If the room is too dry, static electricity may build up. If the humidity is too high, moisture may condense inside the equipment.

Noise induces fatigue, which in turn reduces operator productivity. As electronic parts replace mechanical parts in newer equipment, the noise factors are being reduced. Some equipment, however, is still very noisy. The use of drapes and carpets does a lot to dampen noise, but they are also a source of dust, and carpets can generate static electricity. Sound-absorbing wall panels and wallpaper can be used. Small equipment, such as printers, can be enclosed in acoustical hoods.

PROCEDURES

Part of implementing a new system is the development and writing of new procedures. In Chapter 3 we described a "brainstorming" approach to this. In Chapter 6 we suggested questions whose answers will improve an existing operation. Some equipment vendors recommend specific procedures for the efficient use of their equipment. However you develop them, it is important to have procedures worked out and in writing before a new operation starts.

Procedures serve several purposes. They:

1. Establish uniformity in processing work; everyone does a job the same way.
2. Relieve the supervisor of many operational decisions.
3. Form the basis for productivity standards.
4. Tell users of the operation what to expect.

5. Help to train new personnel.
6. Show temporary-help personnel what to do.

To accomplish these objectives, procedures must be in writing and readily available both to those who perform and to those who use the changed operation.

All of the above objectives except the fourth are aimed at those who work in the new operation. Number four is aimed at the users of the system. Users are not interested in the internal details of how you get work done. They are interested in how to input the work, what type of instructions they should provide, and when they can expect the job to be completed. Therefore, two procedure manuals are required. One is an operations manual that contains the specific operating procedures and is written for those who perform the function. The other is a user's manual that covers what the users need to know.

Operator's Manual

This manual should contain:

1. The specific steps to perform the job, listed in the sequence in which they are done.
2. The productivity, accuracy, and turnaround time standards for the operation.
3. The work input forms, productivity statistics forms, and any other forms in use.
4. The responsibilities of each person in the operation.
5. The filing or work retention procedures.

All these elements were discussed in earlier chapters.

User's Manual

This manual shows the users of the operation:

1. Its purpose and capabilities, unless this is obvious.
2. Its location and working hours.
3. The procedure for putting in work, including the input form and instructions on filling it out.
4. The turnaround time standard.
5. The manner in which work is returned to the originator.
6. The procedure for designating work for priority treatment.
7. The name and phone number of the manager or supervisor.

The user's manual should be brief—not more than six single-spaced pages—or it will not be read.

TRAINING

We have stressed the need for training and for patience while the staff learns the new procedures and becomes proficient. Since productivity will be low until a training program is completed, effective training is important.

If equipment is involved—word processors, PC's, data processing equipment, printers, micrographics, and so forth—the vendor may have a training program for that equipment. Even if an additional cost is involved, it will usually be worth it. Time is important. You want the staff to reach their new productivity levels as soon as possible. You also do not want to overtax the patience of the users, who will tolerate errors and slow output only for a short time. Another source of training is individuals who have gone into the business of training others. The equipment vendor knows who these people are.

After some members of your staff are fully trained, they can be used to train others. But when an operation is starting up and everyone is new to the operation, it is better to bring in an outside expert.

USER ORIENTATION

This is also training, but under a different name. It is best done by the manager or supervisor of the operation that is changing because it introduces the supervisor to the users, and because the supervisor knows more about the new system than anyone else does.

Large meetings are not ideal for orientation. There is little reaction from the audience, and it is difficult for the speaker to know if his or her points have been understood. Many listeners arrive unmotivated to listen and are thinking of other matters while the speaker is talking. Nevertheless, if a new system is being introduced that the entire staff must know about, there is no other way to orient them. How can you increase their chances of understanding?

The orientation talk is an information presentation, but it has elements of a sales presentation as well. Part of its purpose is to sell the listeners on the advantages of the new system. The precepts noted in Chapter 12 apply. Here is how to organize the talk:

1. At the start, appeal to the self interests of the audience. State that the system will save them time, provide faster response, be more accurate, etc., and briefly show them how it provides these benefits.
2. Describe only the parts of the policy and procedure that the listeners need to know. Do not discuss your internal procedures or problems.

3. Use overhead view graphs to illustrate the main points and to show the forms that the audience will use.
4. Invite questions as you go along, but don't get bogged down in detail. If a lot of time is being taken on one issue or by one person, offer to discuss it further later or to see the person after the meeting.
5. Keep the meeting brief—15 minutes for a simple change, 30 minutes for a complex one.
6. At the end of the meeting, hand out copies of the view graphs, a user's manual, or the procedures so that attendees have a written reminder of what they must do after the new system is implemented.

Identify the individuals who are heavy users of the operation being changed, and talk to them individually before the orientation meeting. If there are people with special problems or who you know will be antagonistic, talk to each of them individually.

START-UP

Everyone must know the date on which the new system goes into effect. If it is being phased-in one department at a time, a full implementation schedule should be published. Be prepared to help the users at the start. Despite the use of orientation meetings, some people will have missed the talk, or forgotten the procedures you covered, or mislaid the manual you handed out.

If the changeover involves a period of downtime while equipment is being installed, while files are being converted, or for any other reason, give plenty of warning. Two weeks notice is minimum, and a month is preferable so that users can plan their needs around the shutdown. Keep the downtime to a minimum. A day or two can usually be accommodated by users; longer than that may generate ill will. Use weekends for conversion, if possible. The overtime pay involved is usually less costly than the disruption caused by a multi-day shutdown.

Assure that the operating staff handling the new system has been trained on it before the start-up. If the change is in the operating procedures, talk to the staff a couple of weeks ahead of time and explain the "why" and the "how" of the new method. Allow the staff to study the new methods during the week before changeover. Give them time to try the new procedure on one or more tasks they have just completed the old way. In this way, questions will be raised and answered before the changeover occurs, and you will have a slight start on climbing up the learning curve. If the change is more drastic (e.g., involving the use of new equipment), provide time for the operators to train on the equipment before the changeover day.

If a phased implementation is used, start with a department whose reaction to the change is known to be favorable and whose needs and problems are already well known.

SUMMARY

Any change evokes anxiety, even a change for the better. Feelings of anxiety are related to fear of losing one's job, loss of a familiar routine, loss of status, change in personal relationships, the need to learn new skills and procedures, fear of failure, and the possible elimination of a chosen career path. To overcome these feelings, their existence must first be recognized. Some actions that can be taken have been identified in this chapter.

The changed system must be sold not only to management but to those affected by the change and those who will use the new system. Their involvement in planning the change helps achieve a positive attitude.

Selection of equipment for automating a function should be done by the person who will be responsible for the function. Equipment selection involves determining the work load, the equipment configuration, the equipment features, and each vendor's service and support record, financial condition, and commitment to future products. Visit companies using equipment being considered. Have vendors demonstrate their equipment using work examples you provide. Have the supervisor or someone who will work on the equipment try it out. Eliminate from consideration all equipment that lacks a mandatory feature and whose vendor has a poor service and support record.

Be concerned about electrical needs, poor grounding, and static electricity. Check the heat output, the acceptable temperature and humidity limits, and noise.

Procedures must be written before the new system is implemented. One manual is needed for system operators and another for system users, each showing only what that group needs to know.

Training is necessary for the operators and orientation for the users. Vendors usually have training programs on their equipment and independent training specialists familiar with their equipment. The function's manager or supervisor should conduct the user orientation meetings. Talk to heavy users and those with special problems individually. Distribute an implementation schedule. If downtime is involved, give users warning. If possible, use weekends for conversion. If a phased implementation is used, start with friendly departments.

FOR FURTHER INFORMATION

Resistance to Change

Gaffney, Carol T. Selling Office Automation Internally. *AFIPS Office Automation Conference Digest,* Philadelphia: American Federation of Information Processing Societies, 1981.

Selecting Equipment, Utility Needs and Procedures

Davis, Reba, and Balderston, Jack. Chapter 4, Selecting Word Processing Equipment; Chapter 5, Selecting Dictation Equipment; Chapter 7, Designing a Word Processing Area; Chapter 9, Developing Operating Procedures and Procedure Manuals, in *Word Processing Supervision*. Indianapolis: Bobbs-Merrill Publishing, 1984.

Appendix
Keeping Up With This Field

Books and articles on specific topics have been listed at the close of each chapter. Here are additional suggested sources to keep up with changes in the field of office management. Most of these changes will involve the automation of routine manual tasks. The magazines and meetings listed here keep track of such happenings.

Magazines

Business Week. Weekly. Frequently carries articles on information management and information processing. Write McGraw-Hill, 1221 Ave. of the Americas, New York, NY 10020.

Management World. Monthly. $18 per year (free with membership in the Administrative Management Society). Write AMS, Maryland Rd., Willow Grove, PA 19090.

Modern Office Technology. Monthly. (May be free to qualifying professionals). Write P.O. Box 95795, Cleveland, OH 44101.

The Office. Monthly. (May be free to qualifying professionals). Write 1200 Summer St., Stamford, CT 06904.

Office Administration and Automation. Monthly. Write 51 Madison Ave., New York, NY 10010.

Also, occasional articles in *Fortune* and the *Harvard Business Review.*

Meetings

Administrative Management Society, International Meeting. Annual, usually in May, in different cities each year. Write AMS, Maryland Rd., Willow Grove, PA 19090.

Federal Office Systems Expo. Annual, in March in Washington, D.C. Write National Trade Productions, Inc., 9418 Annapolis Rd., Lanham, MD 20706.

INFO '8x. Annual, usually in October in New York City. Write Clapp & Poliak, 708 Third Ave., New York, NY 10017.

National Computer Conference. Annual, usually in July, in different cities each year. Sponsored by the American Federation of Information Processing Societies, P.O. Box 9659, Arlington, VA 22209.

Office Automation Conference. Annual, usually in February, in different cities each year. Sponsored by the AFIPS (see above).

Syntopican. Annual, usually in June, in different cities each year. Sponsored by the Association of Information Systems Professionals, 1015 N. York Rd., Willow Grove, PA 19090.

Evaluation Services

Advanced Office Concepts. Monthly newsletter, $135 per year. Also market guides on office automation equipment and PC's at $135 per year each. Write One Bala Plaza, Bala Cynwyd, PA 19004.

DATAPRO Reports. Different reports cover computer systems, word processing, personal computers, software, office automation, and other topics. A two- or three-volume manual of information with monthly updates. Costs vary with subject but are about $500 per year. Write DATAPRO, 1805 Underwood Blvd., Delran, NJ 08075.

Seybold Reports. Separate reports on word processing, computers, and other topics. Monthly reviews of new equipment and industry trends. About $100 per year. Write Seybold Report, P.O. Box 644, Media, PA 19063.

Index

Index

Abbreviations, overuse of, 217
Abdication of leadership, 200
Acceptable performance, 222, 230
Accountants, PC programs for, 80
Accounting analysts. *See* Financial analysts
Accounting function, 17, 119, 128, 174, 176, 177, 210
  variation among tasks, 119
Accuracy
  desired, 222, 241
  improved, 243
Achievement as a motivator, 198
Activity chart, 121-123
  form, 122
Adapters for mini- and microcassettes, 50
Address directory, 82, 145
Administrative assistant, 16, 152. *See also* Paraprofessional
Administrative functions, list of, 17-20
Administrative support, 16-20, 152-154, 224-228
  communicating with, 224
Administrative support services manager, 146
Advancement as a motivator, 199
Allocating resources, 208
Alternative costing calculation, 40
American Federation of Information Processing Societies, 147
American Management Association, 181
Analog facsimile, 136
Analog telephone systems, 89, 140-141
Analytical support using PCs, 80-81
Analyzing costs, 190-192
  an example, 191
Announcements on PCs, 82
Annual plan, 185-186, 207, 217
Anxiety, 248
Appearance of inefficiency, 242
Applicant interview, 234
Appointment calendar, 82, 131, 145, 153
Appraisal of employees. *See* Performance appraisal
Archives, 103

Army command style, 200
Articles, clipping, 239
ASAP (as soon as possible), 226
ASCII code, 69, 76
Assigning responsibilities, 199, 207
Attitude, 233
Attrition of personnel, 210, 243
Audio conferencing, 141
Auditor, 242
Authoritarian leadership, 199, 200-204
Authority
  by job title, 199
  delegation, 209
  limits, 26, 222
  line of, 209
Autocratic leadership, 200-202, 203-204
Automated office
  candidate functions, 131-145
  evolution towards, 129
  need for a network, 131
  need for pilot phase, 132
Automatic footnote location, 65
Automatic headers or footers, 64
Automatic hyphenation, 65
Automatic pagination, 64
Automatic repagination, 64
Automatic underlining, 64
Automation study, 145-148
  candidate areas, 147
  cost justification, 148
  implement in stages, 148
  questions to answer, 147
  task force objectives, 146
Automation, implementing
  career changes, 250
  fear of change, 248-251
  implementing in stages, 148
  need for a dedicated champion, 148
  need for new skills, 250
  new procedures, 256-260
  overcoming fear, 251-253
  selecting equipment, 254-256

Automation (continued)
  selling users, 253-254
  training, 260-261
Aversion to taking risks, 241

Badawy, M. K., 205
Balancing work flow, 27, 114-117
Balancing work load, 35-36, 118
Barriers to change, 113, 237-239
Baseband network, 88
Behavior factors affecting work measurement,
  113
Behavior requiring discipline, 229-230
Belongingness needs, 196-197
Benefits for cost-benefit analyses, 243-244
Block move or copy, 65
Book, plan of the, 3-4
Boolean logic, 100-102
Booz·Allen & Hamilton, 1, 5, 6, 11, 16, 105,
  164
Brainstorming, examples, 33-34
Broadband network, 88
Budget, 173-189, 207, 208, 210
  approval cycle, 187-188
  capital, 186-187
  cut backs, 184, 187-188
  effect of reductions in, 188
  forms, 174, 175, 178, 179, 183, 188
  judgmental changes, 187
  monthly spread, 188
  narrative justification, 184-186, 187
  padding, 183
  reviewers, 184
  utilization factor, 176
  work sheet summary, 174
  work sheet summary, completed, 183
Budgeting
  by extrapolating past history, 178
  for additional responsibilities, 186
  for contingencies, 183
  of education and training, 181
  of fringe benefits, 177-178
  of leases and rents, 179
  of materials and supplies, 178
  of occupancy costs, 182-183
  of other costs, 182
  of purchased services, 178-179
  of recruiting, 181-182
  of salaries, 175-177
  of travel expense, 180-181
Building expenses, budgeting of, 182
Bus network, 88

Business graphics, 144
Business Week, 238

Call forward, 91
Camera, reduction, 92
Capital assets, 186
Capital budget, 186-187
Capstan drive, 49
CAR. *See* Computer-aided retrieval
Carbon paper, 128
Career change, 250
Career objectives, 212, 232
Cassette bank dictation system, 47
Cassettes, dictation, 49-51
Central copiers, 91-92
Central dictation networks, 46-48
Central processing unit, 69
Centralized word processing, 59-60
Chairs, ergonomic, 58
Challenging work as a motivator, 199
Change
  automation study, 145-148
  barriers to, 113, 237-239
  cost justification for, 39-42
  decision criteria, 240-242
  fear of, 248-253
  implementing, 248-262
  multi-function, 38-39
  planning for, 22-43
  resistance to, 248-253
  selling management on, 237-246
  within one department, 30-38
Change agent, three scenarios, 22, 237-238
Changed system, start-up of, 261-262
Changeover to new equipment, 261
Character printers, 73
Charting a work process, 113-117
Charting symbols, 114
Charting, cost considerations, 123
Charts: bar, line and pie, 143-144
Chemical Abstracts, 82
CIM. *See* Computer input microfilm
Clerical activities performed by professionals, 8
Cliques, 213
Coaching, 211
Code key, 67
Code translation equipment, 140
Colleague communication, 224
Colleague, defined, 224
Column move, 65
COM. *See* Computer output microfilm
Comfort of word processing operators, 57

Command, 199
Command key, 67
Communicating, 216-235. *See also* interviews
  as part of appraisal, 230
  feedback, 228
  understanding, 216-221
  with administrative staff, 225-228
  with colleagues, 224
  with subordinates, 228-232
  with superiors, 221-223
Communicating word processors, 137
Communication features, word processors, 77
Communication, oral. *See* Oral communication
Company health, 130
Company internal mail, 97-98
Company operational style. *See* Company philosophy
Company philosophy, 23-24, 239, 240-242
Compatibility of dictation systems, problems with, 50-51
Computer graphics, 143-144
  versus hand drawing, 144
Computer input microfilm, 144
Computer mainframe. *See* Mainframe, computer
Computer output microfilm, 144
Computer-aided retrieval of documents, 99-101
  example, 101
Concerns of those affected by change, 248-252
Conflict resolution, 213
Consultant contracts, budgeting, 178
Consultant, role of, 146
Contingencies, 26, 131
Contingency planning in budgets, 183
Continuing education, 3
Control key, 67
Control of costs, 189-192
Controller, 240
Controlling as a management function, 14, 210
Controlling meetings, 167-169
Convenience copiers, 92-93
Convenience, value of, 128, 130
Conversations, rules for persuasive, 244
Cooperation of staff in work measurement, 113
Coordination of work, 209
Copiers, 91-93, 128, 186, 254
  cost per page, 92, 93
  versus phototypesetting, 143
  work turnaround standard, 93
Copy center objectives, 111
Copying, 91-93
Correspondence, archiving of incoming, 103

Cost
  analysis, 190-192
  avoidance, 40, 243
  benefit analysis, 242-244
  control, 189, 192-193
  detail report, 189
  justification, 39-43, 148, 243
  justifying office automation, 148
  problems, 223
  limits to a purchase request, 227
  of facsimile transmission, 136, 138-139
  reduction, examples, 192-193
  report, questioning items, 193
  savings as a benefit, 243
  standards, using to sell change, 238
  status reports, 131, 189-190
  summary report, 189-190
Couriers, 99, 117
CPU. *See* Central processing unit
Creative dictation, 159
Creativity, 230
Criteria for decision to change, 240-242
Cumulative variance of costs from budget, 189
Cursor keys, 66

Daisy wheel printer, 73
Data,
  defined, 87
  value of up to date, 131
Data bases available through PCs, 82, 83
Data hound, 130
Data processing, 86-88
  a regimented discipline, 87-88
  equipment, 254
  function, 19
  manager, 146, 240
  networks, 88
  reports, 87
  terminal for electronic mail, 140
  terminal in professional's office, 134
  terminal rooms, 135
  terminal, cost of moving, 135
  uses of, 86
Deadlines, 160, 162, 226
Decentralized word processing, 60-61
Decision criteria for change, 240-242
Decision makers, 23, 239, 244, 245
Decision meetings, 245
Decision process, 240-246
Decision support using PCs, 81
Decisions, modeling alternative, 130
Dedicated champion, 148

Delay steps in process chart, 114, 118
Delegating authority, 209
Delete key, 67
Democratic leadership. *See* Participative leadership
Department objectives, 31, 110-111, 112, 207
Department records using PCs, 82
Dependability, 230
Depreciation, 182, 187
Desk management
  defined, 145
  secretarial support for, 153-154
  using PCs, 82
Desktop dictation units, 48
Determining needs in automation study, 147
Dictate, how to, 154-159
Dictating
  changes to text, 158
  complex documents, 158
  data for forms, 158
  instructions, 156
  money values, 158
  punctuation, 157-158
Dictation
  advantages of, 44-45
  cost comparison to handwriting, 44
  costs for a 200 word letter, 45
  equipment operation, 155
  improving through secretary's help, 152
  practice, 155
  preparing for, 156
  speed, 45, 156
  techniques, 156-158
Dictation equipment
  advantages of each type, 51
  cassettes, 49-51
  categories, 45
  control consoles, 48
  description, 46-49
  need for standardization, 50
  transcribers, 50-51
Digital facsimile, 136
Digital telephone systems, 141, 147
Digital voice switching, 89
Directing, 14, 211
Disciplining subordinates, 229-230
Disk capacity, 69
Disk drive, 71
Distances, estimating during charting, 117
Distributed logic word processing, 63-64
Document retrieval, 99-102, 144
Document revision, 163-164

Documents, secretary's critique of, 152-153
Dot matrix printer, 73-74
Dow Jones Retrieval Service, 82
Duration of a meeting, 167

Earphones, 50
EBCDIC, 69, 76
Editing features
  electronic typewriters, 53
  word processors, 64
Educating management, 237-239
Education, budgeting for, 181
Effectiveness of other companies, 238
Effectiveness
  defined, 110
  examples, 110-111
Efficiency
  defined, 109
  examples, 109-110
  using measures of, 123, 125
Elapsed time, 109
Electrical problems, 257
Electronic blackboard, 142
Electronic mail, 135-140, 147
  choice of system, 140
  considering using, 135
Electronic office. *See* Automated office
Electronic typewriters, 52-54
  and word processors, choice between, 133
Employee
  accomplishments, 223, 228
  ambitions, 231, 232
  expectations, 221-223, 228
  goals, 231, 232
  objectives, 222
  performance, 197, 212-213, 222, 223, 230-232
  roster, 82
  satisfaction, 197-198
  skills, changes required, 147, 250
  strengths, 231-232
  weaknesses, 231-232
Employee relations function, 19, 34, 176, 182, 230
Endless loop dictation tank, 46-47
Engineering company, 12
Engineering function, 206, 225
Engineering Index, 82
Engineers, PC programs for, 80
Envelope feeder, 75
Equipment
  adequacy of, 28

changeover, 261
configurations, word processing, 59, 254
cost justification techniques, 39-40
demonstrations, 255-256
depreciation, 182, 187
dictation, 46-51
features, 255
noise, 258
purchases, compatibility issue, 148
selecting, 254-256
site visits, questions for, 255
temperature limits, 258
vendor support, 255
Ergonomics, 57-59
Escape key, 67
Esteem needs, 196
Ethernet, 88
Executive job security, 241-242
Expectations, 228, 232
Experience of other companies, 238
Extended retention of word processing disks, 163
External memory, 69
Extrapolating budget numbers from past history, 178

Facilities function, 19, 226
Facsimile, 136-137, 138-139
Failure, fear of, 250
Faster operation as a change benefit, 243
Fatigue time, 58, 121
Fatigue, reduction of, 57
Fear of
    change, 113, 248-253
    job loss, 113, 248-249
    security analysts, 241
    stockholders, 241
Feedback in communications, 228
Files management, 99-104
Filing
    computer-aided, 99-102
    filing systems, 99-102, 147
    manual, 102
    personal files, 102
    using a PC, 102
    word processing disks, 162
Financial analysts, 146, 176, 180, 181, 182, 183, 187, 193. See also Accounting analyst
Financial function, 187, 240
Flexibility of operation, 241
Floor plan, 117-118
Floor space, budgeting, 182
Floppy disk, 69-70

Flow charts, 114, 116
Flow of work, 27, 35-36, 114, 116, 117-119
Follow-up by secretary, 152
Footers, automatic, 64
Footnote location, automatic, 65
Forecasting needs, 207
Formal meetings. See Decision meetings
Format key, 67
Forms
    activity chart, 122
    appraisal, 230-231
    attributes of good forms, 123-124
    budget. See Budget forms
    dictating data for, 158
    process and flow charts, 115-117
    using, 27, 37, 113, 151, 225, 227, 259
    work order, 159
Fortune, 238
Freeze frame video, 142
Fringe benefits, 176-178
Full motion video, 142
Functionally decentralized word processing, 60-61
Functions of
    a manager, 13-15, 205-213
    administration, 17-20
    professionals, 15-16
    support staff, 16-17
    the office, 11-12
Furniture, 186
    ergonomic design of, 57-58

Gamesmanship, 185
Glare, 57, 68
Global search and replace, 65
Goals
    for a department, 206
    for the corporation, 207
Grammar, 152, 217
Graphics, computer, 143-144
Group decision, 203

Handwriting speeds, 45
Hard disk, 71
Hard dollar savings, 243
Headers, automatic, 64
Heat, 258
Help key, 67
Herzberg, Frederick, 195, 197, 202, 249, 252. See also Motivation-hygiene theory
Hierarchy of needs (Maslow), 195-197

Historic standards, 125
Hyphenation, automatic, 65

Image as a decision criterion, 241
Implementing change, 248-262
Implementing in stages, 252
Implication of a poor job, 250
Importance of a decision affects leadership style, 204
Improved accuracy as a change benefit, 243
Improving procedures, examples, 33-34
Individual conversations, 244-245
Inefficiency, false appearance of, 242
Inefficient, defined, 109
Inflexible people, 88
Information
  defined, 87
  managing, 87
  selecting appropriate, 130
  value of, 128
Information meeting, 165-166
Information searches using a PC, 82, 83
Informing management, 237, 239
Initiative, 230
Ink jet printer, 74
Input, 109, 112, 124
Insert key, 67
Inspection, 114, 226
Instant decision, 204
Intangible worth, 213
Integrated office, 104
Interaction, 230
Interface of two functions, problems at, 38-39
Internal memory, 69
Interviews
  about existing operation, 25, 116
  applicant, 232-234
  appraisal, 231
  by task force, 147
Inventory, 82, 131
Involve employees, 251
Involvement for good communication, 221

Jargon, 217
Jealousy, professional, 224
Job
  accomplishments, 223
  accuracy, 222
  applicant interviews, 234
  assignments, 35
  attributes, 210, 233
  candidates, 210
  cost status, 223
  enhancement, 252
  expectations, 228
  experience, 210, 213, 233
  function, 208
  importance affecting leadership style, 212
  improvements in, 113
  performance. See Employee performance
  quality of work, 222
  responsibilities, 208, 222
  satisfaction, 197-198
  schedule, 223
  skills, 212, 233
  title, 208
  value of, 212
Judgment as part of performance appraisal, 230
Jurisdictional disputes, 38
Justification of document margins, 65
Justifying
  additional staff, 41-42, 185-186
  budget levels, 184-186
  capital assets, 187
  efficiency improvements, 41
  electronic typewriters, 132-133
  entry into automation, 131, 148
  materials, 186
  personal computers, 134
  word processors, 132-133

Keyboard
  ergonomic, 57
  word processor, 66
Key word searching, 100, 145
Key words by speaker, 217
Keys, word processors, list of, 66-67
Knowledge, 210, 230, 233
Knowledge workers
  functions of, 5-11
  time distribution of, 7

LAN. See Local area networks
Laser printer, 74, 93-94, 143
Layoffs, 113, 248-249, 252
Layout of work flow, 36
Leader
  roles, 13-15
  using hierarchy of needs, 196-197
  using motivation-hygiene theory, 198-199
Leader's personality, 203
Leadership, 195-213, 230, 233
  defined, 199

Leadership
  authoritarian, 201
  factors in using, 203
  flexibility needs, 200
  for best motivation, 205
  participative, 202
  styles, 200-203
Leases, budgeting, 179
Less productive activities, 6-8
Line item budget, 173, 189
Line of authority, 209
Line printer, 74
List processing, 65
Listen-talk ratio, 234
Listeners
  interpreting the message, 220-221
  involvement, 221, 224
  motivation, 224, 260
  problems in understanding speakers, 216, 218-220
  taking notes, 220
  tuning out, 218, 220
Lists, maintaining, 147
Literature searching, 82-83, 147
Local area network, 88-89, 141, 147
Logical thought progression, 217, 218
Loss of job, 113, 248-249, 252
Loss of routine, 249
Loss of status, 249

Mail, 97-99
  electronic. See Electronic mail
Mainframe compatibility to PCs, 84-85
Mainframe computer, 80, 81, 84-87, 135
  availability when needed, 134
Maintenance agreements, budgeting, 178
Management's goals, 14, 31, 205, 206, 240-242
Managers
  functions of, 13-15, 187, 205-213, 224
  inconsistency of, 222
  using information, 130
  what is important to, 240-242
Manager's expectations of subordinates, 232
Manager-secretary relationship, 249
Managing conflict, 213
Mandatory job attributes, 233
Manual filing, 102
Manuals
  originator and user, 259-260
  policy and procedure, 24, 26
Manufacturing function, 111, 206
Margin justification, 65

Marketing, PC programs for, 81
Marketplace, 130
Maslow, Abraham, 195, 197, 199, 202, 249. See also Hierarchy of needs
Materials and supplies, budgeting, 178
Math programs, 65
Measurement of work. See Work measurement
Measuring performance, 210
Meeting leader
  do's and don'ts, 168-169
  leader, roles of, 166-169
Meeting room, 168
Meetings, 9, 121, 164-170, 261
  agenda, 145, 167
  attendees, 166-167
  control, 167-169
  cost of, 165
  duration, 167
  formal, 165, 245. See also Decision meetings
  necessity of, 165
  reasons for, 165
  scheduling, 147, 153
  start time, 168
  time wasted in, 9
  visual aids, 169-170
  work assignments, 169
Memory, word processors, 53, 69
Message operator, 91
Messages, oral, 216-220
Messages, telephone, 91, 141, 152
Microcassettes, 50
Microfiche, 95
Microfilm, 95
Microfilm equipment, selecting, 254
Microfilm reader, 95
Micrographics, 95
Microphone handset controls, dictation systems, 48
Milestone reports, 9-10
Minicassettes, 50
Mixed word processing configuration, 61
Modeling alternative decisions, 81, 130
Modeling using PCs, 82
Monotonous speaker, 217-218
Monthly spread of budget, 188-189
Morale, 130
Motivation, 195-199, 211, 213, 224, 260
  for listening, 221
  practical examples of using, 196, 198
Motivation-hygiene theory
  description, 197-199
  practical uses of, 198

Multi-function change, 38-39
Multi-function keys, 67
Multiple objectives, 31, 111

Naming persons assigned to tasks, 208
National Industrial Conference Board, 238
Needs
  communicating, 225-227
  analysis (feasibility study), 147
  forecasting, 207
  hierarchy of (Maslow), 195-197
Negative prefixes, 217
Network
  data processing, 140
  personal computer, 82, 84
  types of, 88-89
New York Times, 82
Noise, 258
Nomogram for facsimile costs, 138-139
Nonproductive activities, allowance for, 121

Objectives
  accomplishment of, 110-112
  of automation task force, 146-147
  of departments, 31, 110-111, 207-208
  hierarchy of, 112
  knowing your, 112
  multiple, 31, 111
Observation of procedures, 116
Occupancy costs, budgeting, 182
OCR. See Optical character reader
Office Automation Conference, 147
Office automation. See Automation
Office functions
  cost of, 1-2, 5
  defined, 11-12
Office of the future, 128
Office support functions, 19-31
  integration of, 104-105
Office-less professional, 17
Open discussion as a leadership style, 202
Operation, knowing the present, 22-30
Operational steps in flow charts, 114
Operator posture, word processing, 58
Operator's manual, 259
Optical character reader, 75-77
Optimizing, 111-112
Oral communication, 216-235
Oral presentation, 244-245, 260
Organization chart, 18, 82, 145, 209, 239
Organization of integrated support functions, 104
Organization's style, 203

Organizational changes, 147
Organizational power and politics, 213
Organizationally decentralized word processing, 60
Organizing, 14, 208-209
Orientation of new users, 260-261
Output, 109, 110, 124-126, 222
Outstanding performance, 222
Overcoming fear of change, 251-253
Overhead rate, 242
Overhead viewgraphs (transparencies), 245, 261
  rules for preparing, 169
Overtime, 244, 261

Pacing, 117
Pagination, automatic, 64
Paperwork, 1-2, 11, 111, 151
  cost of, 1
Paraprofessional, 16, 152, 154, 166, 211, 249
  defined, 3
Participative leadership, 200, 202-203, 204-205
Patent, being first to file for, 130
Patience, 253
Payback (payout) calculation
  electronic typewriters, 132-133
  personal computers, 134
  procedure, 39-40
  word processors, 132-133
PBX network, 88
PC. See Personal computer
Penalty, disciplinary, 229
Performance appraisal of employees
  forms, 230
  interview, 231-232
  procedure, 230-232
  reasons for, 211-212
Performance of other companies, 238
Performance reviews. See Performance appraisal
Performance on job, measuring, 210
Performer of a service, 225-228
Periodic reports, 9
Permanent retention of word processing disks, 163
Personal computers, 79-86
  and mainframe computer, choice between, 134
  criteria for selecting, 84, 86, 254
  software availability, 85
  use as telex terminals, 136
Personal files, 102
Personal time, 121
Personal work habits, 145

Personnel department. *See* Employee relations
Personnel roster, 82
Persuasive presentations, 244-245
Philosophy of the operation, 23-25
Phosphors, 68
Photocopiers, 91-93
Phototypesetting, 94-95, 143
Phrase memory, 54
Physiological needs, 196-197
Pilot phase for automation, 132, 148
Plan of action, 185, 208
Plan of action meetings, 165, 166
Planning, 13-14, 205-208
Policies
  changes to, 147
  defined, 12
  establishing, 207
  purpose, 12-13, 207
  questions about existing, 25
  review of, 31
Policy manuals, 24, 26
Politics, power, 213
Portable dictation units, 48-49
Position description. *See* Job description
Post office box, 98
Power and politics, organizational, 213
Present operation, knowing the, 22-30
  key questions about, 30
Presentation, persuasive, 244-245
Presentation, written, 245-246
President of the company, 240
Primary department, estimating work load, 185
Printers, 71-74
  matching word processors, 71
Printing, 91
Priority work, 162, 226, 259
Problem resolution meetings, 165, 166
Procedure manuals, 24, 26
Procedures
  defined, 12
  developing new, 258
  enforcing, 35, 229
  establishing, 32-33, 208
  obsolete, 26
  maintaining, 34-35
  principles for establishing, 32
  questions about existing, 25
  reducing complexity, 34
  review of, 32
  secretary's knowledge of, 151-152
  use in charting, 116
Procedures of other companies, 238

Process chart
  defined, 114-115
  gathering data for, 116-117
  symbols, 114
  using, 118-119
  variation in activities, 118-121
Production line, 109
Productive steps in charting, 114
Productivity, 108-109, 110
  effect of change on, 252
Productivity improvement
  from automation, need for faith in, 148
  potential size of, 5
  through ergonomics, 59
  with electronic typewriters, 54
  with use of word processors, 55
  using measures of, 123-125
Professional jealousy, 224
Professional meetings versus teleconferences, 142
Professionals, 152, 159, 211, 224, 242
  roles of, 15-16
Profit-oriented groups, optimizing the, 111, 225
Programmable keys, 67
Programs, software for PCs, 85
Programs, word processor and PC, 69
Progress reports, 9
Project department, estimating work load, 185
Project manager, PC programs for, 80
Pronunciation guide, 157
Proofreader marks, 164
Proofreading, 153, 163-164
Protecting vital records, 103
Punched cards, 128
Punctuation, dictating, 157, 158
Purchased services, budgeting, 178-179
Purchasing function, 19, 31, 33, 110, 112, 178, 206, 225, 226
  variation in activities, 120

Quality circles, 24
Quality of work, 111
Quality standards, 210
Quantity of work, 108, 230
Quasi-professional activities, 8
Questions for job applicants, 233-234
Questions, open-ended, 233

Random access memory (RAM), 69
Rating form for appraisals, 230
Rating job applicants, 234-235
Rating job attributes, 233
Rating scale, performance appraisals, 230-231

Ratio of support staff, 242
Recognition as a motivator, 198-199
Records management, 99, 103-104, 147
Records retention schedules, 103
Recruiting, budgeting for, 181-182
Reducing administrative staff, 240
Reducing overhead costs, 240
Reference searches using PCs, 82-83
Relationships, change in, 249-250
Rents, budgeting, 179-180
Repagination, automatic, 64
Replacement of staff, 210
Reporting relationships, 208
Reports
  as a part of communications, 222
  presently generated, 29
  time involved in creating, 9-10
  types of, 9-10
  unnecessary, 37-40
Reprographics, 91-95, 226
Requester of a service, 225-228
  notification to, 228
Resistance to change, 248-253
Resolving conflicts, 213
Resources, allocating, 208
Responsibilities
  as a motivator, 199
  budgeting additional, 186
  delegation, 35
  of employees, 26-35, 113, 208, 259
  of managers, 205-213
Retention of vital records, 103
Retention schedules, word processing disks, 162-163
Return on investment, 240, 241
Revising a document, 163-164
Rewarding employees, 212-213. See also Salary increases
Rewards, based on survey results, 112
Ring network, 88
Risk, aversion to, 241
Rivalries, 213
Roles. See Functions
Roster of personnel, 82
Routine, loss of, 249
Rules, enforcing, 229
Ruprecht, Mary M., 55, 133
Rush work. See Priority work

Safety and security needs, 196-197
Salaries, budgeting, 175

Salary
  as a motivator, 198
  grades, 212
  increases, 176, 212, 230, 250
  plans, 212
  theory, practical considerations, 212
Satisfaction of personal needs, 195-196
Saving time, value of, 128, 130-131
Savings, hard dollar, 243
Savings, soft dollar, 243
Schedule of work, 208, 210
Schedules, using PCs, 82
Scheduling
  a request for support, 226-227
  implementation of change, 147, 261
  meetings and conference rooms, 147
Schmidt, Warren, 200, 203, 204
Scratch pad, 145
Screen, ergonomic, 57
Screen, word processor, 67-68
Screening job applicants, 210, 233-235
Search techniques for documents, 100-102
Secretary, 3, 16, 44, 82, 91, 102, 131, 145, 160, 167, 170, 249
  functions assignable to, 154
  variations in the job, 120
  ways to aid professionals, 151-154
Secretary-manager relationship, 249
Selecting equipment, 254-256
Selecting from job applicants, 234-235
Self-actualization needs, 196-197
Selling a change, 237-246
Selling a decision, 201
Selling change to those affected, 253-254
Sentence structure, 217-218
Shared decision making, 202
Shared logic word processing, 55, 63
Sheet feeder, 74-75
Short-term profit, 241
Signature limits, 26
Skills required, fear of change in, 113, 250
Slides, 144
  rules for preparing, 169-170
Small business computer. See Personal computer
Social conversation, 121
Soft dollar savings, 243
Software
  available for PCs, 85
  errors, 86
  problems with homemade, 86
Sorting, 65

Sorting mail, 97-98
Sound-alike words, list of, 157
Speaker, 217-218, 221, 224
  faults, 217
  improving understanding, 218
  motivation, 224
Specialization of work, 27
Specification, 226
Speed for dictating, 156
Speed of response, 241
Speed up of work, 113
Spelling checker, 66
Spindle drive, 49
Staff
  additions, justifying, 185-186, 244
  additions, selecting personnel, 234-235
  changes, effects of, 35, 209
  cooperation, 113
  hiring, 210-211
  needs, planning for, 207
  reduction, fear of, 113, 248-249
  size of, 29
  skills, 29
Staff assistant, 240
Staff meetings, 165
Staged implementation, 252-253
Stand alone word processing, 55, 61
Standard cassettes, 49
Standard work turnaround times
  copiers, 93
  word processing, 160
Standardization of dictation equipment, 50-51
Standardization of PCs, 84
Standards
  defined, 125
  control to, 210
  for work output, establishing, 126
  historic, 125-126
  industry-wide, 125
  productivity, 258
  review of, 126, 207
  work turnaround time, 93, 160
Star network, 88
Start up of changed system, 261-262
Static electricity, 257-258
Statistical tables, dictating, 158
Statistics, dangers in using, 29
Status, fear of loss, 249
Steps, charting work process, 113-119
  questions about, 118
Storage, permanent, in process charts, 114
Storage, temporary, in process charts, 114

Stored formats, 64
String search, 54
Studying automation, 146-147
Suboptimizing, 111-112, 225
Substitute words, 217
Supervisor. See Manager
Support department, estimating work load, 185-186
Support staff, roles of, 16-17
Surveys of other organizations, 112
Switchboard, programmable, 140
Systems analyst, 113, 146
Systems and procedures group, 24, 240

Tannenbaum, Robert, 200, 203, 204
Tape recorder for telephone messages, 91
Task budget, 208
Task force, 24, 146-148, 238, 251
  approach to the study of change, 24
  automation study, members of, 146
Task Group. See Task force
Team decision, 203
Telecommunications, 88-91
Teleconferencing, 141-142
  versus professional meetings, 142
  versus travel, 142
Telegraph, 135
Telephone, 88-90
  directory, 82, 145
  equipment, 89
  messages, 91, 141, 147, 152
  operating costs, 89-90
  systems, 140, 147
  tag, 90-91, 131, 141
  tape recorder, 141
Telex, 135-136
Temporary help personnel, 244, 259
Temporary help agency costs, budgeting, 178
Temporary retention of word processing disks, 163
Temporary storage in process charts, 118
Ten-key pad, 66
Thimble printer, 73
Thought pattern, 217-218
Tickler list, 145, 153
Time
  a request is needed, 226-227
  allowed for processing a request, 226
  elapsed, 109, 112
  provided vendor for delivery, 227
  savings possibilities, 10
  value of saving, 128, 130

Time and material contracts, budgeting, 179
Time and motion standards, 125
Timing the steps in an operation, 117
Title of job, 208
Training, 2, 121, 152, 165, 166, 170, 181, 210, 211, 231, 232, 252, 259, 260
Transcribers, dictation, 50
Transcription speeds, 45
Transportation steps in process charts, 118
Travel expenses, budgeting, 180
Travel time, 6-7
Travel versus teleconferencing, 142
Turnaround time, 93, 111, 160, 226, 259
TWX, 135
Typeset versus typed copy, 96
Typewriter
  electric, 28, 52, 128, 186
  electronic, 52-54

U. S. mail, 98, 128, 135
Unanswered telephone calls, 90
Underlining, automatic, 64
Understanding, 216-221, 225, 260
Undo key, 67
University, 2-3
Unnecessary steps, 113
Unproductive activities, 6-8
User orientation, 260-261
User's manual, 259-260
Utilities. *See* Electrical needs
Utilization factor, budgeting, 176-177
Utopia, 253

Variances of costs from budget, 189-192, 210
Variations in some office tasks, examples, 119-120
VDT. *See* Word processing or personal computers
Verbal communication. *See* Oral communication
Vice-president administration, 240
Video disk storage, 144
Video teleconferencing, 142
Viewgraphs. *See* Overhead viewgraphs
Visiting other organizations, 255
Visual aids, 169-170, 245, 261
Vital records protection, 103
Voice mail, 91, 141
Voice networks, 89

Waiting time, 7-8
Waiting steps in work process charts, 114
Wall Street Journal, 238

Warning, documenting the, 229
WATS, 90
"What if" modeling, 81, 130
"What if" programs using personal computers, 81-82
What is needed, communicating, 225-226
When is something needed, 226-227
Whiz kids, 250
Wide Area Telephone Service, 90
Window display, electronic typewriters, 53
Word processing, 54-77, 147
  advantages, 54-56
  disks, filing of, 162
  disk retention schedules, 162-163
  ease of original input, 55-56
  ease of revision, 56
  editing features, 64-66
  entry point for office automation, 132
  equipment categories, 61-64
  equipment configurations, 59-61
  equipment design principles, 57
  keyboard, 66-67
  input to phototypesetters, 95, 143
  manager, 146, 159
  on personal computers, 83-84
  output cost per page, 55
  printers, 71-75
  special terminology, 57
  turnaround time standards, 160
  user instructions, 159, 259-260
  using, 159-160
  work order form, 161
  working conditions, 58
  work turnaround time standards, 160
Word processing equipment
  capital asset, 186
  communicating, 135, 137
  selecting, 254-256
  use as telex terminal, 136
Word processor or PC for a secretary, 83-84
Word wrap, 54
Work
  breaks, 58, 121
  charting, cost considerations, 123
  coordination, 14, 209
  decription, 208
  flow, 14, 27, 35-37, 113, 209, 251
  habits and use of automated programs, 145
  hours, 109-110, 112
  layout, 36, 117-119
  measurement, 112-118
  order form, 161
  output, 124-126, 222

process, improving, 118-123
processing time, 226
relationships, 209
responsibilities, 14, 208
schedule, 208, 210
specialization, 27
speed up, 113
standards, establishing, 126
transport, 36. *See also* Work flow
Work load
  balance, 35-36

estimating future, 13-14, 185-186, 207
  use in selecting equipment, 254
Work sheet summary, 174, 183
Work turnaround time. *See also* Turnaround time
  copying, 93
  word processing, 160
Workshops, budgeting for, 181
Worry, 249
Written presentation, 245-246

Xerography. *See* Copying